ECONOMIC AND SOCIAL COMMISSION FOR ASIA AND THE PACIFIC

PUTTING
GENDER MAINSTREAMING
INTO PRACTICE

UNITED NATIONS

New York, 2003

ST/ESCAP/2254

UNITED NATIONS PUBLICATION
Sales No. E.03.II.F.30
Copyright © United Nations 2003
ISBN: 92-1-120169-1

PREFACE

Gender mainstreaming was established as a global strategy for the promotion of gender equality in the Platform for Action adopted at the Fourth World Conference on Women (Beijing, 1995). The mainstreaming mandate was reinforced in the ECOSOC Agreed Conclusions 1997/2 and at the twenty-third special session of the General Assembly in June 2000. ECOSOC resolution 2001/41 calls for intensified efforts to ensure that gender mainstreaming is an integral part of all its activities, including through follow-up to the implementation of the ECOSOC Agreed Conclusions 1997/2.

All entities within the United Nations are encouraged to give greater attention to gender perspectives in their work programmes and to support the efforts of Member States. Experience from both the United Nations and Member States has shown that the provision of opportunities for the exchange of ideas, experiences and good practice on gender mainstreaming is a fruitful means of increasing awareness, commitment and capacity to implement the strategy.

The Office of the Special Adviser on Women and Gender Issues and the Division for the Advancement of Women of the United Nations, therefore, decided to organize a series of regional symposia on gender mainstreaming in collaboration with the five Regional Commissions of the United Nations. The present volume is the proceedings of the first of these symposia, organized with the Economic and Social Commission for Asia and the Pacific at Bangkok in December 2001.

The Asian and Pacific regional symposium brought together 80 representatives of Governments, intergovernmental organizations, civil society organizations and United Nations bodies for a constructive dialogue on gender mainstreaming in the region. The symposium programme included six substantive sessions covering the theme of the forty-sixth session of the Commission on the Status of Women, "Eradicating poverty, including through the empowerment of women, throughout their life cycle in a globalizing world"; institutional change; gender mainstreaming in national budgets; responsibilities and accountabilities; case studies; and gender mainstreaming in intergovernmental processes.

The symposium covered presentations on gender mainstreaming practices that had been tested in the field, interactive discourse to identify and address potentials and constraints of the utilized approaches, and intensive working group sessions. This publication is a compilation of the presentations made at the symposium and the communiqué and recommendations adopted unanimously by the participants.

The organizers would like to thank the moderators and participants who so generously shared their expertise and experiences. We would also like to express our appreciation to the Governments and organizations that sponsored presentations, and to the Government of Japan and the Japan International Cooperation Agency which provided financial and technical support for the symposium and for this publication.

CONTENTS

CONTENTS *(continued)*

CONTENTS *(continued)*

PART II: REPORT OF THE SYMPOSIUM

LIST OF TABLES

ACRONYMS

ACW	ASEAN Committee on Women
ADB	Asian Development Bank
AFTA	ASEAN Free Trade Area
AIT	Asian Institute of Technology
APEC	Asia-Pacific Economic Cooperation
ASEAN	Association of South-East Asian Nations
AWP	ASEAN Women's Programme
BRAC	Bangladesh Rural Advancement Committee
CAA	Constitutional Amendment Act, India
CAPWIP	Centre for Asia-Pacific Women in Politics
CBO	community-based organization
CCA	Common Country Assessment
CEDAW	Convention on the Elimination of All Forms of Discrimination Against Women
CENWOR	Centre for Women's Research, Sri Lanka
CIDA	Canadian International Development Agency
CLC	Community Learning Centres, Indonesia
CROP	Council of Regional Organizations of the Pacific
CSO	civil society organization
CSW	Commission on the Status of Women
DAW	Division for the Advancement of Women
DBM	Department of Budget and Management, Philippines
DFID	Department for International Development, United Kingdom
DILG	Department of Interior and Local Government, Philippines
DLS	Department of Livestock Services, Nepal
DOF	Department of Forest, Nepal
ECOSOC	Economic and Social Council
EFA	Education for All
EHM	Environmental Health Motivator, Viet Nam

ACRONYMS *(continued)*

EGM	expert group meeting
ESCAP	Economic and Social Commission for Asia and the Pacific
ETTA	East Timorese Transitional Administration
FAO	Food and Agriculture Organization of the United Nations
FWCW	Fourth World Conference on Women
FWPR	female work participation rate
GAD	gender and development
GAU	Gender Affairs Unit, UNTAET
GBAA	Gender Budget Analysis and Advocacy, Philippines
GDP	gross domestic product
GDI	Gender-related Development Index
GEM	Gender Empowerment Measure
GFP	Gender Focal Point
GIA	Gender Issues Advisor, Pacific Islands Forum Secretariat
GIAE	Gender Impact Assessment and Evaluation, Japan
GIS	Gender Implications Statements, New Zealand
GO/IGO	Governmental Organization/Intergovernmental Organization
GSF	Gender Support Facility, Tonga
HDI	Human Development Index
HIV/AIDS	human immunodeficiency virus/acquired immunodeficiency syndrome
HLFFDP	Hills Leasehold Forestry and Fodder Development Project, Nepal
ICPD	International Conference on Population and Development
ICT	information and communication technology
IFAD	International Fund for Agricultural Development
ILO	International Labour Organization
IMCW	Inter-Ministerial Committee on Women, Fiji
INWID/INGAD	Information Network for Women in Development/Gender and Development, Pakistan
IWEP	Integrated Women's Empowerment Programme, India

ACRONYMS *(continued)*

IWRAW	International Women's Rights Action Watch
JICA	Japan International Cooperation Agency
LGU	Local Government Unit, Philippines
MOC	Ministry of Construction, Viet Nam
MOGE	Ministry of Gender Equality, Republic of Korea
MOW	Ministry of Women, Social Welfare and Poverty Alleviation, Fiji
MWA	Ministry of Women's Affairs, New Zealand
MWCA	Ministry of Women and Children Affairs, Bangladesh
MWVA	Ministry of Women's and Veterans' Affairs, Cambodia
NACGAD	National Advisory Committee on Gender and Development, Tonga
NCRFW	National Commission on the Role of Filipino Women, Philippines
NEDA	National Economic and Development Authority, Philippines
NGO	non-governmental organization
NPC	National Planning Commission, Nepal
NWAC	National Women's Advisory Council, Fiji
ODA	official development assistance
OSCE/ODIHR	Office for Democratic Institutions and Human Rights of the Organization for Security and Cooperation in Europe
OHCHR	Office of the High Commissioner for Human Rights, United Nations
OSAGI	Office of the Special Adviser on Gender Issues and Advancement of Women
PLAGE	Policy Leadership and Advocacy for Gender Equality, Bangladesh
PLAU	Policy Leadership and Advocacy Unit, Bangladesh
PIFS	Pacific Islands Forum Secretariat
PPA	Pacific Platform for Action
PRIA	Participatory Research Institute of Asia
SAARC	South Asian Association for Regional Cooperation
SAP	structural adjustment programmes
SEWA	Self Employed Women's Association

ACRONYMS *(continued)*

SHG	self-help group
SPC	Secretariat of the Pacific Community
SRSG	Special Representative of the Secretary General of the United Nations, UNTAET
TAG	Technical Advisory Group
TNCWA	Thai National Commission on Women's Affairs
UNDAF	United Nations Development Assistance Framework
UNDP	United Nations Development Programme
UNESCO	United Nations Educational, Scientific and Cultural Organization
UNFPA	United Nations Population Fund
UNICEF	United Nations Children's Fund
UNIDO	United Nations Industrial Development Organization
UNOPS	United Nations Office of Project Services
UNTAET	United Nations Transitional Administration for East Timor
UNV	United Nations Volunteers
VO	village organization
VPWSP	Vietnam-Australia Five Towns Provincial Water Supply Project
VWU	Vietnam Women's Union
WDC	Women and Development Centre, Tonga
WFP	World Food Programme
WID	Women in Development
WOSED	Women's Social and Economic Development Programme, Fiji
WPA	Women's Plan of Action, Fiji
WSC	Water Supply Company, Viet Nam
WTO	World Trade Organization

COMMUNIQUE

Asia-Pacific Regional Symposium on Gender Mainstreaming

Gender mainstreaming was recognized as a global strategy for the promotion of gender equality in the Platform for Action from the Fourth World Conference on Women (Beijing, 1995). The ECOSOC agreed conclusions (1997/2) provide a clear definition of gender mainstreaming as the "process of assessing the implications for men and women of any planned action, including legislation, policies and programmes in all areas and at all levels..."

A regional symposium on gender mainstreaming in the Asia-Pacific region was organized by ESCAP in collaboration with the United Nations Office of the Special Adviser on Gender Issues and Advancement of Women and the Division for the Advancement of Women, from 10 to 13 December 2001. The meeting brought together 80 representatives of Governments, regional-level intergovernmental organizations, NGOs and civil society groups, the private sector and academia, and United Nations personnel for a constructive dialogue on gender mainstreaming in the region. The discussions focused on identifying entry points, approaches, methodologies and tools to support gender mainstreaming at the local, national, subregional and regional levels. Potentials, good practice and remaining challenges were also identified.

The participants first discussed the issue of gender mainstreaming in the context of efforts to reduce poverty in a globalizing world, one of the two themes of the forty-sixth session of the Commission on the Status of Women (March 2002). There is increasing evidence that the ongoing processes of economic and political restructuring in the region have heightened women's vulnerabilities and led to an expansion and intensification of poverty among women. National governments have responded through women-specific poverty programmes and interventions for the empowerment of women. However, some of these programmes usually address income poverty in isolation and do not recognize the fact that poor women face human poverty through multiple deprivations and violations of their equal rights and entitlements. This approach may have hindered the incorporation of gender perspectives into mainstream sectors, which are critical for gender-responsive poverty eradication strategies, such as agriculture and manufacturing. While acknowledging income as one of the means to reduce poverty, there was also recognition that it does not always lead to gender equality. A human poverty perspective should be incorporated into the design and implementation of all mainstream programmes for poverty reduction.

The participants expressed concern at the continuing gaps between macroeconomic policies focused on economic growth and social policies focused on the larger goals of gender equality and social justice. Advocates of gender equality need to engage with and influence processes of macroeconomic policy-making. Women's groups and gender-responsive NGOs and development agencies in countries of the region have evolved alternative approaches, which can provide valuable lessons for policy makers.

In many cases, there are wide gaps between policy commitments to women's empowerment and gender equality and resource allocations to meet the goals set. Budgets are one of the most powerful instruments for bridging this gap, promoting women's equitable access to public resources and mainstreaming a gender perspective into national development. Experiences of incorporating gender perspectives into budgeting also demon-strate the need for clarity in the responsibilities and accountabilities of the organizations and individuals involved. The involvement of economic and planning bodies, finance and budget departments and the legislature, and oversight by an informed and committed group of gender advocates, both inside and outside government, are critical to the process of making budgeting processes gender-responsive. To be effective and sustainable, gender mainstreaming in budgets has to be supported by an active constituency for gender equality, both within government and in civil society. The role of the national machinery is important in ensuring political and technical support in terms of gender auditing and budgeting.

Challenges in institutionalizing gender mainstreaming approaches within organiza-tions were discussed. Gender-biased institutional norms often operate below the level of awareness but are embedded in the hierarchies, work practices and beliefs of organiza-tions and constrain efforts to implement gender mainstreaming. While there has been progress in setting up the infrastructure to support gender mainstreaming, there is a need for strategic action to combat deeply-embedded organizational values and institutional structures that discriminate against women in subtle and insidious ways. Experiences shared at the meeting included the need for an informed and vocal constituency that could demand change and hold public agencies and authorities accountable for addressing the interests of women as well as men. The importance of developing accountability mechanisms, including sanctions for behaviours, which perpetuate discrimination against women, was highlighted.

The responsibilities of government machinery in gender mainstreaming should be clearly spelt out and supported by relevant policies. Accountability at the highest levels, while difficult to build, is critical for activating similar mechanisms down to the grass-roots level. Policy-making bodies and institutions that control resources have their respective roles to play in strengthening accountability mechanisms. International donors can help to strengthen accountability mechanisms by incorporating a gender perspective into the framework for their assistance and the component programmes and projects which they support.

Recommendations

The meeting urged national Governments, regional intergovernmental bodies and civil society actors, with the support of international bodies and donors as appropriate, to work towards the following goals:

- Ensuring that the principles of gender equality and a rights-based framework, as embodied in CEDAW and other relevant international instruments, are mainstreamed into the policies, programmes and activities of all actors in development.

- Incorporating gender perspectives into the conceptual frameworks and processes of macroeconomic planning and decision-making, in order to address the multiple dimensions of poverty among women and the adverse impact of globalization on women's lives.

- Helping gender equality advocates to gain an understanding of macroeconomics, including the planning and budgeting processes, to better enable them to engage in informed dialogue at all levels on economic issues and national policies from a gender perspective.

- Supporting gender-responsive budgeting by mainstreaming gender into the processes of formulating budgets through developing skills and disseminating methods and tools that build on existing experience and good practices.

- Promoting people-centred analysis of government policies and programmes that make visible their economic and social impacts and outcomes, particularly in terms of their congruence with larger national goals of gender equality and social justice.

- Ensuring that the principles of gender equality and non-discrimination, as embodied in Security Council resolution 1325 (2000), are mainstreamed into United Nations peace support operations, including conflict prevention, peace-building and post-conflict reconstruction.

- Paying particular attention to the capacity- and strategy-building of the national machineries in States affected by armed conflict.

- Strengthening linkages between women's movements and other civil society movements to incorporate gender perspectives into governance, through promoting participation, transparency and accountability.

- Developing capacities to address the political dimensions of promoting and sustaining gender mainstreaming and providing the necessary technical support to initiate and expand gender mainstreaming in strategic sectors and issues.

- Enhancing and strengthening the range of mechanisms for supporting and implementing gender mainstreaming, including high-level advisory groups, gender focal points and task forces; training-including for top management; strategies for making gender analysis mandatory; action plans; accountability mechanisms and monitoring and reporting mechanisms.

- Building new constituencies to deepen and sustain gender mainstreaming, including men and youth.

- Continuing to mainstream gender concerns in multilateral agencies including the United Nations, World Bank, Asian Development Bank, International Fund for Agricultural Development and regional forums, as well as to strengthen cooperation between agencies.

13 December 2001
Bangkok

PART I

Statements and Presentations

SESSION 1:

OPENING OF THE REGIONAL SYMPOSIUM

OPENING STATEMENT

Mr. Kim Hak-Su

Executive Secretary
Economic and Social Commission for Asia and the Pacific

It gives me great pleasure to welcome all of you to the Asia-Pacific Regional Symposium on Gender Mainstreaming. ESCAP is pleased to host this symposium, the first of five regional symposia that the Office of the Special Adviser to the Secretary General on Gender Issues and Advancement of Women plans to hold jointly with the five regional commissions of the United Nations.

In the United Nations, concern for the advancement of women and gender equality began with the Charter signed in 1945. In the Preamble, faith in fundamental human rights, in the dignity and worth of the human person, and in the equal rights of men and women were declared. A half century later in 1995, the Beijing Declaration and Platform for Action striving for the goals of Gender Equality, Development, and Peace, was adopted. The commitment was further reaffirmed in the outcome document of the twenty-third special session of the General Assembly held in June 2000 (popularly known as Beijing plus 5). In the historic Millennium Declaration in 2000, the heads of States and Governments pledged "to promote gender equality and the empowerment of women as effective ways to combat poverty, hunger and disease and to stimulate development that is truly sustainable".

In spite of the long history of efforts to promote the advancement of women, many obstacles remain to prevent women in the region from attaining gender equality. The plight of the women of Afghanistan reminds us starkly that some women in the region still do not enjoy their human rights and fundamental freedoms, and are subjected to gender-based violence. Many women continue to face *de jure* and *de facto* discrimination. The feminization of poverty is increasing in the region while the differential impact of globalization on men and women needs to be analysed and the adverse effects managed. The low level of women in decision-making deprives women of a voice in shaping their lives.

It is therefore important to intensify our efforts to promote the elusive goal of gender equality through a two-pronged approach. The first approach is the empowerment of women, through their economic and political empowerment, and through the promotion and protection of their human rights and fundamental freedoms. The other complementary approach is to mainstream a gender perspective in all sectors of development and integrate gender concerns in the public policy agenda in line with the ECOSOC Agreed Conclusions 1997/2 and the recent ECOSOC resolution 2001/41.

It is very opportune that this Symposium is being convened today to discuss the very important subject of gender mainstreaming to promote gender equality. ECOSOC defines mainstreaming a gender perspective as "the process of assessing the implications for men and women of any planned action, including legislation, policies of programmes, in all areas and at all levels". This definition was supplemented at the ESCAP regional preparatory meeting for Beijing plus 5, where in addition to assessing the implications, gender mainstreaming was also seen as a process that should lead to transformative changes.

ESCAP's current priorities include assistance to countries in managing the challenges of globalization, to reduce poverty (including the new poor), and to tackle emerging social issues. I am very pleased that at the first plenary session you will be discussing the theme of the forthcoming forty-sixth session of the Commission on the Status of Women on "Eradicating poverty including through the empowerment of women throughout their life cycle in a globalizing world", a topic which addresses one of the top priority concerns of ESCAP.

Earlier this year, at the fifty-seventh ESCAP session, the Commission adopted resolution 57/3 on follow-up to the Beijing Conference and the outcome of its global review. In this resolution, I was requested to assist members and associate members to "promote gender mainstreaming and the integration of gender concerns into public policy..." I am very glad that you will be taking up the issues specifically mentioned in resolution 57/3 such as gender budgeting, and responsibility and accountability measures.

This Symposium will discuss strategies for gender mainstreaming. I note with interest that you will be drawing from best practices in the region on important issues such as education, political participation, and sustainable development among others. The work on gender mainstreaming in the intergovernmental process is also very topical in the light of the growing importance of subregional and regional cooperation. In the case of ESCAP, it has been possible to utilize the intergovernmental structure of ESCAP to reach policy makers in specific sectors and at very high levels.

I look forward to your deliberations which I am sure will provide all of us with further guidance on establishing and strengthening institutional mechanisms and procedures, building competency and capacity, and working with strategic partners and support groups to link participatory processes with policy making. It is my hope that the outcome of this symposium will lead to strengthened national capacity to mainstream a gender perspective into policies and programmes. The Symposium should also enhance national capacity and regional cooperation for the empowerment of women.

I would also like to take this opportunity to thank the Government of Japan for its funding generous support, to FAO and UNESCO for sponsoring presenters, and to all other donor countries and agencies for their support of this Symposium.

I wish you a constructive and successful Symposium and a pleasant stay in Bangkok.

* * *

OPENING MESSAGE

Ms. Angela E.V. King
Assistant Secretary-General and Special Adviser to the Secretary-General on Gender Issues and Advancement of Women, United Nations

Delivered by

Ms. Carolyn Hannan
Director, Division for the Advancement of Women, United Nations

I am delighted to send a statement of support to the opening of this first Regional Symposium on Gender Mainstreaming organized by the United Nations. The regional symposia which will be held annually in different regions over the next five years are being organized in response to increasingly clear intergovernmental mandates on gender mainstreaming. From the Beijing Platform for Action in 1995 and the ECOSOC agreed conclusions in 1997, to the Security Council resolution in October 2000 and the ECOSOC resolution (2001/41) this year, the importance of incorporating gender perspectives into all areas of societal development has been highlighted by Member States of the United Nations.

It is highly appropriate that this first symposium is being held in the Asia-Pacific region since so much innovative work on promoting gender equality has been carried out in this region. I recall in particular the path-breaking Regional Plan of Action prepared for the Fourth World Conference in Beijing in 1995.

I wish to congratulate ESCAP, in particular the Executive Secretary, Mr. Kim Hak-Su for his support to this process and to Ms. Thelma Kay, Chief of the Women in Development Section, and her staff for their efforts to make this symposium a success.

Throughout the United Nations system concerted efforts are being made to implement gender mainstreaming. Many organizations have developed policies and strategies for promoting gender equality, based on the gender mainstreaming strategy. Institutional arrangements to support achievement of the goals set, such as gender units and gender focal point systems, have been established. Initiatives are undertaken across the system to develop the capacity to identify and address relevant gender perspectives in all areas of work, at both normative/policy and operational/programme levels. Gender perspectives are being incorporated into planning, budgeting and reporting processes, and guidelines and other materials to support staff are being developed to ensure gender perspectives are taken into consideration in data collection and research, analysis, support to legislative change, policy and programme development and monitoring and evaluation.

Organizations in the United Nations system support governments to develop gender-sensitive policies and strategies and to take gender perspectives into consideration in planning, implementing and monitoring development interventions in all areas of collaboration. Considerable support is given to capacity development. Non-governmental organizations and groups and networks in civil society are supported to play critical advocacy roles in relation to gender mainstreaming and monitor the adherence to all commitments made by governments. Efforts are also being taken to involve more men in promoting gender equality through gender mainstreaming.

Within the United Nations, my office has been charged with promoting, supporting, facilitating and monitoring gender mainstreaming across the system. This has been done through advocacy, particularly with senior managers, and provision of advice and support. In addition, guidance materials have been produced – fact sheets, briefing notes and inventories of intergovernmental mandates; competence development programmes have been developed; and assessments of progress have been carried out, leading to concrete recommendations for change. Examples of many of the materials developed are provided here.

The Interagency Meeting on Women and Gender Equality has also worked consistently to ensure greater collaboration and coordination in promoting gender mainstreaming. The work of the inter-agency group is organized through taskforces, which have focused on carrying out inventories of good practices in gender mainstreaming, of gender focal points and of training materials. Methods have been developed to incorporate gender perspectives in programme budgets. Collaborative efforts have been undertaken to influence processes such as CCA/UNDAF, the implementation of the Security Council resolution 1325 and preparations for the International Conference on Financing for Development to be held in Monterrey in Mexico in 2002.

The Commission on the Status of Women (CSW) plays a catalytic role in relation to gender mainstreaming – advocating for, promoting and monitoring progress on gender mainstreaming among Member States, as well as within the United Nations itself. Attention was given to gender mainstreaming during the discussions of the future working methods of the Commission at its last session. These discussions will continue at the next session in March 2002 and I am certain that the outcomes of this symposium will make an important contribution. That Member States are also making advances in implementation of gender mainstreaming at the national level is increasingly evident in the national statements during the Commission on the Status of Women, as well as in the panel discussions around the themes being addressed by the Commission each year.

Increasingly, efforts have also been made to incorporate gender perspectives into other intergovernmental processes. To give one concrete example, in the preparations for the International Conference on Financing for Development, attention has been given to gender perspectives in relation to all areas of the financing for development agenda: domestic resource mobilization (including credit and savings, national budgets and expenditure reviews, taxation and social security systems); foreign direct investment; trade; debt; and ODA. These positive steps are due to the commitment of Member States, as well as to the efforts of the United Nations Inter-agency Taskforce on Gender and Financing for Development. Critical inputs are also being made by NGOs working individually or in coalition, to raise awareness and promote the incorporation of gender perspectives into the preparatory process.

Another particularly important example concerns the United Nations Security Council. In response to the Security Council resolution 1325, which calls for gender mainstreaming in the area of peace and security, a study of the United Nations Secretary-General on women, peace and security is currently being prepared, which will form the basis for a Secretary-General's report to be presented to the Security Council. It is expected that this will lead to further practical recommendations on how gender perspectives can be incorporated into the work of the United Nations on peace and security, both as a means to increase gender equality and ensure more effective peace support operations.

The purpose of this regional symposium is to stimulate exchange of knowledge, experience and good practice on gender mainstreaming within the region, particularly between governments. We know that there are many good ideas and initiatives in this region and that many of these have not yet been adequately documented. We anticipate that this symposium will bring these experiences to the fore.

In order to achieve this goal we hope that the examples provided will be very concrete and the discussions practically oriented, so that by the end of the symposium we will have some very practical recommendations and good practice examples to disseminate on a broad scale. Given the wealth of knowledge and experience among the participants at this symposium, I am certain we will have a very positive outcome.

* * *

Keynote address by

Ms. Sochua Mu

Minister, Ministry of Women's and Veterans' Affairs, Cambodia

WOMEN'S ECONOMIC EMPOWERMENT: MAINSTREAMING GENDER IN NATIONAL PLANNING IN CAMBODIA

Challenges of a post-conflict economy

As Cambodia emerges from years of conflict and isolation, it faces many challenges of reconstruction and development. Fighting depleted our human resources, which has to be replenished. However, our financial resources are not adequate to make up for the serious loss caused by so many years of conflicts. Incidence of poverty is high, with 36 per cent of households living below the poverty line. Most of the population, or 85 per cent of it, lives and works in rural areas. Cambodia continues to be primarily dependent on agriculture. And particular to the post conflict situation impacted by the military conscription, death and disability among men, women have to take on increasing economic responsibilities in addition to their family caregiver role, although most were engaged in unskilled and low-paying positions. 20 per cent of our households are headed by women.

Cambodia has the highest female labour force participation rate in the subregion.	
Cambodia	73.5%
Thailand	64.2%
Indonesia	51.5%
Singapore	50.0%
Philippines	50.0%
Malaysia	41.8%

As our social and political situation is getting stabilized, new kinds of challenges are emerging. There are growing pressures on land because of an increasing population and increasing demand for land in a market economy. Loss and lack of land represents the loss of means of production, and is the first step in a well-known vicious cycle that leads to migration, employment in highly exploitative jobs, and further poverty. Cambodia is facing land scarcity for the first time in its history and landlessness is a growing concern. There is also a need for viable alternatives to agriculture.

In addition, as we rejoin the global economy, the pressures of globalization and regionalization make it imperative that we increase our capacity to compete. Cambodia is now a full member of ASEAN and is to become a member of WTO. The transition from central economic planning to participation in a free market global economy has been rapid and dramatic over the past five years. Cheap, better quality and more marketable products are flowing into local markets, particularly from neighbouring countries. Import tariffs have been lowered and will continue to go down especially for agriculture and agro-processing products. Cambodian farmers are losing their market share at an alarming rate. Rural production and food security is being adversely affected.

In order to take up on these challenges, consideration on the following gender and women's issues is imperative.

Women in the development of Cambodia

Women are actively engaged in economic activities in Cambodia. Women comprise 53 per cent of the economically active population in Cambodia.[1] In the most important sector of our economy, agriculture and fisheries, 53.9 per cent of the workers are women.[2] 66.8 per cent of the primary labour force in manufacturing, and 74.5 per cent of the primary labour force in wholesale and retail trade are also women. However, women hold less than 25 per cent of professional and technical positions and less than 9 per cent of senior managers and national decision makers are women.[3]

Women and health

Access to health services is severely constrained. An estimated 47 per cent of the population have inadequate access to health care services. For example, 45 per cent of the births given were not assisted by trained birth attendants, while only 51 per cent of mothers received ante-natal care. Women also suffer from food shortage and malnutrition, which is manifested in 41 per cent of pregnant women being underweight. Consequently, the maternal mortality ratio is among the highest in the subregion at 470 per 100,000 births.

---

[1] General Population Census of Cambodia 1998, National Institute of Statistics, Ministry of Planning.

[2] Socio-economic Survey 1999, National Institute of Statistics, Ministry of Planning.

[3] Ibid.

The situation is getting aggravated by the growing HIV/AIDS epidemic, which affects women particularly harshly. One out of 30 pregnant women is found to be HIV positive; on the other hand, when family members are HIV positive, the responsibility for caring for the members is shouldered primarily by women.

Health care expenses consume approximately 30 per cent of household expenditure. Those who are in debt cite the cost of health services as one of the main causes of their having fallen in indebtedness, and this tendency is acutely noticeable among the poor and vulnerable. Often the poor are compelled to sell their land and other assets to meet health care costs, thus losing their primary source of livelihood. Female heads of household who are the sole source of household livelihood are particularly vulnerable in this regard.

Women and education

Low levels of educational attainment and skills are formidable constraints for women in Cambodia. Nearly half of all Cambodian women over the age of 25 are illiterate. A further 38 per cent have completed less than primary school education. Only 6 per cent have more than primary school education, whilst 16 per cent of men have. This situation is even more serious in rural areas. The gender gap is being perpetuated by a low retention rate of girls in formal education, with 50 per cent greater male enrolment in schools at age 15.

There are also very few sources of market-oriented skills training in the country. An added difficulty is that training opportunities which respond to the constraints faced by women in their multiple roles as caregivers and economic providers are scarce.

Such poor access to education and training leaves women with few marketable skills and inability to participate in the modern sector of the economy or to build businesses in the informal sector. There are also very few early childhood education services. This means that many women, particularly young female heads of households, have added difficulties in getting engaged in economic activities as they simply cannot leave their young children at home.

In rebuilding the society in the post conflict situation and preparing it for the future, the Ministry of Women's and Veterans' Affairs (MWVA) works as the National Machinery for the Promotion of the Status of Women of Cambodia and in partnership with multisectoral stakeholders to incorporate gender perspectives in development efforts.

Ministry of Women's and Veterans' Affairs
The National Machinery for the Promotion of the Status of Women

Vision

The vision of MWVA is that the Cambodian people, both men and women, are united and moving forward to build a prosperous and peaceful nation, upholding law and order, through a just and transparent system of good governance which leads to social, economic and political stability.

Four priority areas are Education, Women's Health, Economic Empowerment, and Legal Protection. The Ministry's five-year plan, "Neary Rattanak (Women are Precious Gems)", identifies the issues which need to be addressed both in terms of capacity building within the Ministry itself and the policies and developmental approaches to meet goals in the four priority areas.

Gender mainstreaming strategy

The strategy of MWVA is to integrate gender concerns into policies and programmes throughout the Kingdom so that all national and local governmental institutions, the civil society, the private sector and communities are effectively responding to the critical needs and concerns of women. The gender mainstreaming strategy has five main components:

1. Building commitment and capacity

   - Advocacy with senior decision makers

   - Establishing and strengthening gender focal points in national and local development structures

2. Influencing policies to be gender-sensitive and responsive

   - Advocacy for gender-responsive legal reform

   - Organizing policy forums

   - Strengthening the women's forum as our partner in policy advocacy

3. Increasing the participation of women in national and local development planning and governance

   - Leadership training for women

   - Promoting women leaders as role models

4. Enhancing capacity for gender planning, monitoring and evaluation

   - Expanding the information base and using information more effectively in monitoring and advocacy

5. Increasing public awareness and support

   - Establishing and strengthening gender focal points in national and local development structures

   - Fostering gender-friendly media practitioners, disseminating information through community outreach activities

In addition to gender mainstreaming in economic development, MWVA complements and strengthens the initiatives of other governmental agencies through its mandate to ensure that gender concerns are addressed and through its networks of women at the community level.

For example, MWVA works with the Ministry of Justice, the Ministry of Interior, the courts and the National Assembly to secure gender equality in legal reforms in the civil code, the criminal code, the land law, labour laws, and the anti-human trafficking law. MWVA also work with these institutions to draft the law on the prevention of domestic violence. On the other hand, MWVA disseminates information on legal issues to the population and provide guidance and training to women so that more women enter the judiciary.

Advocacy in reproductive health and HIV/AIDS related issues

Young adults as a group have emerged as having the highest HIV positive cases. Among this group, women, especially young female factory workers, are found to be particularly vulnerable as a group. The vulnerability is due to traditional beliefs and prevailing discriminatory attitudes towards them in the society, and low access to health services and counselling. To reduce the vulnerability and risks of infection among young women, we have to address gender and HIV/AIDS as a cross cutting issue and take on a multisectoral approach.

We have taken on enhancing the understanding and commitment by decision makers in the Ministries of Education, Youth and Sports (MOEYS); of Health (MOH); of Social Affairs, Labour, Vocational Training, and Youth Rehabilitation (MOSALVY) and National AIDS Authority (NAA) in support for multisectoral programmes, as well as strengthening the capacity of selected governmental institutions and NGOs in advocacy efforts and skills in support of multisectoral programmes. MWVA further strives to increase the understanding and commitment by the mass media to report on multisectoral programmes. Through the enhanced support for multisectoral programmes, we envision reducing the vulnerability of youth, especially young women and young female factory workers, to HIV/AIDS, and promoting responsible male behaviour.

Mobilizing women for local politics

Ensuring that half of the population is represented in decision-making fora is an important task. MWVA worked with Ministry of Interior to engender the election law while it continues to work with women local NGOs in establishing special programmes for female candidates and women leaders. MWVA lobbies political parties to put women on the parties' lists of candidates. These efforts have led to 12,000 women registering as candidates representing eight political parties for the next local election.

Monitoring progress

In celebration of the International Women's Day 2001, the Government of Cambodia officially launched the Cambodian National Council for Women. This council brings together senior officials from 13 ministries to develop strategies and plans, and monitor progress in responding to gender concerns. Basic indicators on the status of women can be monitored from national census and survey data. Further research is needed to enable us to better understand the specific needs and concerns of women in our economy and society as a guide for the government in formulating policies and programmes to address needs, and monitor progress.

Building for the future

MWVA is committed to working together with partners in the public and private sectors, the civil society and the international community in developing and implementing programmes directed at alleviating poverty, and promoting economic growth and the political empowerment of women in Cambodia.

The Ministry is relatively new and is only just beginning to put into place mechanisms for gender mainstreaming. In this regard, we very much appreciate opportunities to learn from the experiences of other countries and look forward to continuing to learn from and work together with our colleagues and friends in the region in our efforts to mainstream gender in national economic planning in Cambodia.

* * *

OVERVIEW ON GENDER MAINSTREAMING

Ms. Carolyn Hannan

Director, Division for the Advancement of Women, United Nations

Introduction

The strong focus on the advancement of women and gender equality through the United Nations over the past three decades has led to increased international recognition that there are important gender perspectives in relation to the overall goals of development. Poverty eradication, human rights, good governance, environmentally sustainable development and peace and security are among them. As a result of this understanding, the 189 Member States attending the Fourth World Conference on Women in Beijing in 1995 endorsed gender mainstreaming as a key strategy for promoting equality between women and men. The United Nations and other international organizations were called upon to implement the strategy in their own work and support the efforts of Member States.

Governments and the United Nations made commitments in the Beijing Platform for Action (1995) to implement gender mainstreaming: that is, to consider the realities of women and men and the potential impacts of planned activities on women and men, before any decisions on goals, strategies, actions and resource allocations are made.

Clarity on certain aspects of gender mainstreaming

There is considerable clarity on certain important aspects of gender mainstreaming today. We know, for example, that there are very strong and explicit intergovernmental mandates. We can point to the Beijing Platform for Action, the ECOSOC Agreed Conclusions of 1997, the twenty-third special session of the General Assembly to follow up the Beijing Platform for Action in 2000, and even more recently in ECOSOC resolution

2001/41, which calls for attention to gender perspectives in the work of ECOSOC and all its functional commissions, as well as in the integrated and coordinated follow-up to global conferences. In addition to these more generic mandates for gender mainstreaming, there are also very specific recommendations for all areas of the work of the United Nations, such as poverty eradication and national budget processes, the areas which this symposium will be focusing on. The recent Security Council resolution 1325 on women, peace and security is one good example of a very specific intergovernmental mandate on gender mainstreaming.

We understand that gender mainstreaming is not an end in itself, but a means, an approach, a strategy for achieving gender equality. There is also increased awareness that bringing gender perspectives to the centre of attention not only supports the promotion of gender equality but also contributes effectively to the achievement of other development goals. It has been clear for decades that women in many parts of the world make key contributions in areas of development such as agriculture and water resources management. Neglecting women in these areas often led to less than optimal effects of development inputs, and at worst negative impacts. Development goals will not be met unless the needs and priorities of all stakeholders are identified and addressed. Even in areas where gender perspectives were normally considered irrelevant, such as trade and macroeconomics, it is increasingly recognized that sound development must be based on a clear assessment of the contributions of women as well as men, and the potential impact of planned interventions on both women and men and on their productivity. There has been a steady accumulation of evidence that gender differences and inequalities, directly and indirectly, affect the impact of development policies and strategies and hence the achievement of overall development goals.

Some warnings have, however, been raised about the risks of using gender mainstreaming simply as a strategy to achieve other goals, while neglecting the promotion of gender equality itself. Gender equality is a development goal in its own right. Gender mainstreaming must be seen as a process for promoting equality between women and men, which in turn can facilitate the achievement of other developmental goals, including economic goals.

Gender mainstreaming is not simply about integrating or including women in development agendas already decided upon by others. Gender mainstreaming involves a transformative process. It can reveal a need for changes in goals, strategies and actions to ensure that both women and men can influence, participate in and benefit from development processes. This can require changes in organizations – structures, procedures and cultures – to create organizational environments, which are conducive to the promotion of gender equality.

We also know that while representation of women is an essential element in gender mainstreaming, increasing the numbers of women is not enough. The mainstream agenda can only be transformed when the perspectives of both women and men inform the design, implementation and outcomes of policies and programmes. This requires analysing the gender perspectives in each and every area of development. It further requires examining the institutional mechanisms through which development is done.

While we recognize today that gender mainstreaming is a critical strategy for gender equality, at the same time we acknowledge that gender mainstreaming does not eliminate the need for targeted activities to promote the advancement of women and gender equality. Women- or gender-specific activities are still required to address serious gaps which must be urgently tackled to support women's empowerment and develop women's leadership capacities and to test ideas and approaches which may then be applied to the mainstream development process.

Similarly, it is also very clear today that gender mainstreaming does not do away with the need for gender experts. On the contrary, improving the implementation of gender mainstreaming at national level by Member States, and within the United Nations, over the coming decade will require the strategic inputs of such experts, working in a catalytic manner to deepen the awareness, knowledge, commitment and capacity of all professional staff. Additional, not fewer, resources will be required to support the important work of gender specialists and gender focal points.

Some key misconceptions

Two important and pervasive misconceptions of gender mainstreaming need to be dealt with here. Firstly, gender mainstreaming is not about gender balance within organizations, although this is an important element of overall efforts to promote gender equality. Every organization must have a dual strategy – efforts to promote gender equality within the organization itself, combined with efforts to promote attention to gender perspectives within the work of the organization. Gender mainstreaming is focused on the work programmes of organizations – the goals, strategies, resource allocations and planning and implementation processes.

Secondly, separate specially targeted activities for women are not gender mainstreaming activities but a necessary complement to gender mainstreaming. As the term "mainstreaming" implies, gender mainstreaming means bringing gender perspectives into regular "mainstream" activities – research, analyses, policies, programmes, etc. – which are not specifically targeted to women. Gender mainstreaming is the strategy utilized in programmes where the principal objectives are related to other development goals than gender equality – such as improvements in health status, greater agricultural productivity, improved transport, more efficient energy consumption. Gender mainstreaming involves linking the goal of gender equality to these other development goals, in the context of "mainstream" development policies and programmes.

Implementation of gender mainstreaming

Although gender mainstreaming is now well established as a global strategy for promoting gender equality, we still have considerable work to do before gender perspectives are routinely incorporated into all areas of development. While it is relatively easy to secure agreement that gender mainstreaming is an important strategy, implementation of the strategy has proven more difficult than originally anticipated. Implementing gender mainstreaming can require significant changes in how business is done. Trying to bring the realities of both women and men – their contributions, perspectives, needs and priorities – to bear on data collection, analyses, policy development, planning, implementation and monitoring in all areas of development, requires specific knowledge and capacity. There can be a need for changes in awareness (and in some cases even in terms of attitudes), in knowledge on gender issues and in methods and approaches. Ability to work with gender mainstreaming should be regarded as a professional competence required of all staff.

(a) Definition of "gender mainstreaming"

Two key obstacles are a lack of real understanding of what gender mainstreaming actually means and the fact that the practical implications of gender mainstreaming are not fully understood in many areas of development, for example, in economics or in more technical areas.

An authoritative definition of gender mainstreaming is contained in the ECOSOC agreed conclusions 1997/2:

> "Mainstreaming a gender perspective is the process of assessing the implications for women and men of any planned action, including legislation, policies or programmes, in all areas and at all levels. It is a strategy for making women's as well as men's concerns and experiences an integral dimension of the design, implementation, monitoring and evaluation of policies and programmes in all political, economic and societal spheres so that women and men benefit equally and inequality is not perpetuated. The ultimate goal is to achieve gender equality."

Gender mainstreaming involves bringing relevant gender perspectives to the centre of attention in substantive work – both in more socially-oriented sectors or issues such as health, education, agriculture where the gender perspectives are relatively well understood and accepted, and in sectors and issues where the linkages to gender equality are less well recognized, such as economics, energy, transport, disarmament. Gender mainstreaming further involves ensuring that these gender perspectives, once identified, are incorporated into the many different types of activities through which development objectives are achieved. This requires explicit, systematic attention to gender perspectives in all types of activities.

(b) Practical steps to be taken

An important starting point in the implementation of gender mainstreaming is ensuring that the initial definitions of issues and or problems across all areas of activity are done in a manner that allows for the identification of gender differences and disparities. Assumptions that issues and or problems are neutral from a gender perspective should never be made – gender analysis should always be carried out, separately or as part of existing analyses. All analytical reports and recommendations on policy or operational issues should take gender differences and disparities fully into account. Plans and budgets should be prepared in such a manner that gender perspectives and gender equality issues are made explicit and can be specifically addressed.

The first step required is an assessment of the *linkages between gender equality and the issue or sector being worked on,* that is, to identify the gender implications of, for example, poverty elimination, good governance, enterprise development, and peace and security issues. This involves understanding *why* promotion of gender equality is important from the perspectives of human rights and social justice, as well as for achievement of other development goals.

The lack of implementation of gender mainstreaming in many areas can often be directly related to the fact that relevant gender perspectives have not been identified. Important questions about the linkages between gender and different sector areas or development issues need to be raised. For example:

- What are the differential impacts of trade development on women and men?

- Are the existing contributions of women as well as men taken into account in development of peace processes?

- What potential contributions could women make to disarmament processes, if given a little more support?

Gender mainstreaming cannot be achieved unless such questions are raised and the full implications of the roles, responsibilities, contributions, priorities and needs of women as well as men are taken into consideration in all areas.

Secondly, once these gender perspectives have been identified in different areas of development, the *opportunities* and *entry-points* for addressing these in the regular processes and procedures should be identified.

Thirdly, an *approach* or *methodology* has to be identified for successfully incorporating gender perspectives into these work-tasks in a manner which facilitates influencing goals, strategies, resource allocation and outcomes. Different strategies will be required for different types of activities, such as research and data collection, policy development, planning and implementation of programmes, training. These can include the systematic use of gender analysis, sex-disaggregation of data, and commissioning of sector-specific gender studies and surveys if necessary. Efforts to ensure equal representation of women are also important elements.

(c) *Institutional development*

Institutional development, in terms of clarifying roles and responsibilities, establishing accountability mechanisms, developing guidelines, utilizing gender specialists, providing competence development for all personnel, etc., is also required to support gender mainstreaming. Overall responsibility for implementing the mainstreaming strategy should rest at the highest levels within governments and other organizations. Management levels should be responsible for developing accountability mechanisms to monitor progress with mainstreaming. One means of ensuring accountability is to establish clear indicators of progress, which can be monitored over time by management.

(d) Assessing progress in gender mainstreaming

To monitor progress in implementation of gender mainstreaming within an organization, it is necessary to look at:

- The institutional environment, including structures, cultures, procedures and processes;

- The explicit attention to gender perspectives in the work programme – in all areas of the work of the organization;

- The extent to which progress is monitored and evaluated, through both regular and special processes, especially in relation to how the work of the organization impacts on the situation of women and men on the ground.

Some key elements which must be present in a conducive **institutional environment** include:

- Explicit elaboration of goals, strategies and expected outcomes in a *policy statement.*

- Explicit *management commitment* – promoting, demanding and monitoring attention to gender equality issues in the work programme.

- *Common understanding among staff* on what the organization should be seeking to achieve with respect to gender equality issues – the overall goals.

- Adequate understanding among staff, in relation to their specific areas of work, of the relevant gender perspectives – *how and why gender is a factor* which should be taken into account at policy and programme levels; the potential *entry-points in the work programme* – where and how gender perspectives can be given attention; and the *methods* required to address the gender perspectives identified.

- Perception of work with gender equality issues as a *professional responsibility* shared by all staff, and the knowledge and capacity required to address gender equality issues is seen as a professional competence in the organization.

- Inclusion of gender perspectives in *guidelines, manuals and management instructions* which guide the work of professional staff.

- Adequate access to *information resources and contacts (specialists),* both within and outside the organization, needed to work effectively with gender equality issues – knowing where to go for support.

- Explicit attention to the need to incorporate gender perspectives in work programmes in all *job descriptions* for staff and long-term consultants.

Elements required in relation to the work programme include, but are not limited to, the following:

- Gender perspectives are taken into account in *project planning processes*, including problem identification, data collection and consultation exercises as well as *implementation, monitoring and evaluation*.

- Efforts are made to increase the *participation of women*, alongside men, in decision-making processes.

- Statistics are *sex-disaggregated* and efforts are made to ensure that *collected data cover all issues of relevanc*e from a gender perspective.

- Gender perspectives are raised in *meetings, seminars and training.*

- *Reports and publications* incorporate gender perspectives as relevant.

- There is explicit reference in the *Terms of Reference* for all projects and consultant assignments to the need to incorporate gender perspectives in the work.

Critical elements in relation to *monitoring and evaluation* include the development and application of indicators of progress on gender mainstreaming, including indicators to measure the extent to which all the efforts of the organization are *contributing towards greater* equality between women and men.

Conclusion

In conclusion, I would like to emphasize that implementing the mainstreaming strategy at national level by Member States, and within the United Nations system, is one of the most important means to further the advancement of women. and promote gender equality throughout the world. Gender mainstreaming should be promoted both because it is a matter of equality and human rights and because it provides an important means of ensuring that development goals are achieved in an effective, sustainable and people-centred manner. Leaving out 50 per cent of the population – ignoring their contributions and neglecting their needs – can never be considered an effective strategy for sustainable development in any area.

SESSION 2:

ERADICATING POVERTY, INCLUDING THROUGH THE EMPOWERMENT OF WOMEN THROUGHOUT THEIR LIFE CYCLE IN A GLOBALIZING WORLD

Moderated by
Ms. Pawadee Tonguthai
Thai WomenWatch

In line with the forty-sixth session of the Commission on the Status of Women in March 2002, this session focused on the issue of gender mainstreaming in the efforts to alleviate poverty in the globalizing world. Ms. Rashmi Chowdhary of the Department of Women and Child Development of the Government of India, which had hosted the United Nations Expert Group Meeting in preparation for the CSW on the theme of "Eradicating poverty, including through the empowerment of women throughout their life cycle in a globalizing world", made a presentation on the deliberations at the EGM. Her presentation was followed by presentations from practical efforts on the ground by Mr. Salehuddin Ahmed, Bangladesh Rural Advancement Committee, Ms. Kalyani Menon-Sen, UNDP, India, and Ms. Wang Xinxia, Ministry of Foreign Affairs, China. A summary of the discussion based on the presentations in this session is available in the report of the symposium in Part II.

EMPOWERMENT OF WOMEN THROUGHOUT THE LIFE CYCLE AS A TRANSFORMATIVE STRATEGY FOR POVERTY ERADICATION: SUMMARY AND THE RECOMMENDATIONS OF THE UNITED NATIONS EXPERT GROUP MEETING

Ms. Rashmi Chowdhary
Deputy Secretary
Department of Women and Child Development, India

The Government of India has declared the year 2001 as Women's Empowerment Year, with the purpose of ensuring that women take their rightful place in the mainstream of the nation's social, political and economic life which should also lead to their improved well-being, equitable distribution of resources and a just social order.

Part I: United Nations Expert Group Meeting

The Commission on the Status of Women adopted a new programme of work in March 2001, with the eradication of poverty through empowerment of women as the first thematic issue of its next annual session. The first part of this presentation focuses on the summary and recommendations (see box) from the United Nations Expert Group Meeting

Box. United Nations Division for the Advancement of Women Expert Group Meeting on Empowerment of Women Throughout the Life Cycle as a Transformative Strategy for Poverty Eradication

The expert group meeting adopted the following recommendations:

A. Economic liberalization and poverty eradication

a. Undertake analysis of the impact of economic liberalization on women living in poverty based on region-specific data and information disaggregated by sex and age.

b. Review macroeconomic policies and strategies for financing development to incorporate the objectives of gender equality and empowerment of women.

c. Identify ways and means to increase the participation of women in the norm setting and decision-making processes regarding macroeconomic issues, including the areas of trade, finance and investment.

d. Acknowledge that women have emerged as major bread-winners in many countries and support them in these roles by ensuring that financial and trade liberalization and economic policies do not undermine women's choices to engage in gainful employment under conditions and on terms that enhance their capabilities, self-respect and dignity.

e. Monitor the quality of employment, as well as wage levels, gender gaps in wages, health and safety standards at work, skill creation, retraining and social insurance in order to promote the well-being of women.

f. Conduct sectoral analyses within the context of trade liberalization, including in goods, services, intellectual property rights, the environment, competition, investments in order to identify any possible effects on the livelihoods and prospects of empowerment for poor women.

g. Integrate market assessment and outreach as an integral part of livelihood interventions for effective income generation and poverty eradication among women.

h. Provide assistance to women's groups, which are often marginalized within larger social movements engaged in the processes of economic liberalization, to facilitate the analysis, formulation, implementation and monitoring of economic liberalization policies and programmes, with a view to ensuring that such policies are gender-sensitive and have greater potential to reduce poverty among women engaged in both formal and informal employment.

i. Inform women's groups and individual women about the internal functioning of all markets (including labour markets) as well as the international trade regime through organizing economic literacy training in relevant areas.

j. Improve poor women's access to productive resources such as land, credit, technology and marketing techniques to facilitate their entry into viable self-employment opportunities that can provide a decent standard of living for themselves and their dependents.

k. Promote partnership between the private sector and women entrepreneurs in order to enhance their ability to market their products and improve their economic opportunities.

20

l. Identify and address the gendered dimensions in existing and new trade agreements to facilitate the eradication of poverty while promoting both economic growth and social development goals.

m. Work with relevant United Nations agencies and regional and national institutions to assist the members of the WTO to clarify those aspects of the new trade agreements that may marginalize poor women as workers and negatively affect their livelihood strategies. For example, Article I: 3 (ii) c of the GATS, may be harmful to the livelihood strategies of women and their families living in poverty because it impacts on the provision and distribution of health services to poor women, and may result in the increase in prices for specific services.

n. Encourage, through appropriate economic and social policies, the balanced distribution of the gains from trade liberalization including through taxes, employment and re-training programmes.

o. Encourage developed countries to share the burden of poverty eradication in the developing world, including through the provision of international public goods.

p. Ensure that the design and implementation of taxation policies do not disproportionately affect women, especially women in poverty, by, *inter alia*, increasing the participation of women in these processes.

q. Ensure the mainstreaming of a gender perspective into decisions and agreements emanating from the forthcoming International Conference on Financing for Development (in Mexico, March 2002) regarding the mobilization of financial resources for development, private and public, domestic and international.

r. Regulate short-term capital flows to protect the livelihood strategies of poor women and men taking into account the adverse social and economic effects of financial liberalization.

s. Intensify efforts to reflect women's unpaid work in households in national statistics and in poverty eradication policy formulation, implementation and monitoring, and ensure that the design and implementation of strategies for financing development recognize unpaid work.

B. Social policy within the context of globalization

Reinforce the role of the national and local government as actors in production and delivery of adequate and affordable social services for women and women in poverty, especially in such areas as health, education, child and elderly care and access to water and sanitation.

Education and training

a. Extend and expand educational programmes to include girls and women of all ages who have been excluded from education during their childhood and adolescence, recognizing that adult literacy, non-formal education, awareness building and skills training are some of the ways to ensure empowerment of poor women to participate in the labour market.

b. Undertake analysis of the impact of economic liberalization on women living in poverty based on region-specific data and information disaggregated by sex and age.

c. Develop educational and training policies and programmes to enhance the capabilities of girls and women through formal and non-formal education, and ensure that these policies and programmes aim at breaking the gender-stereotyped provision of knowledge and skills and promote images of women and girls in positions of power, value, prestige and public presence.

d. Identify and strengthen training and re-training, as well as vocational education in non-traditional areas to expand women's employment opportunities with empowering implications, and promote vocational training in sectors with growth potential, especially for young women.

Health

a. Recognize the close link between health and poverty, and ensure that effective, accessible and appropriate health services are available to women in poverty.

b. Adopt a holistic life cycle approach to the design and implementation of health policies and programmes and ensure that issues, such as tuberculosis and HIV/AIDS are not addressed in an isolated way.

c. Design and implement health programmes, specifically those concerning reproductive health and reproductive rights, in partnership with civil society.

d. Guarantee the provisioning of free and universal basic health and nutritional services, including health and nutrition education, in partnership with NGOs and other civil society organizations throughout the entire life cycle of women.

e. Ensure that any genuinely empowering social and economic policy for women contains the basic, minimum, bodily demands for women's nutritional well-being, and meet any absolute calorific gap amongst adolescent girls and women through direct state provisioning of supplemental feeding, and especially through initiating core feeding programmes.

f. Consider the right to bodily safety and physical privacy of women as an inalienable and fundamental right of special importance to poor women and promote adequate sanitary facilities and basic physical infrastructure for women and allocate adequate resources to that end.

Older women

Design and implement policies and programmes for active ageing that ensure economic independence and social security, equality and participation of older women, especially older women in poverty.

Social security

a. Shift from residual and crisis related safety nets to the development of permanent and sustainable social security systems through the different stages of the life cycle of women, especially in developing countries.

b. Increase the role of the state in the design, implementation and monitoring of more progressive social policies and gender-sensitive social policy models concerning poverty eradication, including social protection.

c. Strengthen the proactive role of the government and its collaboration with civil society, including women's NGOs, working women's forums, in providing appropriate social security systems that reduce risks throughout the life cycle of poor women, including the provision of unemployment insurance when wage labour and public works programmes are insufficient.

d. Review the macroeconomic policy approach to full employment as the sole basis for state-based entitlements and extend entitlements to those who are engaged in informal or part-time work as well as for the providers of unpaid caring work.

Caring services

Promote, including through education and mass media, the notion of equal sharing of family responsibilities between women and men and provide extensive, affordable and quality social services such as day care facilities, pre-school day care facilities, static and mobile crèches etc. to allow both women and men, especially in poverty, to utilize their employment opportunities and build their capacities.

C. Microcredit and microfinance

a. Review all types of microcredit and microfinance programmes to determine whether these programmes enhance women's capabilities, status, bargaining power and promote their empowerment, and ensure that these programmes do not reinforce women's traditional roles within households and communities.

b. Develop microcredit and microfinance programmes that effectively reach the poorest and most vulnerable of the poor women.

c. Go beyond microcredit and microfinance policies and programmes to develop various comprehensive strategies to better address the needs of diverse groups of women in poverty, and ensure that these strategies assist women in the building of their own assets (savings, land) and strengthen social insurance, especially during economic shocks and adversities.

D. Empowerment of women as a transformative strategy for poverty eradication

a. Review existing poverty eradication policy frameworks and strategies from a gender perspective and incorporate an empowerment approach.

b. Evaluate poverty eradication policies and programmes in terms of their impact on the economic, social and political empowerment of women throughout their life cycle.

c. Ensure that poverty eradication policies and programmes combine an empowerment approach with gender mainstreaming initiatives and are explicit about the meaning of empowerment in the particular context.

d. Implement a bottom-up approach to poverty eradication policies and strategies to ensure women's ownership of poverty eradication initiatives and their involvement at all stages of decision-making by enhancing women's capacities through, *inter alia,* economic and political literacy training, mass media and new information and communication technologies.

e. Identify and address, through designing and implementing policies and programmes, the factors inhibiting women's empowerment such as violence, lack of resources, lack of access to information, traditional norms and attitudes negative to gender equality, and discriminatory laws and practices.

f. Design and implement awareness raising campaigns regarding gender equality and women's empowerment at the national, local and household levels targeting all sections of the population.

g. Make existing institutions and mechanisms more accessible to poor and marginalized women through e.g. adjusting meeting hours and venues.

h. Explore the potential of women's informal associations, enhance their capacity to strengthen women's subjective sense of empowerment and the objective access they have to a diversity of resources and decision-making.

i. Design and implement new models for organizing women around livelihood strategies, in particular in the countries where women are more restricted culturally.

j. Promote the context-specific and culturally sensitive agendas for women's empowerment.

k. Intensify dialogue among all actors, including government, development agencies and civil society, to develop and implement concrete and successful methods and approaches for changing attitudes and norms detrimental to women's empowerment and gender equality, and design methods for facilitating the empowerment of women.

E. Measurement of poverty and empowerment of women

a. Collect, compile and disseminate timely and reliable data disaggregated by sex and age to assess and monitor poverty among women and men.

b. Create national and international databases on essential sex disaggregated indicators to evaluate and monitor poverty among women, including income poverty and human poverty, to facilitate the formulation of more successful gender-sensitive poverty eradication strategies.

c. Encourage and support the work to develop quantitative and qualitative indicators to measure poverty among women and men throughout their life cycles, and to monitor the impact of poverty eradication policies and programmes on both women and men.

d. Develop methods and indicators to measure progress in terms of empowerment of women that are both qualitative and quantitative, both context and culturally specific and universal, and cover both process and impact, and determine the correlation between women's empowerment and poverty eradication.

F. Governance and women's participation

a. Develop or strengthen the mechanisms facilitating women's full and equal involvement in decision-making processes at all levels and in all areas, that affect their life chances, choices and opportunities throughout their life cycle.

b. Engage women and women's groups in global, national and local governance processes and mechanisms through building new alliances and partnerships, especially with men, trade unions, alternative trade groups, etc. and facilitate this process by providing necessary resources, assistance and information.

c. Ensure women's efficient engagement in social and economic decision making through organizing economic literacy training, providing access to mass media and new information and communication technologies.

d. Undertake, if necessary, affirmative actions to ensure equal participation of women in decision-making processes at all levels and areas.

e. Identify and implement measures to increase the participation of women in the conceptualization, design, implementation and evaluation of poverty eradication programmes and policies.

f. Strengthen national capacities of governments, in particular those promoting gender equality and the empowerment of women, to address effectively women's empowerment and poverty eradication concerns in policy analysis and dialogue at local, national and global levels.

g. Mobilize and allocate public resources to meet the social and economic needs of both women and men, especially those in poverty, and ensure that the design and implementation of all budgetary processes promote women's economic opportunities and equal access to productive resources and address the basic needs of women, especially those living in poverty.

h. Ensure that gender budget initiatives take account of the contributions made by the care, or reproductive economy, to the nation's economic output.

i. Strengthen economic and financial governance and promote accountability and equality through the implementation of gender-responsive budget initiatives at the national and local levels.

j. Conduct gender analysis of sectoral funds allocations, tax policies, labour and industrial policies, as well as other tools of fiscal and macroeconomic policy, in collaboration with researchers and women's NGOs.

k. Establish appropriate mechanisms to monitor gender-sensitive allocations and policies and to ensure their implementation, including in the Ministries of Finance, Budget Management Offices and other financial structures.

l. Organize regular and comprehensive impact assessments of empowerment policies and programmes, in particular for poverty eradication.

m. Empower women by allocating and mobilizing domestic resources to support microfinance programmes that provide poor women with the requisite credit, knowledge and tools to enhance their economic capacities, and to promote the establishment of reliable, convenient savings, insurance and remittance facilities that serve the financial needs of women, especially from poor households.

on Empowerment of Women throughout the Life Cycle as a Transformative Strategy for Poverty Eradication, which India hosted from 26 to 29 November 2001. The findings and conclusions of the expert group meeting would be the basis for preparation of the report of the United Nations Secretary-General to the Commission on the Status of Women. It was an honour for India that the expert group meeting on this critical issue was held in India in the Year of Women's Empowerment. The second part focuses on poverty eradication efforts in India.

Part II: An Indian perspective

The principle of gender equality is enshrined in the Indian Constitution, which not only grants equality to women but also empowers the State to adopt measures of positive discrimination in favour of women. The Committee on the Status of Women was created in 1971 to comprehensively examine all questions relating to the rights and status of women. The Committee pointed out that gender, class, and urban bias was marginalizing a large majority of women in the economy and leading to their neglect and devaluation by the society and the State, and that the Indian development plans had to adequately acknowledge the involvement of millions of women in the major sectors of the economy.

The Department of Women and Child Development was established in 1985 under a Minister accountable to Parliament. As the national machinery for the advancement of women and children, the Department formulates plans, policies and programmes; enacts and amends legislation; guides and coordinates the efforts of governmental organizations (GOs) and NGOs; and implements innovative programmes in such areas as welfare and support services, training for employment and income generation, and awareness generation and gender sensitization. It developed a *National Perspective Plan for Women* (1988-2000) for economic development and integration of women into the mainstream of the economy, equity and social justice. These and other efforts led to identifying operational tools for gender mainstreaming, including:

- Gender Focal Points: Establishing cells within sectoral development planning agencies.

- Women's Component Plan: Earmarking a share (a minimum of 30 per cent of the development funds) for women in various sectoral allocations. 18 Ministries and Departments are obliged to identify and allocate a separate budget for women in all their programmes and to follow this up by monitoring and review.

- Promoting women's organizations at the grass-roots.

That empowered women are agents for social change and development are recognized in the Ninth Five-Year Plan (1997-2002), which incorporates these strategies, signifying a shift in perspective from a women in development approach to a gender approach.

Strategies for eradication of poverty in India

Over the period from 1951 to 2001, there has been a steady decline in the number of people living in absolute poverty from around 43 to 26 per cent. Because of the sheer size of the population, 26 per cent still translates into a large number, but the observed decline shows that various poverty eradication efforts have been paying off. Among the efforts, the State policy to eradicate poverty includes the following components: economic growth, land reforms, basic minimum services, public distribution system and employment generation. The employment generation component contains wage-employment and self-employment; employment schemes for the unemployed, and creation of rural economic infrastructure, training and capacity building and provision of microcredit.

UNITED NATIONS

ECONOMIC AND SOCIAL COMMISSION FOR ASIA AND THE PACIFIC

READERSHIP SURVEY

We are conducting a survey on the usefulness of the publication titled **"Putting Gender Mainstreaming into Practice"** (ST/ESCAP/2254).

Please complete this questionnaire within two weeks of receipt of this publication and send it to us, by air mail (or fax), at the following address: ***Director, Emerging Social Issues Division, UNESCAP, United Nations Building, Rajadamnern Nok Avenue, Bangkok 10200, Thailand. Fax: (662) 288-1018.***

QUESTIONNAIRE

1. Please circle your rating of the quality of the publication on:	Excellent	Very good	Average	Poor	Very poor
(a) Presentation/format	5	4	3	2	1
(b) Readability	5	4	3	2	1
(c) Timeliness of information	5	4	3	2	1
(d) Coverage of subject-matter	5	4	3	2	1
(e) Analytical rigour	5	4	3	2	1
(f) Overall quality	5	4	3	2	1

2. Please circle your rating of the usefulness of the publication on:	Very useful	Quite useful	Useful	Nearly useful	Not useful
(a) Information	5	4	3	2	1
(b) Identification of issues	5	4	3	2	1
(c) Findings	5	4	3	2	1
(d) Recommendations	5	4	3	2	1
(e) Overall quality	5	4	3	2	1

3. Comments on the issues covered in the publication

....
....
....
....

4. Suggestions for improvement of the publication

....
....
....
....

Your name: _____

Affiliation: _____

Mailing address: _____

■ *Thank you for your kind cooperation in completing and returning this questionnaire to us.* ■

Readership Survey [ST/ESCAP/2254]

Director

Emerging Social Issues Division
UNESCAP, United Nations Building
Rajadamnern Nok Avenue
Bangkok 10200
Thailand

Gender dimensions of poverty

Women suffer from the double burden of discrimination and insufficient income. For Indian women, human poverty, especially due to the stark and revealing discrimination against women, is much more serious than income poverty. Although the lack of sex-disaggregated data, especially poverty data, is a problem that accentuates the real problem of female poverty, micro studies show that 70 per cent of the people living below the poverty line are female and that 30 per cent of rural households are female-headed.

As to the impacts of globalization, it is true in India as elsewhere that globalization has created new and non-traditional jobs, such as agro-exports, apparel, electronics. However, again like elsewhere, globalization is also accompanied by a reduction in traditional sector employment, which, in combination with the absence of safety nets, can lead to pauperization. Globalization has also brought about depletion of the depository of women's indigenous knowledge systems.

There is no national level data or analysis of the net effect of globalization. The available findings and data are based on micro studies, which show that women have been displaced from traditional occupations. A project supported by ILO conducted more macro-oriented studies but were concentrated on a few areas. A more comprehensive exercise at the national level to find out the effect is necessary.

New initiatives to address women's human poverty

Although it is often argued that globalization would also cause a decline of the welfare state, social sector expenditure has not declined in India after structural adjustment programmes (SAP). Rather, India initiated several new India-based nationwide programmes during this period: such as, Universal Elementary Education, Integrated Child Development Services, Reproductive and Child Health, Integrated Women's Empowerment Programme (IWEP), and National Nutritional Mission. These programmes have been initiated with substantive allocations of funds. With these allocations made in the budget, the basic problem is with the utilization of allocations. In another words, this is an issue of governance and implementation

Among the new initiatives, three made really significant impacts: (1) Decentralization of power and resources to elected women representatives; (2) Voluntary sector involvement; and (3) Self Help Group (SHG) movement. The 1993 Amendments to the Indian Constitution provide for reservation of one third of elected seats for women at different levels of local governance in both rural and urban areas. Women have captured seats of power in local governance in large numbers, often exceeding the reserved quotas, with significant impacts.

The SHGs movement of women in India is a silent revolution that is slowly but steadily changing the landscapes of many parts of the country. Small SHGs have proven an effective strategy for empowering women, and are the principal and most successful strategy in poverty alleviation, driven by their realization that the initiative to utilize and seek State resources and services for their own progress is primarily their prerogative. Across the country, more than 700,000 groups work on a range of issues such as literacy, health, nutrition, agricultural extension services, forestry, in addition to undertaking income-generation activities and accessing microcredit. IWEP mentioned above has 53,000 SHGs at the base of the structural pyramid, with 26,500 Village Societies and 650 Block Societies above, and benefits 930,000 women. As an important strategy of eradicating poverty among women, these groups are engaged in issues relating to health, education, employment, and others; network with each other and attain confidence and negotiation skills; learn to design activities for their own benefit; and monitor and evaluate activities through a participatory process. As the end result, we would like to see poor women empowered to access assets and resources.

Over the past five decades, multisectoral interventions have brought about perceptible improvement in the status of women and increasing awareness on gender issues. However, certain grey areas remain: violence against women, the unfavourable sex ratio, and a lack of attention to the contribution of women farm workers and homemakers. Developing and establishing systems to collect and analyse data, disaggregated by sex, age, and location is a priority concern. Resource mobilization in the national budget is crucial for sustaining and expanding the efforts for gender equality. Greater efforts will also be needed to sensitize policy makers so that gender impact analysis is incorporated into the development of economic and social policies.

* * *

POVERTY ALLEVIATION AND EMPOWERMENT OF WOMEN: THE BRAC EXPERIENCE

Mr. Salehuddin Ahmed
Deputy Executive Director

Mr. Mohammad Rafi
Senior Research Sociologist
Bangladesh Rural Advancement Committee (BRAC)

Gender is socially constructed roles ascribed to males and females. These roles, as learnt, change over time and vary widely within and between cultures. Gender is also a socially constructed definition of the relationship between the sexes and contains an unequal power relationship with male domination and female subordination in most spheres of life. Men and the tasks, roles, functions and values attributed to them are valued higher than women and what is associated with them. It is increasingly recognized that society is characterized by male bias: the male norm is taken as the norm for the society as a whole, which is reflected in policies and structures, and that such gender inequality is widely prevalent in many societies. It often happens that gender inequality is unintentionally reproduced through policies and structures. As a strategy to attain gender equality, therefore, mainstreaming of gender perspectives in policies and structures was proposed.

Gender equality has both quantitative and qualitative aspects. The quantitative aspect implies an equal distribution of women and men in all areas of the society, such as education, work, recreation, and position of power. The qualitative aspect implies that the knowledge, experiences and values of both women and men are given equal weight and used to enrich and direct all social areas and endeavours.

Gender mainstreaming is a strategy for making women's as well as men's concerns and experiences an integral dimension of the design, implementation, monitoring and evaluation of policies and programmes in all political, economic and societal spheres, so that women and men benefit equally, while preventing inequality from being reproduced. The ultimate goal of gender mainstreaming in simple term is the achievement of gender equality.

Bangladesh

Bangladesh won a hard-fought victory to become an independent nation in 1971. At its independence, the country's economy and basic infrastructure had been devastated. However over the decades there have been many positive changes. Between 1975 and 1992 food production almost doubled;[4] life expectancy increased by 30 per cent between 1970 and 1996; and under-five mortality rate decreased by 55 per cent between 1960 and 1996.[5] Bangladesh also achieved impressive results in many other fields. The contraceptive prevalence rate has risen to nearly 50 per cent from under 10 per cent in the mid-1970s, and total fertility rate declined from over 6 in the 1970s to 3.2 in the late 1990s. Net enrolment in primary schools increased to 77 per cent.[6] The percentage of poor households identified by their calorie intake declined from 63 in 1983 to 47 per cent in 1995.[7]

In spite of these achievements, considerable gender inequalities still exist. NGOs like BRAC cannot be indifferent to gender inequalities and are making serious efforts in gender mainstreaming in the development efforts.

Bangladesh Rural Advancement Committee

BRAC has evolved over time in its effort to become more effective in achieving its development objectives. BRAC started its journey in 1972, just after the liberation of Bangladesh, as a relief organization to help refugees returning from India to their homes in Sulla, a remote and inaccessible village at the northeastern border. Shortly thereafter, it adopted the community development approach in order to have a sustainable impact. Finding the outcome of that approach unsatisfactory, in 1976 BRAC adopted the target group approach to development. In this approach, BRAC works with households that have less than half-an-acre of land and at least one of their members selling manual labour for not less than 100 days a year as the targets of development efforts.

---

[4] Government of Bangladesh 1996, *Food and Agriculture in Rural Bangladesh.* Country position paper presented at the World Food Summit, Italy.

[5] UNICEF 1998. *State of the World's Children* 1998. Oxford: Oxford University Press.

[6] Chowdhury A.M.R. 1999. "Success with the DOTS strategy". *Lancet*, 353:1003.

[7] Bangladesh Bureau of Statistics 1997. *Bangladesh Household Expenditure Survey 1995-96,* Dhaka.

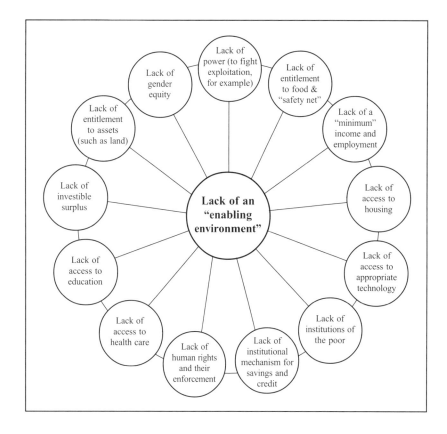

The twin objectives of BRAC are poverty alleviation and empowerment of the poor. BRAC works particularly with women and poorer families whose lives are dominated by extreme poverty, illiteracy, disease and malnutrition. Although the emphasis of BRAC's work is at the personal and village levels, the sustenance of development depends heavily on a pro-poor policy environment and BRAC is committed to playing a role at the policy level through its research and advocacy work, working in partnership with like-minded organizations, governmental and donors to achieve its ends.

To alleviate poverty BRAC takes a holistic approach, whereby poverty is defined as not merely a lack of income or employment but also a complex syndrome, with many different manifestations. As expressed by Amartya Sen (1995), "The point is not the irrelevance of economic variables such as personal incomes, but their severe inadequacy in capturing many of the causal influences on the quality of life and the survival chances of people".[8] To empower the poor BRAC premises that every person, regardless of wealth or sex, is capable of improving one's destiny if given the right opportunity. BRAC believes in the creativity of the poor.

BRAC therefore strives to create opportunities for the target group to improve their conditions. Such creations in term of the target group are divided into three overlapping categories by BRAC: "conscientization", utilization of material resources, and capacity development to make good use of the resources.

BRAC also works to develop institution of the poor: conscientization, health, gender equity, training and so on. Central to these activities is the creation of an "enabling environment" in which the poor can participate in their own development and perform to their fullest potentials. All of BRAC's efforts are geared to creating such an environment.

---

8 Sen, A. 1995. "Mortality as an indicator of economic success and failure", Paper 66, London School of Economics, Development Economics Research Programme.

Different from many existing institutions at the village and the national levels, which have been controlled by the traditional power elite and none of which voiced the needs or opinions of the poor, BRAC has been trying to create new organizations of the poor for the poor to cater to the need of its members.

The nuclei for all BRAC development activities for the poor is the Village Organization (VO). A VO consists of 35-40 female members and has Management, Social action and Law implementation committees to conduct its activities. Through VO the target group plans, initiates, manages and controls group activities, both in social and economic domains. BRAC assists VOs by providing them with training, credit and logistics support. Presently BRAC has 4.3 million members, of which 95 per cent are female, forming 109,135 VOs in 70 per cent of the villages throughout the country.

BRAC Programmes

The major development interventions of BRAC are performed in three broad areas – poverty reduction, health care, education and capacity building. Accordingly development programmes have been set in these areas to empower the poor especially women and children. The following and other programmes of BRAC are implemented in partnership with the national government.

BRAC Development Programme (BDP) is operated based on the belief that microcredit can play a pivotal role in improving life and in reducing poverty. BDP provides collateral-free loans to its VO members to develop their income-generating capacities. BRAC has so far disbursed to its 4 million female members US$ 1.31 billion (Tk 6,197 crore) in loans. A part of this microfinance programme is the savings accumulated by the members, which is an important service in its own right. As of June 2001, the members had saved US$ 7.4 million (Tk 397 crore). BDP has a number of income-generating programmes encouraging VO members to engage in six major income-generating activities (IGAs): namely, sericulture, poultry, livestock, agriculture, social forestry and fisheries. These are the sectors where VO members may make productive use of BRAC loans. Some examples of unconventional IGAs that VO members are involved are restaurants, grocery stores, tailoring shops, and laundry shops. BDP provides back-up services for these activities with training and technical and management support mainly through BRAC staff and paraprofessional workers.

BDP also organizes a social development programme, which is to develop the inherent skills of VO members to resolve their day to day problems and to enable them to take charge of their lives. The Programme includes Human Rights and Legal Education (HRLE), Community Leaders' Workshop and Popular Theatre contributing to knowledge, conscientization and awareness building of the members. HRLE is the most important of these social development activities. The goal of HRLE is to empower VO members through educating them on human rights and on some essential laws.

Given the urgent needs of the poor in Bangladesh, however, BRAC felt that credit without education was insufficient. In 1985 BRAC initiated a Non-Formal Primary Education (NFPE) programme under the supervision of BRAC Education Programme

(BEP). The students in these schools came from the target group and other poor households and had either never been to school or dropped out before acquiring any meaningful education. Presently BEP has a large number of schools of various types (for example, NFPE, pre-primary school, community primary school, hard-to-reach school) and libraries in villages throughout Bangladesh. With 34,000 schools and over 1.1 million enrolments BEP is the largest private primary education programme in the world. The schools are operated by 34,000 teachers overwhelmingly representing the target group and have been trained in teaching at these schools by BRAC. About 70 per cent of the students and 75 per cent of the teachers are female. Over two million students have already graduated; 90 per cent of them have moved to formal schools at higher levels.

BRAC also realized that development programmes could not achieve their intended goals without ensuring that basic health needs of the community were met, leading to the introduction of the Health, Nutrition and Population Programme (HNPP). The Programme empowers women by teaching them how to engage in health-care activities and provides essential health care, family planning, reproductive health and diseases control services to the poor. HNPP also endeavours to improve health and nutritional status of women and children by offering integrated maternal and child health services. The programme serves 31 million people in 33,116 villages. The programme has 106,753 female health para-professionals from VOs who were trained in health to assist the poor in their localities.

Responsiveness to need of the rural poor

In recognition of the importance in achieving its objectives of capacity building of both BRAC staff and VO members, BRAC established the BRAC Training Division (BTD). The primary objective of BTD is to enhance the knowledge, skills and attitudes of the staff and VO members. BTD employs 150 trainers who provide training at 12 residential Training and Resource Centres and two Centres for Development Management created in different locations throughout Bangladesh.

BTD offers three types of human development courses:

- *Skills development training* to enhance the capacity and skills of the members so that they can manage their development enterprises more effectively and efficiently. Poultry and livestock are the most important of these training. By the end of 2000 a total of 106,604 VO members had received a variety of poultry and livestock training.

- *Awareness building training* to make members more knowledgeable and conscious about the social environment which they live in and to enable them to combat certain social problems they often face. These training are directed towards social mobilization of VO members. HRLE is the most important of these training. As of 2001, a total of 197,229,901 VO members have received this training.

- *Management training* to facilitate the members to run their VO more effectively. The training is offered primarily to the VO management committee members.

BTD contributes to the human resource development of the members mostly by training a cadre of paraprofessionals who in turn train other members in their locality. This cascade method of training allows the dissemination of training to a larger number of members within a shorter period of time. At the bottom of this cascade of training are the overwhelming majority of the female poor targeted for empowerment and poverty alleviation.

Besides the BTD training, the members also have other venues for capacity development. The VO as part of their routine activities holds weekly and monthly meetings. In monthly meetings local problems and their solutions are discussed. BRAC staff routinely informs them about the technical know-how which they can apply in their development initiatives and opportunities within the reach that they may avail for development. The meeting empowers the members with knowledge that is very much needed. In the weekly meetings members share experiences and knowledge related to development projects they are involved in. It is both formal and informal knowledge gaining process for the members. The training and meetings, in fact, build the knowledge and skills of the members as required for development.

Gender quality action learning

Presently BRAC has 25,378 full-time workers, of which 27 per cent are female. BRAC's expansion, together with its interest in recruiting more women staff and its commitment to women's empowerment, pose considerable challenges organizationally and programmatically. In early 1990s BRAC developed specific policies in response to women's staff-related issues and problems as they came up. The policy shortly resulted in the formation of a Women's Advisory Committee to advise on women's staff issues and staff gender training programme.

In 1995 BTD developed the Gender Quality Action Learning (GQAL) programme and has been implementing it across BRAC. The goal of the GQAL programme is to improve gender relations within the organization and to improve programmes with gender related issues among the poor. Underlying this approach is the need for BRAC to build an organizational culture, which will attract and retain highly skilled and dedicated women and men staff and allow them to become most productive.

A large number of staff is involved in a process of defining gender and organizational change issues in three areas: individual attitudes and behaviour, programmatic outcomes and organizational systems. GQAL programme has imparted training to 15,000 regular BRAC employees. It is important to note that some changes were already underway.

Promotion of women in the development process

From its very inception, BRAC has been sensitive to the question of gender equity. All efforts, be they in credit, children's education or health, are designed to benefit women thereby reducing the gender gap in the society. Women who have been empowered now exercise greater influence and control than before within and outside their households.

BRAC has been promoting a new culture in the development field with women in the forefront of all activities. Breaking the barrier of a predominantly conservative traditional Muslim society, BRAC has even succeeded in training female workers to use motorbikes in performing their duties. Women are now running rural restaurants, vaccinating chicks, treating patients, doing carpentry, teaching, studying in schools – occupations and activities that traditionally fell in the male domain.

In a recent study on the impact of BRAC programmes on gender relations, members and their husbands were interviewed to understand the changes that may or may not have happened in the lives of the women. The following comment of the husband of a VO member gives an idea of the impact that the programme is having on women's control over resources.

> *My wife has the right to buy toiletries and cosmetic jewellery of her own from the income of her loan, even though it is utilized by me. Last month she bought a cooking pot which cost Tk 80. She said that it was essential for her kitchen. I do not argue with her about this necessity. But she would not have done this before receiving loans.*[9]

Hashemi et al.[10] found that 60 per cent of borrowers in new BRAC villages had "full" control over their enterprises.

Change in the status of women in the eyes of the greater community has been rather slow. However, the following comments by a group of VO members reveal a beginning of important changes:

> *In the past we used to sit on the ground, with other poor people. And now we are offered to sit on the bench. We don't have active participation in Shalish (village court), but we can make plea against the decision if it is taken wrongly.*[11]

These changes are not without backlash from the vested groups. BRAC has managed to take effective measures against these obstacles and so far came out winner. The efforts for poverty alleviation and empowerment complement each other. BRAC believes that poverty cannot be eradicated without reconstructing existing gender roles in the society. The empowerment of women is a necessary precondition for sustainable poverty alleviation. Underneath the objectives of BRAC lies the motive of gender mainstreaming. Given the situation in Bangladesh the mainstreaming effort is directed towards elevating all round positions of women and make them equal to those of male counterparts.

* * *

---

[9] Mustafa, S. L., Ara, D. Banu, A. Hossain, A. Kabir, M. Mohsin, A. Yusuf and S. Jahan 1996. *Beacon of Hope: An Impact Assessment Study of BRAC's Rural Development Program.* Dhaka: BRAC.

[10] Hashemi, S.M. S.R. Schuler and A.P. Riley 1996. "Rural Credit Programme and Women's Empowerment". *World Development.* 24:635-653.

[11] Mustafa et al. 1996.

BEYOND THE FEMINIZATION OF POVERTY

Ms. Kalyani Menon-Sen

Gender Advisor
United Nations Development Programme, India

Since the Beijing Conference in 1995, the notion of the "feminization of poverty" has almost attained the status of development dogma, leading to the centre-staging of women's empowerment as an essential element in national strategies for poverty reduction. This recognition is often based on an understanding that women are disproportionately represented among the poor, and constitute the majority of the "poorest of the poor" category.

In India, for instance, this argument is a central element of the National Policy for Empowerment of Women, as in the following:

Since women comprise the majority of the population below the poverty line and are very often in situations of extreme poverty, given the harsh realities of intra-household and social discrimination, macroeconomic policies and poverty eradication programmes will specifically address the needs and problems of such women. There will be improved implementation of programmes that are already women oriented with special targets for women. Steps will be taken for mobilization of poor women and convergence of services, by offering them a range of economic and social options, along with necessary support measures to enhance their capabilities.[12]

At one level, this might seem like a validation of efforts by Indian women's movements to draw attention to the needs and priorities of poor women. Ironically, however, the strongest criticism of these policy responses to women's poverty has come from women's movements themselves. The critique is two-fold: first, that most of these policies and programmes are premised on a simplistic and mechanical understanding of empowerment and second, that they are based on an inadequate and inappropriate understanding of poverty.

Empowerment: complex and non-linear

The understanding of women's empowerment that emerged from women's movements is rooted in the lived realities of millions of women, and reflects a complex and multi-layered process. Most feminist writings speak of empowerment as a process of challenging existing power relations, and of gaining greater control over the sources of power. Batliwala defines empowerment as "... a process which must enable women to discover new possibilities, new options ... to independently struggle for changes in their material conditions of existence, their personal lives and their treatment in the public sphere".[13] Village-level activists of the Mahila Samakhya programme refer to the process of

---

[12] Department of Women and Child Development, Ministry of Human Resource Development, Government of India. 2001. "National Policy for the Empowerment of Women".

[13] Batliwala, Srilatha. 1993 "Empowerment of women in South Asia: Concepts and Practices". FAO-Freedom From Hunger Campaign, New Delhi.

empowerment as a *"jalebi"*,[14] a twisted circle that sometimes turns in on itself. Kabeer categorizes empowerment as "power to" make one's own decisions; "power over", or the capacity and freedom to put issues on the agenda; "power within", or the awareness that an issue is an issue and "power with", that comes from uniting with others for collective action.[15]

By contrast, government programmes appear to be premised on a simplistic view of women's empowerment that equates it primarily, or solely, to economic empowerment. Even if policy documents speak of empowerment as a process of acquiring rights and choices, programmes focus exclusively on increases in income. Thus, the major national projects for women's empowerment under the Department of Women and Child Development are based on the formation of women's self-help groups. To quote one of these documents:

> *Self Help Groups (SHGs) of women in India have been recognized as an effective strategy for the empowerment of women in rural as well as urban areas: bringing women together from all spheres of life to fight for their rights or a cause. Since the overall empowerment of women is crucially dependent on economic empowerment, women through these SHGs work on a range of issues such as health, nutrition, agriculture, forestry, etc. besides income-generation activities and seeking microcredit.*[16]

Despite the reference to other issues, the focus in implementation of programmes that purport to combine women's empowerment and poverty alleviation is on promoting savings and credit for women to take up microenterprises. These programmes are also monitored exclusively on economic criteria.

Anti-poverty programmes: women fall through the gaps

A gendered analysis of mainstream approaches to poverty alleviation and gender equality reveals few indications of erosion in the barriers that keep poverty issues separate from wider gender equality concerns. At the national level, a "two-track approach" to development is still evident, with economic policies and social policies proceeding on separate tracks. As the UNDP Poverty Report 2000 points out,[17] these tracks rarely intersect and it is usually women who fall into the gaps between them.

This divergence between economic and social priorities is clearly visible in the design of many anti-poverty programmes. These programmes are premised on an income-focused view of poverty rather than the notion of human poverty, where poverty is defined not only

---

[14] An Indian sweetmeat of a convoluted shape.

[15] Kabeer, Naila. 1994. "Reversed Realities: Gender Hierarchies in development Thought". Kali for Women, New Delhi.

[16] Information brochure on Women Empowerment Project. 2001. Government of India.

[17] UNDP Poverty Report 2000. (op. cit.)

in terms of reduced access to resources but as denial of choices and opportunities. The bulk of resources under anti-poverty programmes are devoted to individual or family-based economic initiatives for families below the poverty line. Even where these have led to income increases for target groups, they have not always translated into equitable improvements in non-income parameters of human development.

For instance, there are practically no rigorous studies of changes in the income and expenditure patterns of SHG members before and after they took up economic activities using microcredit. Similarly, there are very few studies that explore the extent to which microfinance programmes have been able to facilitate non-economic dimensions of empowerment for women members of SHGs. The success of microcredit programmes, for both government and NGOs, is gauged by the amount of money saved, the size and frequency of loans and the rate of loan repayment, rather than by the extent to which the economic environment has changed or which the exploitation of women has been reduced.

In particular, poverty alleviation programmes have proved inadequate to address situations where multiple vulnerabilities exist within a group. During the last decade, it has become increasingly clear that certain categories of poor people have been consistently marginalized. These include women, landless agricultural workers, tribal communities, people with disabilities, bonded and child labourers, migrants and displaced people. Poverty statistics show an increasing stratification of these groups at the bottom of the ladder. Ironically, the same social and cultural subordination that lies at the root of their poverty also contributes to their exclusion from poverty alleviation programmes. Thus, microcredit programmes aiming to build the asset base of poor women have been found to exclude the poorest category of women, who cannot save the minimum required amount.

Mainstream poverty alleviation programmes are also reflective of some neo-liberal biases that inevitably limit the extent to which women can benefit from them.[18] These include:

- A "male breadwinner" bias, or the assumption that men contribute the major share of the family's income and women's economic activities are subsidiary. Where this bias prevails, women are not entitled to resources in their own right, but only by virtue of their relationship to an adult male, thus limiting their access to resources.

- Deflationary bias, leading to cuts in social sector spending which impact women disproportionately. Development interventions including many poverty programmes are therefore premised on the successful transfer of social costs from the public sector to the "care economy", thus increasing the burden of women's unpaid work.

---

[18] Elson, Diane and Nilufer Cagatay. 2000. The Social Content of Macroeconomic Policies. World Development Vol. 28, No. 7.

- Commodification bias. Since markets cannot recognize the value of goods and services that are not monetized, they cannot take into account the unpaid work that is mainly done by women in caring for families and reproducing the labour force. The invisible subsidy provided by women's unpaid work, which subsidizes the larger economy, is ignored in macroeconomic calculations and cost-benefit analyses of specific programmes. Market-based entitlements, which increasingly form the underpinning of poverty programmes, are thus inherently male-biased.

Apart from biases in the frameworks and designs of many poverty programmes, their impacts are also distorted by biases in implementation. There is considerable evidence to show that discrimination against women operates even in those programmes that incorporate specific measures for women. For instance, food-for-work programmes pay women only half the wage paid to male workers. Similarly, women trying to access credit under poverty programmes have to counter the attitudes of male bank staff who discourage them from operating their own accounts.

The premise that women's poverty can be best addressed through microenterprise development is also open to question. For example, without corresponding changes in the larger macroeconomic policy context, the degree to which this approach can enable the poor to address their own poverty is limited. Experience shows that, to become financially viable, microenterprises need support in the form of subsidies on raw materials and marketing assistance, whether from the government or from a well-connected NGO. Ironically, as part of the economic restructuring package, the state is retreating from providing this kind of support to cooperatives of traditional artisans. With government policies favouring the entry of multinationals into the rural market, the extent to which microenterprises can provide a viable base for rural entrepreneurship is being questioned at many levels. The recent spate of suicides by debt-ridden traditional artisans, like the handloom weavers of Andhra Pradesh, corroborates this critique.

Women in agriculture programmes: unreal assumptions, ungendered frameworks

Given the fact that the majority of poor women in India are agricultural workers, it would seem logical to target poverty at least in part through programmes designed to strengthen women's position as agricultural workers. In fact, however, programmes for women in agriculture often appear to be based on some unreal assumptions.

- Most of these programmes reflect the assumption that women play a subsidiary role in agriculture as helpers to the men in their families, rather than being farmers in their own right. This assumption flies in the face of reality: women perform the majority of tasks in agriculture and constitute the core of agricultural competence in the country. These programmes are designed within a patriarchal framework where ownership of the land defines who is a farmer. Because the majority of women do not have titles to the land they work on, they are categorized as "farm women" rather than farmers. Programmes for women in agriculture have an overwhelming focus on off-farm activities and do not address the core issue of women's access to and control of resources.

- Mainstream agriculture programmes also assume that so-called "modern methods", which involve high-input and chemical-intensive techniques, are essential for increasing production. They ignore the growing body of researches indicating the economic and ecological potential of low-input methods of subsistence agriculture, the methods that women have traditionally practiced.

- A related assumption is that it would be cheaper in strategic terms to buy food than to grow food. Thus, programmes put emphases on encouraging women to move from cultivation of low-value food crops to high-value cash crops. Such strategies would ignore the devastating consequences of chemical-intensive agriculture on lands that are already degraded. Also, these programmes do not capitalize on the fact that women often have far more control over agricultural produce from homestead or marginal lands, which they can use to directly meet their food needs, than cash incomes.

- A central focus in programmes for women in agriculture is on transfer of technical skills and knowledge, reflecting the assumption that women lack technical competence in agriculture. The fact that women are in fact repositories of a huge wealth of skills and knowledge in agriculture is ignored, along with the possibility of building on this resource-base to address critical issues of sustainability and regeneration of the environment.

The overwhelming acceptance of these assumptions by successive generations of agricultural policy planners has resulted in such critical issues as the increasing rate of unemployment in agriculture, degradation of the natural resource base, and consistent denial of land rights and wage entitlements to women farmers being pushed off the agenda. Going by the lack of a coordinated policy response, there is little awareness that these are all central determinants of women's condition and position.

Against these rather grim backdrops, however, several strong alternative approaches to women's poverty and empowerment have emerged in recent years, from the struggles and experiments of women's collectives.

Alternative approaches

Many of the alternative approaches have been hailed as development "best practice" models. Several features they have in common include a political and gendered analysis of the causes and consequences of poverty and an understanding of macroeconomic processes and their impact on women's lives. The work of organizations such as the Self Employed Women's Association (SEWA) and Mahila Samakhya, where seasoned collectives of women are focusing on building an organized strategy to enter and influence processes of macro-economic decision-making is noteworthy in this regard. An important component of these initiatives is an intensive process of building economic literacy at the grass-roots.

Women's movements in India are unfamiliar with the tools and frameworks of macroeconomic analysis. State actors are often trapped within patriarchal perspectives with the growing body of work by feminist economists remaining marginal to mainstream policy-making. Creative and strategic collaborations between these diverse groups can strengthen the alternative discipline of "socio-economics" (to use the term coined by Diane Elson). An emerging partnership between State and civil society actors around the issue of gender budgeting, a partnership through which they address the challenge of bringing macro-economic policy within the realm of public debate, gives cause for hope.

* * *

CHINESE PRACTICES TO MAINSTREAM GENDER IN POVERTY ERADICATION

Ms. Wang Xinxia

Deputy Division Director
Department of International Organizations and Conferences
Ministry of Foreign Affairs, China[19]

Since the Fourth World Conference on Women, which was held in Beijing, the Government of China has placed emphasis on implementing the Beijing Platform for Action, especially the strategies to eradicate poverty among women. China completed a five year programme from 1995 to 2000, with a specific task to bring down the number of women living in poverty by one million. This objective was basically fulfilled. China is now implementing a new ten-year programme (2001-2010). This sets forth strategies and measures to ensure equal rights and access to economic resources and social services between women and men, aiming to reduce the number of women living in poverty.

China is a developing country with 1.2 billion people. In the country, poverty, especially women's poverty, is a complex and multidimensional problem. Women's poverty has many causes. For example, women's disadvantaged position in resource allocation and in developing and utilizing their potentials can cause their poverty. At the same time, poverty can have different meanings, such as inadequate income or resources. Lack of education or lack of access to other social services, health problem, living environment, as well as gender discrimination and women's inadequate participation in decision making and social and cultural activities can lead to poverty.

Facing with poverty as described above, the Government has taken several measures. First the Government keeps increasing financial input to provide special support for the poorest counties that are so identified by the national government. In China, there are basically three categories of poor counties, of which the "national category counties" are the poorest with approximately per capita income below 600 yuan per year.[20] By 1999, the

---

[19] Summarized from transcript of presentation.

[20] Other categories of counties that have less severe poverty conditions are the "provincial category" and the "regional category".

national government had allocated 130 billion yuan for poverty alleviation in these counties, with an annual increase of 14.2 per cent in Government input. I think this is a good example of incorporating women's development programme into the overall national strategy to ensure more adequate resources allocated to poverty eradication, as this measure responds to the usual dearth of resource allocation to alleviate women's poverty.

Secondly, the Government uses various channels as a means to help the development of poor areas. According to the local conditions, the government developed "exchange of labour". Usually there is less land and more labour force in the south, while there is more land and less labour in the north. Responding to this specific situation, the Government would encourage the farmers in the south to go to the north to work during the harvest season. This is the "exchange of labour". The Government also encourages people living in the areas with harsh natural conditions, such as the areas stricken with natural disasters, drought, floods or desertification, to move to areas with better conditions.

Third, microcredit is proved to be one of successful strategies for women's economic empowerment. Women are the major recipients and beneficiaries of microcredit. In addition, the Government allocated more loans that were earmarked for poverty eradication on preferential terms, with the interest rate at 3 per cent. From 1995 to 1999, 43.5 billion yuan was allocated as credit to farmers' households, many in the rural areas. For effective loan programmes, international cooperation with the World Bank and other international financial development institutions is important.

The fourth is a measure targeted for urban areas: the Government conducted a major reform in social relief system in urban areas in 1995. The Government gradually established a minimum living expense mechanism, including unemployment insurance. In 1999, the government raised the relief safeguard and began to provide more aid to city residents with low incomes.

The fifth measure to point out is use of sex-disaggregated data on poverty. The measure is necessary to give priority to eradication of poverty among women. It is now in practice in some provinces. For example, in Shanxi Province, the provincial government made it a principle not to approve a poverty alleviation programme that did not cover women.

Education is another important element of poverty eradication measures. In China, many social relief activities and programmes to improve female education are under way. For example, a programme called springboard was started in 1992 to help girls to complete their nine year compulsory education. Since 1992, this programme has helped one million girls to finish their education. Despite successful programmes like this, however, there are still some obstacles, which require further measures to overcome so that girls can complete their compulsory education.

Even with so many years of hard work, there are still 20 million people living in poverty in China, including women. There are still people living in the poor areas with bad conditions. The Government makes further efforts and gives more resource inputs to enhance the efficiency of fund utilization and to expedite infrastructure improvements in poor areas. It also endeavours to improve local conditions and environment, improve education and social insurance systems and develop social welfare schemes. Through these measures in China and international cooperation, we are confident that the objective set forth in the 10-year programme for the development of Chinese women will be fulfilled.

SESSION 3:

INSTITUTIONAL CHANGE FOR GENDER MAINSTREAMING

Moderated by
Ms. Aruna Rao
Gender at Work Collective

Ms. Aruna Rao moderated the discussion on developing conducive institutional environments for gender mainstreaming. Experience was shared from a number of different country contexts by Ms. Govind Kelkar (IFAD gender mainstreaming project in Asia and AIT), by Ms. Sherrill Whittington on building a new institution in post-conflict East-Timor (now Timor-Leste), by Ms. Yoko Suzuki on the Basic Law for a Gender-equal Society of Japan, by Ms. Banuve Kaumaitotoya on the efforts of the Government of Fiji and by Ms. Khair Jahan Sogra on Bangladesh experience of building institutional mechanism through a bilateral project. Ms. Sogra's presentation was originally given as a case study in the Strategies session.

INSTITUTIONAL CHANGE FOR GENDER MAINSTREAMING: A CASE STUDY OF IFAD'S ASIA DIVISION

Ms. Govind Kelkar

Coordinator, Gender Mainstreaming Project
International Fund for Agricultural Development and World Food Programme

Refining Goals to Incorporate Gender Mainstreaming

Institutions, their structures, procedures and cultures embody certain goals and understanding about the way to achieve these goals. Therefore, in order to change an institution, the first necessary task is to change its goals or the understanding of the way to achieve the goals. In the case of an institution that was established for poverty alleviation, as IFAD was, changing the institution has to begin with a change in its understanding of the process of poverty alleviation.

If poverty alleviation were merely a matter of service delivery, that could be achieved by a top-down delivery system. But if poverty alleviation is a matter of enhancing the agency of women, then a different type of institutional structure, procedure and culture is required. Agency, defined as the capacity for autonomous action in the face of constricting social sanctions and inequalities, offers a framework in which constraint is seen as constitutive of gender norms and relations between women and men. Gender norms and relations are entrenched and durable but not unchanging.

From goals to interventions

Once goals and processes are refined, it is then necessary to proceed to identifying the interventions that are likely to achieve those goals. The introduction of gender mainstreaming brought to the institutions for poverty alleviation the shift of the subject of intervention from households to individuals. These are the strategic interventions in critical areas that have ripple effects across many sectors of social activity.

At the Asia Division of IFAD these have been identified broadly as:

- A proportion of the community budget for the main project activities to be earmarked for women's organizations to plan and implement.

- Separate women only groups for execution of key (mainstream) portions of the project.

- To move up the scale from Self Help Groups (SHGs) for microfinance to non-bank financial intermediary; to move to larger scale credit schemes and up the technological ladder (for example, into long-distance marketing).

- Women's ownership of productive assets – land, trees, water bodies, housing, fishponds and so on.

- Sharing and social provision of childcare and domestic work.

- Increased recruitment of women at professional levels – in decision-making roles in IFAD, UNOPS and project offices.

Structures

In order to take up or continue the process of gender mainstreaming, new organizational structures need to be built. A core organization for gender mainstreaming is needed, along with the supplement of gender officers in various units. This means that both vertical and horizontal links are necessary in the gender mainstreaming set up.

In the case of an academic institution like the Asian Institute of Technology (AIT), where I spent 10 years in establishing the GenDev degree awarding programme) this meant that a core gender degree programme had to be established, along with subsidiary gender modules in various academic programmes. The central, core gender unit should be equal in status to the various other technical units within the organization. At the level of an academic institution this translates into the equal status of gender studies with other degree-awarding, academic disciplines as a field of study. True institutional change further requires that commitment for gender equality and incorporation of gender issues in technology fields is recognized at the top and implemented throughout every programme of the Institute. This is the matter of responsibility and accountability.

For the horizontal link, the academy and industries need to build gender competence. Present development discourse tends to emphasize: (1) widespread and higher levels of education for women in science and technology; and (2) empowerment of women through their participation in decision-making and control of resources. With the institutionalization of WID/GAD, there has emerged a demand for gender experts in the region. These experts can help to develop national gender equality policies and design institutional mechanisms to implement policies as well as facilitate equality based work environments for industry, conducive for efficiency and higher productivity.

Along with the above internal structures, having regular and systematic inputs from outside the regular organization, whether it be from academic institutions or individual researchers, is beneficial. This organization input is needed for bringing critical inputs and the latest results of research into project design and implementation. In the case of the gender mainstreaming project for Asia of IFAD, though funded by IFAD the project is outside of the regular IFAD structure, having been housed at AIT (Bangkok) and then at the WFP (Delhi). Along with the above, smaller "Indigenous Women's Resource Centres", independent institutions in Shillong and Bastar in India and in Lijiang, Yunnan in China, have been set up with IFAD funding.

Procedures

Working with individual projects the gender mainstreaming concerns can then be translated into detailed, local interventions. These suggested interventions, in order to lead to gender mainstreaming, need to be put into the project implementation procedures through writing in official documents, such as in the aides-memoire of supervision mission reports. This is a critical step for gender mainstreaming because, unless put in an official documents followed by efforts to implement them, gender studies and suggestions remain mere pieces of paper.

Over the course of the last two years the concrete suggestions have come up in relation to IFAD projects in Asia. The following is based on an analysis of the case studies of some IFAD projects undertaken under the "Gender Mainstreaming" project. The gender studies of these projects point out many complex forms of a structure of constraints based on gender relations and men's control over knowledge and resources. These in turn play a crucial role in maintaining gender inequality and in reinforcing neglect of women's needs and interests in developmental and technological benefits. To deal with this structure of constraints, to move beyond window dressing and to operationalize gender mainstreaming, the following generic gender issues emerged in IFAD projects in Asia:

(1) The village and community has become the main agency in managing village development funds.

- Women's participation in community management structures, for instance, in the natural resource management groups in north-east India or other village management groups in Ha Giang in Viet Nam, has become an important issue.

(2) Women's individual and direct (not through men) access to productive resources.

- Except microfinance, women's access to productive resources in other areas, particularly land and common property, like trees and water, is rarely addressed.

- Transfer of control of household ponds to women in the aquaculture development in Bangladesh was implemented.

(3) Advancing from microfinance

- Formation of women's bank or non-bank financial intermediaries was proposed in north-east India.

(4) Marketing:

- Women's separate market centres section, as proposed for Bangladesh

- Marketing success in the Lao People's Democratic Republic, with felt impact on various aspects of gender relations.

(5) Training of women in new agricultural and other technologies, livestock management, literacy, and accounting and management skills, electronic fat tester in all women dairy cooperatives.

- The means of access or entry to new technologies tend to weaken the structure of constraints and delegitimize patriarchal power in knowledge systems, particularly in the field of technology. The technology question for women is, therefore, not whether technology represses or liberates, but how to restore and carry forward a creative and empowered participation of women in technology development.

(6) Project organization and functioning

- Appointment of gender advisors and/or officers in central project staff.

- Representation of women in all levels of project staff, particularly in local level project management and monitoring and evaluation (M&E) system.

- Gender sensitization of project staff and concerned NGOs.

(7) Incorporation of gender analysis and indicators in M&E and impact assessments.

(8) Overcoming cultural constraints and sanctions

- Necessity of being innovative.

- Increase women's mobility, participation in decision-making, acquiring management skills and knowledge and reduce women's subordination.

- A rights approach to strengthen women's agency.

- Address the burning issue of violence against women in the home and community.

(9) Women's agency

- Develop agency in women through putting local women's groups in charge of project implementation and related issues, involving them in non-traditional roles (mobility, marketing), and building literacy and confidence in dealing with external staff.

(10) Project design

- Access to land, and other productive resources, like fishponds.

- Community management structures and possibility of women's organization's management of specific portion of overall community fund (energy project in Midu County, China).

- Marketing organization.

- Small and medium-scale enterprises.

- Bank or non-bank financial intermediaries.

- Knowledge centres with multiple functions (M.S. Swaminathan Research Foundation, India).

- Gender indicators in M&E.

- Ongoing gender impact assessment.

- Formation of women's groups with broader functions relating to violence and other social and cultural constraints and sanctions (Anhui Province, China).

Examples from Bangladesh, Cambodia and Indonesia studies show that, in order to implement these gender mainstreaming interventions, gender indicators need to be written into relevant terms of references for various posts and functions in the projects during implementation. Experience with gender mainstreaming in the Asia Division of IFAD, however, shows that mere procedures are necessary but not sufficient. At various levels there needs to be a commitment to gender mainstreaming and an organizational culture that values gender equality. For gender mainstreaming to be effective, changes have to come from within the organizations.

Organizational cultures

Various types of organizational attitudes exist that are an obstacle to gender mainstreaming:

- Accepting cultures as limits to what can be done, not as flexible behaviour patterns that can be changed in many ways. A fundamental problem is the way in which reality is perceived so that even the existence of constraints is not recognized. "The order of things" is most placable of all hidden forms of persuasion. The unrecognized nature of these cultural/social constraints mean that steps are not taken to remove them and the constraints are instead accepted as being unchangeable aspects of institutional culture.

- Playing the "numbers game", focusing only on the numbers of beneficiaries without any regard for the strategic importance of the activities.

- Being satisfied with token gestures, rather than taking it as a beginning.

- Continuing to believe that poverty alleviation reduction is a matter of service delivery with the household as a unit, rather than individual capability enhancement.

46

Areas of major concern are: cultural sensitivity; continuing, or increasing, violence against women; mixed results of market on women; close relationship between poverty and gender inequality. Gender sensitization of staff, along with training in gender analysis, needs to be carried out within organizations to enable the organization staff to accept gender equality as a value in itself, and not merely as instrumental in achieving some other goal.

United Nations organizations, like IFAD, deal with international public funds. Such public money should be utilized to foster the achievement of goals of gender equality, which may otherwise not be given sufficient importance by countries or localities where projects are located.

Institutionalization of gender equality, with external linkages and networks, in development organizations is needed to change their organizational culture. The management should provide room for growth of representation and self-esteem of the excluded people (largely women), instead of playing judge and jury only to perpetuate various inequalities.

The essential issue for gender mainstreaming is transformative change of culturally sanctioned institutional resistance to women's advancement, including women's complicity. It is important to set up local, regional, national and international organizations which formulate and implement programmes addressing patriarchy. In this regard, examples can be drawn from good practices in rural and indigenous Asia.

* * *

EXPERIENCE AND LESSONS LEARNED IN UNITED NATIONS TRANSITIONAL ADMINISTRATION FOR EAST TIMOR

Ms. Sherrill Whittington

**United Nations Transitional Authority for East Timor
(UNTAET)**

I arrived in Dili March in 2000 to see the most incredible destruction I had ever seen in my life. It was not simply the destruction of buildings. The destruction of the people was so visible. UNTAET was established in exactly that situation. It faced one of the biggest challenges of any peacekeeping operation had ever faced: to set up a government from the very beginning, a government that had to be established right across the board.

In peacekeeping operations or missions, there are a number of areas: there are the military or peacekeeping side, the civilian component, and the humanitarian pillar. UNTAET was slightly different from the usual form, as it had the humanitarian pillar only for over 12 months, which lasted until the end of 2000. It also had the civilian component, which was called the Governance and Public Administration (GPA) pillar. GPA became, and is still becoming, and evolving into the independent government of East Timor. It was that part of the mission that carried out the transitional administration mandate. It became the East Timorese Transitional Administration (ETTA) at the end of 2000, and after the election of 30 August 2001 became the East Timor Public Administration, and will become the independent Government of Timor Leste on 20 May 2002.

The transformation from what was fundamentally a pillar of the peacekeeping operation, into the transitional government, to the independent Government of Timor Leste, has been very challenging, particularly when we look at the area of gender.

Gender mainstreaming in East Timor by UNTAET[21]

A major challenge we have faced is that the majority of the people who were in the mission were either people who have worked in peacekeeping mission after peacekeeping mission, or who came in from outside the United Nations system. Some of them had little understanding of the United Nations mandates or resolutions. Even though the mission was pulled together and put on the ground to become operational rather quickly, awareness and consciousness that we were really United Nations had to be raised among all, and it has been a challenge.

Another challenge was caused by a lack of understanding of gender issues. In the original organogram of UNTAET there was a gender affairs unit. This was to be located in the office of the Special Representative of the Secretary-General of the United Nations (SRSG). However, on the ground of East Timor, the gender unit was taken out because it was deemed not necessary. The Gender Affairs Unit (GAU) was established gradually during the months of April through July 2000. The reason that the unit was taken out seemed to be a lack of understanding of what the issue was and how it was necessary in this particular type of missions. GAU finally regained the status as a functional unit and was established within the GPA pillar.

The incident of removing the planned gender unit from and putting it back in the organogram itself caused challenges. The posts that had been assigned to the originally planned unit had been given to other areas. Fortunately with the help from officers in charge of civilian services and personnel who were personally committed to gender issues, GAU was established with some posts after many requests and negotiations. However, the absence of posts was not the only issue. The Unit did not have a budget line, nor did it have any resources. As the Unit was not on the organogram, it did not "belong". This posed significant difficulty initially as we had the reporting line to the office of Deputy SRSG but that was not a direct line. It was very difficult for us to access computers, desks, a car, all those basic things that you would have access to if you are on an organogram. This is a lesson learned. This should never happen again to any unit established in the United Nations peacekeeping mission.

---

[21] A comprehensive report of the efforts by UNTAET/ETTA on gender issues is available in *Report to DPKO on the implementation of Security Council Resolution 1325*, issued by UNTAET on 25 May 2001 and distributed at the symposium.

Drawing upon the personal experience of working on the Beijing Conference and at UNICEF, I decided to establish mechanisms and processes to very quickly put in place both a taskforce at the headquarters and a mechanism that would be operational in the field. In East Timor there are 13 districts, with Dili being the largest district. A letter signed by the Deputy SRSG, who headed the GPA pillar, was sent out to all districts administrators asking to appoint Gender Focal Points, who could work with the office and who could develop various types of programmes or activities to enhance the works of the headquarters at the district level.

The establishment of GAU and operational mechanisms in districts was received with overwhelmingly positive responses. Many United Nations Volunteers (UNVs), who had participated in many peacekeeping missions, gave particularly positive responses. Some really experienced UNVs, particularly experienced women who have been working on gender and development, were very keen to come in and work with the office and support it. That was an extremely successful strategy in terms of mainstreaming gender through out the entire administration, down to at the district level. A number of capacity-building workshops for the District Gender Focal Point Network and for Gender Focal Points within UNTAET/ETTA, within the United Nations agencies and CSOs were conducted. At the first major workshop held in the middle of 2000, we looked at the whole concept of mainstreaming and at the ways by which it could be implemented. All these were done on the run. There was no blueprint, model or text to refer to. We really had to go back to whatever models existed, try to adapt them and carry them forward.

This particular mechanism described above was, and even until now, still remains successful even through the process of "Timorization": that is, handing the administration over to the East Timoreses themselves. At the last gender focal point workshop held recently, an assessment of post UNTAET mechanisms was conducted. There were nine national counterparts for gender focal points for the 13 districts. The presence of these national counterparts in itself was recognized as a significant achievement, as well as the way that it has been carried on and support given at the local level. Of course we have to look at how this mechanism can be sustained after the United Nations pulls down in May 2002. That will be another challenge and I am sure many of these will be, perhaps, supported by United Nations agencies or donors.

There were many lessons learned, which are to be utilized in the way ahead. If we were to do it again, we would do it differently. In my view, the biggest challenges were that there were no models, that the whole thing was transforming all the time, and that the Unit did not belong anywhere.

There were also successful practices, among which was that GAU opened the door to the women of East Timor from the very outset. The women's organizations of East Timor met in June 2000 to have their own National Congress, the first national congress that the women of East Timor ever had, not just since the recent crisis. Major women's organizations came together, under an umbrella group named, REDE, which is a Portuguese word for "organization". REDE developed the "Platform for Action for the Advancement of the Women of Timor Loro Sae", and engaged themselves in promotion, implementation and monitoring. GAU took the platform in and took that up right up to the Office of SRSG. SRSG met with representatives of women's organizations comprising REDE to bring women's concerns and their platform into UNTAET so that this became the basis of our work of the mission.

Among the concerns raised in the women's platform, the women ardently asked for the quota of 30 per cent within the government system: 30 per cent in employment of civil services, 30 per cent of teachers, 30 per cent in nurses, and for women to be represented by at least 30 per cent in all positions in any government appointments. When the election was put on the calendar, the women endeavoured to bring the quota into the first National Constituent Assembly, which was to be elected at the end of August 2001.

The women's organizations requested the National Council, which was the precursor to the National Constituent Assembly, for the 30 per cent quota to be implemented in the election. Although many of the members of the National Council initially positively viewed the request, and although UNTAET supported the idea of 30 per cent quota in principle, a quota in the election caused some controversy. Objections were based on the fear that it would create a precedent: namely, if the quota for the women of East Timor were to be introduced in the forthcoming election, then quotas could be introduced or would be demanded by any group in United Nations monitored elections.

The SRSG, Sergio Vieira de Mello, decided on this matter and that instead of pushing for the quota, affirmative action measures would be introduced and, training should be given to 100 women who would in effect run for a political office or who might think of running for a political office. The UNIFEM regional office and its counterparts in the region brought in a training team consisting of very good trainers and former politicians. Together we ran the workshop, not for 100 but for 150 women, for over six weeks. Out of the training came very interesting development and a very interesting mechanism, which was the East Timorese Women's Caucus. The Caucus was set up by the women themselves, not by UNTAET or any other external organizations. The Caucus went out to the districts and provided economic and moral support to independent women candidates throughout the campaigning period. This can be called as one of the best practices, which can be used as a model. In addition, political parties were given incentives in such forms as more airtime, more assistance in distribution of information, access to vehicles, to guarantee democratic principles of participation and place women candidates higher in winnable positions on their party lists.

The election returns showed that the women of East Timor made a global record. In the first election in East Timor, that came out of a peacekeeping mission, women were returned by 27 per cent to the Constituent Assembly. That was way ahead of the majority of countries in this region, where the average was around 15 per cent. The result came almost as close as to bringing in the quota. The pre-election activities were, perhaps, more affirmative because the quota did not come in. That is something that has to be investigated as a lesson learned. Whether this will be continued in the post UNTAET and post United Nations elections, that is something we have to see.

I think there is something we really should address, particularly coming out of the conflict situation, where women are very much disadvantaged in opportunity, and where the playing field is not level. Peace support operations are very complex operations: they are not just peacekeeping operations but they are also operations for the redevelopment and reconstruction of a society. As such, policies and activities of any peace operation should be grounded on gender analysis and sex-disaggregated data. In East Timor, a major World Bank joint assessment mission was conducted in November 1999 to develop assistance programmes. Regrettably the assessment exercise did not fully incorporate a gender perspective; consequently the programmes by international agencies and bilateral donors based on the resulting assessment did not either. This could have been a good opportunity to put in place in the reality what had been promoted by the development sector as gender mainstreaming, but the opportunity was missed. The need for gender analysis cannot be overemphasized.. Gender mainstreaming in post-conflict reconstruction has to be backed by commitment and resources by all parties concerned, not by a gender unit alone.

We are currently completing a study using all secondary data and all the reports being done in East Timor since November 1999 to investigate the gender responsiveness of the major multi and bilateral actors. Virtually not any of them have done any gender analysis, nor even sex disaggregation. Major reports done on education, on health, on development, or on poverty, have not undertaken gender analysis. This means, for GAU, which is becoming the national machinery for the advancement of women in the Office of the Chief Minister of the Government of East Timor, that much of this information is not worthwhile for policies or programmes or for development. This lesson has to be put in writing and shared, so that meaningful partnership, involving everyone, can be mobilized for gender mainstreaming in post-conflict reconstruction.

The national machinery would be located in the Office of Chief Minister, at the top of decision-making. A woman was appointed to be Advisor for the Promotion of Equality. The Advisor was a former head of an organization that took leading role in the Women's National Caucus. She has also been very active in support of women and women's human rights for the last 25 years. Even with this most qualified leader, however, this office needs support, at the national, regional and international levels. It must be under-pinned and supported with expertise brought into collaboration. Alternatively, support can be envisioned in the form of assistance for internship in women's bureaus or women's organizations or any donors in the region so that the women from the Office can come and work there for a short period of time.

As peace settles in and the memory of conflict is fading away, attention and resources of the international community tend to shift to new hot spots. However, in doing so, we do not overlook the women of East Timor. They also have a right to international assistance, and they also have a right to the commitment at the same level as women anywhere else.

* * *

GENDER MAINSTREAMING EFFORTS IN JAPAN

Ms. Yoko Suzuki

Senior Advisor
Japan International Cooperation Agency (JICA)

The Basic Law for a Gender-Equal Society

Background

The Constitution of Japan guarantees equality before the law regardless of sex and other attributes such as race, creed or social status. A number of efforts towards realizing genuine equality are under way. However, women are often omitted from important decision-making situations and a sense of inequality between women and men remains. Furthermore Japan is experiencing rapid socio-economic changes, such as a shift towards an ageing society with fewer children. In order to realize an affluent and dynamic society in which the human rights of both women and men are respected and which can respond to changes in socio-economic circumstances, a law was called for to clarify the responsibilities of the State, local governments and citizens to form a Gender-equal Society. The Basic Law for a Gender-Equal Society became effective in June 1999.

Purpose

The purpose of the Law is to comprehensively and systematically promote formation of a gender-equal society, by laying out the basic principles, clarifying the responsibilities of the State, local governments and citizens, and stipulating provisions to form the basis of policies related to promotion of the formation of a gender-equal society. A gender-equal society is defined as a society "where both women and men shall be given equal opportunities to participate voluntarily in activities in all fields as equal partners in the society, and shall be able to enjoy political, economic, social and cultural benefits equally as well as to share responsibilities".

The five basic principles of the Law are: (1) Respect for the human rights of women and men; (2) Considerations to social systems or practices; (3) Joint participation in planning and deciding policies; (4) Compatibility of activities in family life and other activities; and (5) International cooperation.

The Law clarifies the responsibilities as follows: The State is responsible for comprehensive formulation and implementation of policies related to promotion of a Gender-equal Society (including Positive Action) pursuant to the basic principles. Local governments are responsible for formulation and implementation of policies corresponding to national measures, and other policies in accordance with nature of the area of local governments. Finally, citizens are to make efforts to contribute to the formation of a gender-equal society, including work places, schools, the local community and the home.

A Council for Gender Equality

The Law holds the State Government responsible to establish a basic plan for gender equality. The Council for Gender Equality was established to advise the Prime Minister in formulation of the Basic Plan for Gender Equality, with the legislative authority in Article 21 of the Law, in the Prime Minister's Office (the Cabinet Office, after the administrative reorganization in 2001). In addition, the Council is tasked to study and deliberate on basic and comprehensive policies and important matters with regard to promotion of the formation of a Gender-equal society in response to the consultation by the Prime Minister or other Ministers concerned. The Council also submit its opinions on these matters to the Prime Minister or concerned Ministers.

The Council is composed of no more than 24 members appointed by the Prime Minister from among persons of learning and experience. The Law requires that both women's and men's representations have a minimum of 40 per cent of the total number of the members. In executing its duties, the Council can seek cooperation from the heads of related administrative institutions and other persons, including the submission of materials, statements of views and explanations.

In preparation for the Council to commence its duty to assess and evaluate the impacts of government policies and programmes on the formation of a gender-equal society, the Office for Gender Equality (the Gender Equality Bureau since 2001, the national machinery for gender equality of Japan) organized the Gender Impact Assessment and Evaluation (GIAE) Study Group. The Study Group developed the basic concepts and the survey methodology of GIAE based on its researches of the survey methodologies that had been in use abroad for the same goal.

Gender Impact Assessment and Evaluation (GIAE)

The Basic Law for a Gender-Equal Society, recognizing the possibility of a non-neutral effect of stereotyped gender roles embedded in social systems or practices on the selection of social activities by women and men, requires the State and local governments to ensure that social systems and practices have as neutral an impact as possible on this selection of social activities. Further, the Law requires the governments to consider formation of a gender-equal society when formulating and implementing policies recognized as having influence on formation. Therefore, in order to promote a gender-equal society, in addition to the programmes directly addressing the need to promote a gender-equal society, the governments must implement programmes with goals and methodology which may not seem to be directly related to the promotion of women's status or a gender-equal society, but the results of which impact the formation of a gender-equal society.

In response to the above requirements set force by the Law, GIAE focuses on both direct and indirect impacts and effectiveness of public programmes on the goal of forming a gender-equal society. The Government must take into due consideration the possible different impacts of public policies on men and women during the entire process of programme planning to implementation process. When a programme is being planned and implemented, the specific roles of women and men, the conditions that they face, and their practical needs must be surveyed, so that the programme is informed of the understanding of the different impact that it might have on women and men.

A gender-sensitive perspective must be incorporated into all government programme planning and implementation processes without being constrained by the fixed or stereo-typical image of the roles of women and men, as defined by their social and cultural environment. The Council for Gender Equality, therefore, conducts GIAE at the national level in close collaboration with the Gender Equality Bureau, the Cabinet Office, other concerned government ministries and agencies and external experts, before programme implementation (planning phase), during implementation, and/or post implementation phase to ascertain the gender impact. When an unintentional and unforeseen negative impact has been identified through GIAE, the policy makers or administrators are expected to review the programme in question and revise it by incorporating the GIAE results.

In addition to the above described benefit of GIAE, that it can identify a positive impact and negative impact, whether the positive impact in one area can offset the negative one in the other area, or whether the negative impact could be eliminated in the near future, GIAE can increase the programme efficiency by expending efforts to ensure that the benefits of programmes can be widely and equally shared among women and men given the budgetary and human resource constraints. GIAE also can increase the transparency of the policy planning process and give a broader range of choices to the citizens, as disclosure of GIAE results is informative to the citizens and could result in securing broad public support or inputs of opinions representing a wide cross section of the society.

These benefits should be underlined as there is some misconception that incorpo-rating a gender equality perspective might sacrifice programme efficiency and inflate the cost or general reluctance to incorporate a gender equality perspective into the programme planning process through GIAE as it is cumbersome and troublesome.

GIAE in practice

The Council for Gender Equality or other relevant body conducts GIAE of the government programmes in the widest sense. In view of the human and other resources constraints, priorities are given to the programmes that are high on the government priority, that are presumed to be strongly gender biased, and that require large resource inputs. Although the exact content of GIAE varies from programme to programme to correspond to their specific contents, GIAE exercise has to contain the efforts (1) to satisfy the practical needs of both women and men; (2) to ensure neither women nor men have the programme benefits deprived of; (3) to solicit opinions of both women and men in the target group all through; and (4) to have equal representation of women and men in the ministries concerned at planning and implementation.

In order to obtain widest support for GIAE, it is important to broadly educate public administrators about the concepts that underlie the GIAE and its specific contents. Further, in order to effectively conduct GIAE, training and education programmes have to be given to various levels of public personnel including both at the working and decision-making levels, while the responsibility of each involved agency and personnel has to be clarified. The organizations of relevant agencies have to be strengthened while mutual cooperation between them has to be promoted. GIAE results have to be open to the public and opinions of a wide cross section of the public, experts and academia to be collected and incorporated.

Gender equality is a prerequisite for establishing a vivacious society that respects the rights of individuals and guarantees that all citizens are equal before the law. GIAE has to be conducted to ensure that public programmes serve the goal of formulation of a gender-equal society through examination of the direction and outcomes of programmes from a gender equality perspective. The Government will be fully accountable by disclosing the GIAE results and by responding to the issues that have been identified by the citizens. The results of GIAE will be drawn upon to improve programmes in the future and efforts to reformulate the policy making processes in the gender mainstreaming framework will serve as a model for reformulating policy planning and implementation processes in other areas. At the end, a gender sensitive perspective will be incorporated into the programme planning and implementation and unintended negative impacts on the formation of a gender-equal society will be reduced or eliminated.

Example of a check list used in GIAE

Planning phase

- Does the necessary sex-disaggregated data exist?

- Is information regarding the target group of a programme and their current condition broken down according to gender?

- Has due consideration been given to problems that are gender related? (security and safety, health-related issues)

- Has due consideration been given to the practical needs of both women and men?

- Will the women and men who are targeted for the programme enjoy the benefits of the programme equally?

- Has consideration been given to the indirect positive or negative impact of a programme on women and men?

- Will the programme widen or narrow the social and economic gap that exists between men and women?

- Has the various roles of women and men in society been taken into consideration? (government, local community, home, school, companies)

- Have the women and men targeted for the programme been consulted, and have their views been heard? Are women and men equally represented among public administrators who are responsible for planning public programmes?

Implementing phase (ongoing)

- Is the programme equally accessible and open to participation of women and men? (provision of information, time of access, other conditions that could restrict access such as child care, care of the elderly)

- When it is necessary to take into due consideration problems that are gender related (safety, health), has the gender of the person responsible for implementing the programme been taken into consideration?

- Are women and men equally represented in the decision-making process and implementation of programmes in the ministry responsible for administering programmes?

Post implementation phase

- Does data exist and is it disaggregated according to gender?

- Has the programme satisfied the medical needs of both women and men?

- What is the actual utilization and level of participation in the programme?

- Are both women and men satisfied with the programme?

- Have both women and men in the target group equally received the benefits of the programme?

- Were both women and men satisfied with the way they participated in the planning and implementation processes of the programme?

- What changed through the participation of both women and men in the programme planning to implementation phases?

- Were there any indirect positive or negative impacts of the programmes on women or men?

- Did the programme widen or narrow the existing social and economic gap between women and men?

- How did the programme change the role of women and men in society? (government, local community, family, schools, companies/enterprises)

- How did the programme impact other areas, or society and economy as a whole

The concept underlying the data collection

- Collection and disclosure of sex-disaggregated data

- Data collection from a gender-equal perspective

- Cooperation between government ministries and agencies with respect to the organization and management of data

- Broad collection of data

- Disclosure of data

* * *

GENDER MAINSTREAMING IN FIJI

Ms. Banuve Kaumaitotoya

Ministry of Finance and National Planning, Government of Fiji

Introduction

Fiji is a republic, located in the Pacific and consisting of 332 islands. Its main industries are sugar production, tourism, gold mining, forestry, fishing, garment and manufacturing. In its development efforts, the Government of Fiji has endeavoured to promote the advancement of women's interest and the achievements of gender equality, so that women can develop their capabilities and potential to the fullest extent possible and their choices are respected and opportunities are available. This will enable women to lead productive lives and contribute fully to development.

The Government has incorporated women and gender issues in its planning and national strategy documents over the last 10 years, such as *Opportunities of Growth* (1993)[22] and *Development Strategy* (1997).[23] The Government of Fiji has also constantly addressed the need to integrate women into planning process. Although the Government has adopted the mainstreaming approach on gender issues, it is recognized that special programmes and projects are still necessary to remove the gender gap in many areas. Certain structural mechanisms and attitudinal barriers, which work against improving the status of women, require continuing action. Therefore the Government is committed to ensuring and promoting the active participation and representation of women in the overall development of the nation as well as the promotion and protection of women's human rights.

Overview of gender mainstreaming in Fiji

The 1999 UNDP *Human Development Report* put Fiji 0.749 on the gender-related development index (GDI) and 0.327 on the gender empowerment and political life (GEM) that assessed women's and men's active participation in the economic and political life, out of a highest possible value of one (indicating perfect gender equality). Although these indicators pointed out that there is a significant degree of gender inequality in Fiji, progress has been made that has improved Fiji's ranking on these global indicators.

---

[22] *Opportunities for Growth* dictates government efforts to involve women and men as equal partners at the national levels; to upgrade women's skills to improve their employment opportunities; to collect data on gender bias for the formulation of new policies; and to strengthen the coordination of activities and examine legislation with the view to safeguard women's human rights.

[23] *Development Strategies* states that government policies and strategies will (1) Ensure a gender-balanced partnership at all levels of decision-making; (2) Strive for equal partnership in political, economic and social development; (3) Promote equal opportunity in employment; (4) Assist disadvantaged women and young women's economic activities; (5) Promote safe domestic and workplace environments for women and children; (6) Examine legislation with the view to safeguarding the human rights of women; and (7) Integrate women's concerns into all planning and policy areas.

Fiji's commitment to mainstreaming gender equality and women's concerns has developed in line with the global development since the United Nations World Congress on Women in 1975, which identified the need to establish the specialized government machinery both to promote the status of women and analyse the specific effects that all policies have on women. The Government of Fiji is a party to many international instruments and conventions on women and gender development, including the Beijing Declaration and Platform for Action, CEDAW, the Jakarta Declaration for the Advancement of Women in Asia and the Pacific and the 1994 Pacific Platform for Action.

At the Fourth World Conference on Women in Beijing, the Government of Fiji made five major commitments to women's advancement, which formed the basis of the Women's Plan of Action (WPA) 1999-2008. These five commitments were:

- To mainstream gender and women's concerns in the planning process and all policy areas

- Review laws that are disadvantageous to women

- Allocation of additional resources to be encouraged to review lending policies to disadvantaged women and young women who lack traditional sources of collateral

- Gender balanced partnership at all levels of government to women on merit as appropriate and encourage the same in the private sector

- Campaign to promote a sound and stable environment that is free of violence, especially domestic violence, sexual harassment and child abuse

Women's Plan of Action, 1999-2008

The WPA was launched in 1998 and identifies a broad direction for action in the following five focal areas: mainstreaming women's and gender concerns, women and the law; women and microenterprise, balancing gender in decision-making, and violence against women. The goals of the WPA is to make, from 2002 onwards, the national budget gender responsive and sensitive; government policies and programmes gender responsive; and all levels in the central agencies and line ministries gender aware and sensitive.

Institutional arrangement for gender mainstreaming

Realizing that the full economic and social participation of women is the responsibility of the whole government, the Government has set up several institutional mechanisms to promote gender equality and mainstreaming, with the Ministry of Women, Social Welfare and Poverty Alleviation (MOW) coordinating governmental efforts and making them focused.[24] The mechanisms include: the National Women's Advisory Council (NWAC),[25]

---

[24] The Department of Women was upgraded to a full Ministry in 1997, with international support. The Ministry's portfolio was further expanded in 2001 to include social welfare and poverty alleviation.

[25] NWAC provides MOW with the opportunity to meet with representatives of women's NGOs and gender specialists within the community. Its main task is to advise the Minister on public sector policies, programmes, projects, legislation, regulation and other issues that impact on women and gender.

the Inter-Ministerial Committee on Women (IMCW),[26] Gender Focal Points (GFPs),[27] five Taskforces to work on the five areas of WPA commitments, a Gender Training Unit of MOW, and the Human Rights Commission.

The Ministry of Women was established as the national machinery to effectively address gender concerns in a systematic and comprehensive way. The roles of MOW are to: analyse the situation of women, identify priority needs, identify constraints and opportunities and formulate strategies for addressing them. Such strategies are to be implemented through the national decision-making and development machinery of government in the process of mainstreaming. It is envisaged that through this process the nature, quality and direction of development will change to favour more broad-based, gender sensitive participation and more equitable distribution of development benefits.

MOW works through IMCW, which is comprised of representatives from different ministries and departments, while the planning mechanisms and GFPs of ministries enhance the effective mainstreaming of women's issues and gender concerns. MOW in working partnership with national civil society organizations and other stakeholders plays a crucial role to deliver the outcomes for women. At the regional level MOW strengthens links with regional and international agencies working in the area of women and gender affairs.

The decision-making machinery of the Government is constructed in such a way as to ensure transparency. The machinery allows input from and consultations with a wide range of interest groups at all levels, from small rural communities, to District, Provincial and Regional Development Committees, and to ministries, the Cabinet and the Parliament at the national level.

Mainstreaming process

The Ministry of Women monitors and regulates but does not implement gender mainstreaming. The task and responsibility of gender mainstreaming is with line ministries. Mainstreaming gender concerns starts with the public sector involving three processes: (1) Using the structure and management of government machinery, which allows concerns of women and of gender to be taken in the mainstream policies, programmes and projects; (2) Consultation with and input from women through direct participation of women in policies, planning, decision-making and implementation of government programmes; and (3) Public advocacy and monitoring, which ensures gender equality in all sectors and encourages positive action by all institutions of the society.

---

[26] IMCW was established in 1998 to oversee and coordinate the implementation of WPA

[27] Government's GFPs at the Deputy Secretary level were established in 17 Ministries and Departments in 1998 to ensure the implementation of WPA. GFPs facilitate and integrate identified priority actions into their respective policies and programmes. In addition the GFPs are to promote the development of gender sensitive policies, programmes and practices in their respective ministries and to provide policy advice to MOW and to respective ministries of the overall needs in the area of gender and development.

Implementing mainstreaming

Clear and practical guidelines for project formulation and simple gender sensitivity indicators for governmental projects are necessary for gender mainstreaming in government decision-making and planning machinery. These have to be agreed on early in the mainstreaming process in consultation with concerned ministries so that they are used regularly.

In Fiji, seven strategic objectives have been outlined to use the structure and management of the government machinery for gender mainstreaming:

- Strengthen an enabling environment for women and gender mainstreaming

- Develop and strengthen governmental processes to be gender responsive

- Enhance sectoral and system wide commitment to mainstream women and gender

- Engendering macroeconomic policies, national budgetary policies and procedures

- Strengthen the institutional capacity of the Ministry for Women for advocacy of women and gender policy and monitoring

- Promote effective consultation of government bodies with key civil society organizations

- Integrate gender training in educational and national training institutions

For the Government's effort of gender mainstreaming to lead to institutionalization, the existing supportive environment needs to be strengthened. A number of initiatives are being undertaken to create an enabling environment for gender mainstreaming. They include gender sensitization training within the public sector; the implementation of a gender budget initiative in several ministries;[28] and gender audit studies in selected ministries that are aimed at examining the differential impacts of sectoral policies and programmes on men and women.[29]

Strengthened women's network is another element of a supportive environment. MOW has enhanced its ties with NGOs through cooperation to mobilize resources for specific issues, such as (1) integration of gender concerns in the law reform process – maternity benefits, day care centres in the work place, domestic violence, rape and sexual harassment; (2) economic sectors – skills enhancement, income-generation and credit programmes; (3) social sector – women's health issues, education, housing; (4) strengthening of support services; (5) political sector – affirmative actions to increase participation of women in decision-making.

---

[28] The Commonwealth Secretariat piloted the initiative in five sectors (education, agriculture, health, commerce and PSC), involving analyses of government expenditure in a gender disaggregated manner. The findings and considerations raised from this exercise would be integrated in the formulation of the national budget.

[29] Ministries of Health and of Agriculture, Sugar and Land Resettlements are implementing gender auditing on a pilot basis.

Major constraints

As stated at the outset, despite extensive efforts by the Government in partnership with the civil society and associated progress, there remains a significant degree of gender inequality in Fiji. Some of the major constraints are: (1) Low consciousness of women and gender issues and needs in almost all sectors; (2) Lack of sex-disaggregated data in some sectors of Government; (3) Inadequate flexibility of bank policies regarding loans to persons without collateral, many of whom are women; (4) High female unemployment rate in the informal sector; (5) Influx of new laws with little regard to the status of women; (6) Prevailing attitudes and culture that individual accomplishment or entrepreneurship does not fall into women's domain, which impede reforms requiring equal participation; and (7) Poverty because of availability of only low paid jobs for women and single mothers.

For example, a major problem area for women in the informal sector is the lack of capital because of the requirement by financial institutions of collateral, regardless of women's educational qualifications and entrepreneurial skills. The Government has adopted affirmative actions, which it utilizes under WPA to facilitate women's access to formal credit, in addition to microcredit, and link credit facilities with the enterprise development. The Government is committed to reviewing the lending and credit policies to ensure that women are not disadvantaged.

The Government of Fiji will continue to implement its affirmative actions to increase women's membership at decision-making bodies, such as boards and committees, to at least 30-50 per cent. By 1999 women's overall membership of boards, councils, commissions and tribunals increased to 17.2 per cent compared to 10.8 per cent in 1996. The Government targets 50 per cent representation of women at all levels in the government and, where applicable, in the private sector, in training, appointments and promotions.

Violence against women, especially domestic violence and sexual harassment, is of increasing concern. Since 1995 the Police Department has introduced some measures to deal with this issue. They include the 'nod drop' policy, gender-sensitized training for police officers, establishment of sexual offences units in two divisions and the introduction of a protocol between the Police Department and the Ministry of Health, the Ministry of Education and the Department of Social Welfare.

Initiatives for future

As described in the above, the Government of Fiji has set up institutional mechanisms for gender mainstreaming and pilot-tested several initiatives such as gender budgeting and gender auditing. Some more noteworthy initiatives are under way.

The Women's Social and Economic Development Programme (WOSED) is one of them. The programme has the economic component, where training is carried out in income-generating activities, and the social component which addresses family and household issues such as a safe water supply, sanitation, proper housing, family nutrition and development of self-esteem. Between 1993 and 1998 about 416 women and their households have been assisted under the scheme. Under WOSED, the availability of microfinance for women has improved.

WPA 1999-2008 has identified the need to further increase women's access to microcredit as well as improving women's access to formal credit. The Government established the Microfinance Coordinating Unit, which coordinate requests from organizations and individuals for microfinance programmes

In order for women and their organizations to develop their capacity and entrepreneurship, the Government, United Nations bodies and other organizations have established a number of training and support agencies. The Ministry of Commerce, Business Development and Investment has the Small Business Advisory Unit, which provides technical advice and training in "starting your business". The Small Enterprise Development programme is a Pacific regional programme funded by UNDP, UNIDO, ILO and provides technical advice and training to develop national support systems for small entrepreneurs. Schools and community organizations also provide women with training and support to develop their potentials.

* * *

POLICY LEADERSHIP AND ADVOCACY FOR GENDER EQUALITY (PLAGE)

Ms. Khair Jahan Sogra

PLAGE, Ministry of Women and Children Affairs, Bangladesh

Since the 1990s, the Government of Bangladesh has set women in development (WID) among its priorities and been committed to redressing widespread gender inequality in the country. The Constitution affirms that all citizens are equal before the law and are entitled to equal protection by the law. Although violation of women's rights, including violence against women, remains a cause for concern, positive changes have been reported in such areas as employment and microfinance, education and the election of women to political offices. Policy initiatives and increased resource allocations in key areas have created a positive climate for further change.

Recognizing that gender equality is a crosscutting issue that relates to all sectors and requires changes in the mainstream of society and in the attitudes and practices of men and women, law and policy makers, planners and institutions, the Government has developed an institutional mechanism to coordinate and facilitate its multisectoral efforts for gender mainstreaming. In the mechanism, women-focused ministry and organizations and women specific projects play important catalyst roles to assist all ministries, organizations and projects in making efforts and opportunities to increase gender equality. The national machinery for the advancement of women has the National Council for Women's Development at its apex. The Council is headed by the Prime Minister and comprises 49 members, including 15 Ministers, 15 Secretaries and 10 prominent women representatives of the civil society.

The Ministry of Women and Children Affairs (MWCA) is a lead ministry in the efforts and responsible for implementing the National Action Plan, which was developed and adopted as a follow-up to FWCW and the Beijing Platform for Action (1995) and the 1997 National Policy for Women's Advancement. MWCA works with the Women in Development Implementation and Evaluation Committee. The Committee consists of the WID Focal Points of all the ministries and civil society members. In all 49 ministries and government agencies, there are WID Focal Points and Associate WID Focal Points. The Focal Points are at the rank of joint secretary or joint chief of any government ministry and agency. Associate WID Focal Points are deputy chief or deputy joint secretaries. Because gender mainstreaming is such a crucial issue for the country, the Government decided that WID Focal Point should be from senior level positions so that policy intervention can be done effectively. At lower levels, there are thana/upazila (Sub Division) WID Coordination Committee at the local administrative level and Sub WID Focal Points in project implementing agencies.

Policy Leadership and Advocacy for Gender Equality project

PLAGE is a joint initiative of the Governments of Bangladesh and Canada. The project commenced in 1997/98 for five years and is implemented by MWCA with US$ 5 million financial assistance from the Canadian International Development Agency (CIDA) and the Government of Bangladesh.

The goal of the project is to mainstream gender equality consideration in policies and programmes of the Government of Bangladesh and all selected sectors of civil society. The project's purpose is to strengthen the capacity of MWCA, in policy leadership and advocacy roles through building its institutional capacity and to strengthen the capacity of the civil society and line ministries to carry out action researches and policy analysis and communicate the results. Further PLAGE aims to institutionalize the linkage between the civil society and government ministries.

PLAGE has four components, which are: (1) to strengthen MWCA; (2) to strengthen the linkage between MWCA and other 14 ministries and line agencies that have been identified in the National Action Plan and that are working in the 12 critical areas in BPfA; (3) to develop linkages between MWCA and the civil society; and (4) Project management. Under this framework, PLAGE focuses on:

1. Strengthening the MWCA by creating the Policy Leadership and Advocacy Unit (PLAU)

2. Enhancing the role of WID Focal Points mechanism

3. Assisting and strengthening the Planning Commission/Ministry of Planning and,

4. Maintaining and strengthening linkages with NGOs, women's organizations, members of the civil society, human rights organizations, professional groups, academia and the media.

MWCA was established in 1972 as Women Rehabilitation Board to serve war victims. With this origin, MWCA had its Allocation of Business[30] which was based on the welfare approach. In 1978 MWCA was established as a full ministry, but the welfare approach was mainstay until the 1990s. After FWCW in 1995, the Government of Bangladesh slowly took the development approach. Since the start of the project, PLAGE has worked with the Government to review the approach and in 2000, with the assistance from PLAGE, the MWCA changed its allocation of business and has taken up the gender mainstreaming approach.

---

[30] Mandate of the ministry.

On the WID Focal Points system, a key element of the institutional mechanism for gender mainstreaming in the Government, PLAGE has been closely working with the mechanism. At the beginning, the terms of references of the Focal Points system was very complicated and time consuming to administer. PLAGE contributed to revising the terms of references. It also assisted to set up a WID Focal Point network among the strategic ministries, namely, the ministries that are referred to in the National Action Plan. PLAGE was also instrumental in launching the WID Focal Point mechanism in the Planning Commission in order to incorporate gender perspectives in the national planning process.

In 2001, PLAGE established the Policy Leadership and Advocacy Unit (PLAU) as a part of the project. Of PLAU, the CIDA funded part has four consultants and the Government of Bangladesh funded part has three senior officers. PLAGE also established the Documentation and Resources Centre (DRC). DRC collects gender specific information, data and all sorts of material related to gender issues. DRC is designed to be the information-clearing house for MWCA to develop a better linkage with the civil society. PLAU and DRC are envisioned to be absorbed in the government structure when PLAGE is completed in June 2003.

PLAGE attended to the issue of the profile of MWCA. In terms of resources and personnel strength, particularly the budget allocation, MWCA had been perceived as a weak ministry with low status. Because of this perception, the media and consequently the public did not pay much attention. The many activities that MWCA conducted were unnoticed. To address this problem and raise the profile of MWCA, PLAGE established a linkage with the media and has had the media give a lot of coverage to MWCA. Whatever the ministry has done, that should be covered. As the linkage with the media is growing and getting stronger day by day, the profile of this ministry has increased immensely. This has a significant implication to the catalyst role MWCA plays among other ministries and CSOs for gender equality.

Another major activity of PLAGE is policy research. So far, PLAGE has conducted 12 policy researches and conducted a wide range of advocacy. PLAGE also worked on a formulation of gender analysis framework. The resulting gender analysis tool was published in June 2001 as *Gender Equality Planning Tools Handbook.*[31]

The Handbook presents five gender analysis planning tools to assist planners to integrate gender equality consideration in government programmes and projects: (1) Gender Analysis Framework (GAF), (2) Sector Specific Gender Analysis Check lists (SSGACs), (3) Violence Against Women Prevention Guideline, (4) Guideline for Integration of Gender Equality in Five-Year Plan, and (5) Gender Analysis Tool for Policy Review. GAF is a generic gender analysis tool that can be used for planning and assessing projects in any sector. It lists eight different areas where attention to gender equality is important, and identifies a number of questions under each. SSGACs were developed from the GAF in response to interest in having analysis tools that identify sectoral issues. Check lists have been developed for eight sectors: Agriculture, Education, Environment, Health, Industry, Mass Media,

---

[31] PLAGE, 2001. *Gender Equality Planning Tools Handbook.* Department of Women Affairs, MWCA, 37/3 Eskaton Garden Road, Dhaka-1000, Bangladesh.

Physical Infrastructure and Communication-Rural Development. Each SSGAC includes a two-page Violence Against Women Prevention Guideline, which highlights the importance and the government responsibility of ensuring that incidence of sexual harassment, discrimination and violence against women be both prevented and responded to in all projects.

The Handbook is aimed to help planners and implementers working to realize the objectives of equal participation and opportunity of men and women and of gender mainstreaming in all policies and programmes, through proactive measures in their day-to-day work. The Handbook provides frameworks, check lists and guidelines to identify areas of analysis, questions and activities that can be included in the design and implementation of projects to increase the participation and benefit of both women and men. This handbook also provides tools for analysing policies from a gender perspective for the planners to ensure that what they are planning and its prospective outcomes are in accordance with the Bangladesh Constitution and other policies and commitments.

Through using the tools in this Handbook, planners are envisioned to: (1) identify and address the needs and priorities of women and men; (2) ensure equal ability of women and men to avail and benefit from programme resources and services; (3) incorporate special measures to reduce inequities and promote women's advancement; (4) promote the involvement of women and men as decision makers and implementers; (5) protect the human rights and security of women and men; and (6) enable women and men to contribute fully to the economy and national development.

Lesson learned

- Achievements in gender mainstreaming do not automatically lead to institutional strengthening.

- Advocacy requires group coordination or it is susceptible to failure.

- Project strategies must take into account local government procedures and processes of institutionalization.

- Project design should have factored in the complexity of the necessary government processes, including approval of the allocation of business.

- No amount of "cosmetic surgery" is going to assist a Ministry to gain credence among other government ministries and civil society. A study foundation is required.

- Regional and international networking is important to strengthen and profile the national agenda.

- In Bangladesh civil society is complex and requires a diversity of targeted approaches to involve them effectively in gender mainstreaming efforts.

- Strategic focus of RPM is necessary to target support and maximize potential achieve project results.

* * *

SESSION 4:

GENDER MAINSTREAMING IN NATIONAL BUDGETS

Moderated by
Ms. Rosa Linda Miranda
Centre for Asia-Pacific Women in Politics

Experience in mainstreaming gender perspectives in governmental budget processes was provided by Ms. Ermilita Valdeavilla of the Philippines and by Ms. Patricia Alailima of Sri Lanka. Ms. Maria Isabel T. Buenaobra shared the experience of GAD budget in local governments in the Philippines. The session also featured a video presentation by Ms. Rhonda Sharp of Australia.

THE PHILIPPINE GAD BUDGET POLICY: BACKGROUND, STATUS AND ISSUES

Ms. Ermilita V. Valdeavilla
Executive Director
National Commission on the Role of Filipino Women, Philippines

The national machinery for women's advancement in the Philippines is called the National Commission on the Role of Filipino Women, or NCRFW. It was created in 1975 and since then, has served as a central catalyst and champion of women's concerns in the country.

What is the GAD budget policy?

NCRFW, in partnership with the Department of Budget and Management (DBM), was responsible for calling attention to the need for resources to support the implementation of the National Plan for Women. Former Senator Leticia Ramos Shahani pushed the advocacy in Congress by authoring the provision under the 1995 General Appropriations Act, which among others, mandated the allocation of no less than five per cent of the total budgets of all agencies to women and gender related programmes and projects. This provision applies to all national line departments and their attached agencies, state universities and colleges, and government owned and controlled corporations.

Local Government Units (LGUs) in the Philippines are autonomous and have their own distinct planning and budgeting processes. Thus, a similar provision, requiring LGUs to allocate a minimum of five per cent of their total budget for gender programmes and projects, is contained in the Local Budget Circular that DBM issues to LGUs annually.

The GAD budget policy, among others, also provides that every agency should develop a GAD Plan, which is to be reviewed and endorsed by NCRFW to DBM. This is an important feature of the policy as it makes planning a prerequisite to GAD budgeting. This element of the policy was introduced after an initial assessment done by NCRFW revealed that the GAD budgets were being used for non-strategic projects, such as aerobics, sports and ballroom dancing.

Another strength of this feature was the power given to NCRFW to review the GAD plans prior to their approval and consideration by DBM, a process that is attached to the review of the agencies' budget proposals for the incoming year. This provision helped strengthen the stature of NCRFW as an authority in determining the legitimacy of contentious charges against the GAD budget.

The most problematic aspect of the policy is implementation. Over the years, several circulars and tools were developed and disseminated to help agencies properly implement the policy. The most recent guidelines consist of a twin Joint Memorandum Circulars, both signed by the NCRFW, the Department of Interior and Local Government (DILG), and DBM. The first set of guidelines was an initiative of DILG and is intended for LGUs and DILG's field staff. The second is an initiative of the budget department, which is for all government agencies. Both guidelines spell out: (a) what programmes and projects are eligible for funding under the GAD budget; (b) the kinds of technical assistance available as well as their sources; and (c) the roles and responsibilities of the oversight agencies, such as NCRFW, DILG and DBM.

The guidelines are accompanied with a tool for the staff of those departments who are involved in the process of helping the agencies and local governments in planning and budgeting. There are also training for planners and trainers as well as a three-day GAD Plan Enhancement Workshop where agencies with problematic GAD plans are invited and directly mentored in improving their plans. These workshops are attended by a planner, a GAD Focal Point and a budget officer from each agency.

The roles of the oversight agencies in gender planning and budgeting are duly delineated as shown in the role delineation matrix (see table). Although many of the roles identified in this matrix are already provided under certain policies, they are periodically reviewed and negotiated to ensure better ownership, coordination and clarity in implementation.

Why do we need a GAD budget policy?

The Philippine's GAD budget policy aims to ensure a stable source of funds for the implementation of the laws and international commitments of the Government of the Philippines on women, particularly the Philippine Plan for Gender Responsive Development (1995-2025). This is a 30-year blueprint for attaining the vision of gender equality in the Philippines. It is our main vehicle for implementing all our international commitments and national laws and policies.

Role delineation matrix

Oversight roles and responsibilities				
	National Commission on the Role of Filipino Women (NCRFW)	*National Economic and Development Authority (NEDA)*	*Department of Budget and Management (DBM)*	*Department of Interior and local Government (DILG)*
1. Formulation, review and update of standards and guidelines and dissemination of gender-responsive development plans, GAD plans, GAD budget and criteria for programmes and projects	• Oversee the formulation, *review and updating* of the *PPGD* at the national level • Continue to sit in various *NEDA* planning committees until such time that the set-up for the formulation of gender-responsive standards and guidelines is in place • Continue with the development of guidelines in the form of GAD primers, memorandum circulars, etc.	• Formulate and disseminate standards and guidelines for gender-responsive development plans at the national and regional level • Formulate *and disseminate* Gender-Responsive guidelines for ODA programming at the national level (RDC's will take on the same function at the local level)	• Formulate and disseminate guidelines for the GAD Budget at the national, regional and LGU level	• Formulate GAD Planning Guidelines for the LGUs • Provide technical assistance via its regular or mainstream training and other capability building functions for the LGUs
2. Screening of gender-responsive plans, GAD plans, GAD budget criteria for programmes and projects	• Continue to take on the task of screening national agency plans as to their gender-responsiveness until such time that an agency or group of agencies relieves it of this function (NCRFW cannot review/screen plans of regional offices because it lacks regional presence)	• Screen and determine the consistency of regional development plans with the national gender plans	• Ensure the agencies earmark for GAD	• Formulate guidelines for LGUs in coordination with NEDA

The GAD budget policy is based on the principle that whoever spends the money of the Government should be responsible for ensuring that gender concerns are addressed. Thus, it is meant to strengthen every agency's accountability in using public resources for addressing gender concerns. In short, it is meant to be a mechanism for strengthening the accountability of the entire bureaucracy to the women constituents.

The 5 per cent minimum requirement is meant to be used to make the remaining 95 per cent of the budget gender responsive. It intends to correct problems related to gender. It could be used for new and special projects or components that address gender gaps, or to strengthen women-only projects so that they could respond not only to the practical but also to the strategic gender needs. These budgets should also advance mainstreaming activities such as building of agency capabilities for GAD and reviewing existing plans, policies, programmes, projects and activities to make them gender responsive.

The GAD budget policy also mainstreams GAD into the budgeting process. For example, GAD has since been part of the annual budget call, which contains the priority of the Government. We have also been trying to improve the budgeting procedures and instructions and had included a form for GAD plan and report. NCRFW also sits in the technical budget hearings wherein the budget proposals of agencies are defended, and sends questions that legislators in Congress could ask the agency heads when their budgets are defended for approval.

How was the GAD budget policy conceived?

The GAD budget policy was driven by disappointment over low level of implementation of gender related initiatives provided under the Philippine Development Plan for Women, the Women in Development and Nation Building Act (Republic Act No. 7192, adopted in 1991), and CEDAW.

Nearly two years after the adoption of RA 7192, the low level of implementation of gender related initiatives was evidenced by the reporting mechanism instituted under Section 10 of this law. The reports submitted by the agencies cited the lack of funds as the main reason for non-implementation. Thus, when NCRFW presented a progress report on the implementation of RA 7192 to then President Fidel V. Ramos, the lack of budget was highlighted as a problem that required executive action. The response of the President was a memorandum instructing DBM to identify budget sources for GAD from existing allocations. This memorandum was the antecedent of the current GAD budget policy.

The Philippine's GAD budget policy was a replication of the policy under RA 7192, which provides that a specific portion of ODA shall be allocated for programmes and projects on women. It was inspired by the GAD budget policy of Australia in the sense that it is based on a similar philosophy. However, it applied an entirely different approach.

What is the status?

The Philippines' GAD budget policy now serves as an important tool for women to lobby and negotiate for resource entitlements. At least, they are now able to negotiate from a position of power by asking for what is rightfully theirs, rather than begging. The policy enjoys strong support from the women's movement. There are groups of women who are prepared to rally whenever there is a threat that the policy would be abolished. Initial positive effects on the lives of women in communities have been documented in a publication entitled, *Breaking New Grounds for Women's Empowerment*.[32]

The policy is an important instrument for drawing attention to GAD as a government agenda. It forces agencies to look at the gender dimension of their work and clarifies the roles of oversight agencies in managing gender mainstreaming. Mayors and local executives who would not even bother to ask what gender is all about are now forced to find out, because "5 per cent" is too huge to ignore.

The policy puts gender in the mainstream of government negotiations for resource allocations. Now, some gender focal points are deemed part of the budgeting process, GAD activities are examined and those who did not care to bother about their activities are forced to listen to the arguments of the focal points.

The policy also helps strengthen the stature of the national women's machinery. NCRFW is better known today than before, and has some power to decide whether submitted plans and programmes qualify for the allocation.

The advancements in the women's sector are also an inspiration and model for other sectors. The youth sector, for example has tried to have a share from the national budget through a similar provision.

Major issues

There have been gains, but a number of issues remain.

Need for sanctions: Many believe that sanctions should be adopted to force the majority of local chief executives to comply. Others believe that sanctions would be counterproductive because the resistance could swell to the point that it may result in the abolition of the policy. Some existing sanctions against non-implementation of government policies could serve as an alternative. Under government policies, an administrative case could be filed against chiefs of offices who fail to implement government policies and rules. There are also less confrontational approaches. For example, DBM's guidelines make the GAD plan and budget a pre-requisite to the review and consideration of the budget proposals of agencies.

---

[32] Ermelita Valdeavilla and Fe Manapat (ed.) 2001. *Breaking New Grounds for Women's Empowerment.* NCRFW: Manila.

Dealing with manoeuvring of politicians: Politicians will support or refuse to support the implementation of the policy on the basis of their own agenda. Some would feign ignorance, some would allocate less than five per cent, some would allocate much more to boost their own propaganda projects, and the like. The effective implementation of the policy greatly resides on the hands of the advocates.

Technical constraints: There are a lot of technical problems in terms of determining the budget sources, the forms and tools, the classification of the programmes and projects, among others. There is a mounting demand for technical assistance because of the increase in the number of complying agencies, which puts a lot of strain on the resources of NCRFW.

Need to strengthen integration in local budgeting process: Since NCRFW does not have a presence at the local level, much remains to be desired in institutionalizing gender budgeting among LGUs. Presently, there is an effort to build a network of professionals, both from among Government and NGOs to look into the strengthening of gender planning and budgeting at the local level. Training and tools for the field staff of DILG have also been developed to address this issue.

Need for better monitoring: Monitoring mechanisms remain limited and inefficient in capturing the needed data for assessment and advocacy purposes. Negotiations are under way for the development of a participatory monitoring system which will be a joint venture of NCRFW and AusAID.

Need for "round the clock" vigilance: The GAD budget policy is connected with the General Appropriations Act, a legal instrument that is negotiated and enacted every year. This being so, there is a need for continuing vigilance in showing that the policy is helpful, and in ensuring that it does not get deleted in the processes of annual budgetary negotiations.

Sustaining factors

Activism of women's movement: The vigilance and activism of the women's movement continues to keep the budget policy in place. Women NGOs serve as catalysts in informing women about the policy, getting the needs of women considered in the planning agenda, and providing technical assistance to government agencies in gender planning and budgeting.

Vision of gender equality: The vision of gender equality is shared by a growing number of gender advocates at the national and local levels.

A broad gender mainstreaming framework: A framework that was developed based on the lessons learned by government agencies during the past couple of decades helps to promote a more systematic approach to gender mainstreaming.

Demonstration of results: The experiences of government and NGOs with the GAD budget policy have been documented in order that these could serve as lessons for others.

What are our plans?

NCRFW is implementing short and long term plans to strengthen and sustain the implementation of the GAD budget policy. Among them is the continuing negotiation with oversight agencies, at the national and local levels, for a more rational and practical sharing of roles and responsibilities in gender planning and budgeting. At the regional level, where NCRFW does not have a mechanism, the national planning body serves as the focal agency on gender. Other mechanisms are also being set up such as the regional Gender Resource Centres that are based in state colleges and universities. The involvement of the Commission on Audit and the Department of Finance in gender mainstreaming is also one of the strategies that will be explored in NCRFW's upcoming project with UNIFEM.

In the short term, immediate plans include the dissemination to strategic partners of the tools and guidelines developed under the Institutional Strengthening Project Phase II, a project assisted by the Canadian International Development Agency (CIDA). A participatory monitoring and evaluation approach will also be developed and tested under a joint project of NCRFW and AusAID. The development of a methodology for assessing the impact of the GAD budget, as well as training of women on budget literacy and advocacy are likewise among the list of interventions being planned in the immediate future.

* * *

ENGENDERING THE NATIONAL BUDGET IN SRI LANKA

Ms. Patricia J. Alailima

Director-General
National Planning Department,
Ministry of Finance and Planning, Sri Lanka

Background

Women are in the forefront of the demographic, epidemiological and agro-industrial transitions that are taking place in Sri Lanka. Due to the small size of the country, a good road network and subsidized transport services, the free education and health services are readily accessible in physical as well as financial terms. The cultural attitude towards female autonomy and the value placed on literacy and education have reinforced accessibility and resulted in a high level of participation of both boys and girls in education. Improved education has contributed to increased mobility of the female labour force, both internal and external. Not only have women been moving out of agriculture (a traditional area of occupation) into industry (particularly the garment industry) and services, but they are also moving abroad for employment. Private remittances, about 75 per cent from women working abroad, financed around 15 per cent of imports in 1997, while women on the plantations and in the free trade zones together contributed 53 per cent to exports.

Despite the increasing women's contribution to the economic growth of the country, little was known of the benefits that they derived from government programmes financed through the budget, the government's most important economic policy instrument. It was recognized that integration of a gender perspective into the national budgetary process would improve the impact of public expenditure and enable women to increase their contribution to nation building. Sri Lanka, therefore, requested technical assistance from the Commonwealth Secretariat and participated in the Commonwealth Secretariat programme as one of the five countries chosen for a pilot study.

Objectives of the study

The purpose of the study was to assess the gender impact of the Sri Lanka Budget by examining actual expenditure in 1996 and using the knowledge gained to improve the gender impact of future budgets. The study covered only the main ministries in the services and production sectors: Ministries of Education, Health, Social Services, Industries, and Agriculture. The gender distribution of employment throughout the Public Services was also analysed.

Procedure

Five research teams, consisting of officials from the ministries involved with an identified leader, started their work on 1 June 1998. The study on employment by sex in the Public Services was handed over to the Department of National Planning. An Inter-Ministerial Committee was set up comprising representatives of the respective ministries and officers from the Ministry of Women's Affairs and the Department of Census and Statistics, to assess the progress and the performance of the project. A consultant assisted the working groups and reported on their progress to this Steering Committee. Two workshops were conducted in order to present the findings of the studies to a wider audience, including donors and other researchers.

Methodology used

The study considered only the recurrent budget of the agencies concerned. An assessment of the gender impact of capital expenditure was desirable but required data on accumulated assets and valuation of their service lifetimes, and these were not available. The recurrent budgetary allocations of the participating ministries were considered in terms of (1) service deliverers and their personal emoluments, travelling expenses, contractual services, and other recurrent expenses which were considered service delivery expenditure, as well as in terms of (2) the impact of total recurrent expenditure on the programme recipients. Although each ministry had its own data base, special surveys had to be conducted to obtain the required information in many instances, because collection and collation of existing data was not sex-disaggregated.

Expenditure on those activities in the education and social services, which have been devolved to the Provincial Councils under the 13th Amendment to the Constitution in 1989, have also been included in this study although they were not funded through the recurrent budget of the central line ministries. In addition, analysis of public sector employment and wages covers the Provincial Councils and semi-government institutions and gives a comprehensive overview of the public service, as well as the relative significance of its different components.

Study highlights
Education sector

Young girls with higher education have become important agents of modernization and increasingly participated in economic activities. More than 86 per cent of the 5-14 age group participate in primary and lower secondary education, with about 38 per cent of the 15-17 age group in the upper secondary level. However, in the primary cycle, there is still an imbalance in entry at Grade 1, with girls accounting for less than 49 per cent of total primary enrolment. As boys drop-out at a higher rate than girls, the disparity tends to be narrowing and reversing in higher cycles: girls account for 50 per cent on average in the secondary cycle; 53 per cent of those sitting the GCE 'O' level and 55 per cent of those sitting the GCE 'A' level. Besides, the percentage of those who qualify at each of these exams is also higher for females. However, at the university level there is still a gender discrepancy in enrolment, varying from 31 per cent in the South-eastern University to 50 per cent in Colombo University. Overall only 42 per cent of University places accrue to females, although 54 per cent qualify at the 'A' level examination. Fields of study also have some imbalance: only 12 per cent of engineering students and 33 per cent of architectural students are women, while over a half of the students in Arts, Law and Veterinary Science are. Taking students as direct beneficiaries, 48 per cent of total expenditure accrues to females.

Although female teachers predominate in the primary and the secondary cycles (84 per cent and 63 per cent respectively) they only represent 45 per cent in the collegiate cycle. The participation of female teachers in management level courses is also lower, resulting in a low percentage of female managers in the education sector: only 20 per cent of principals are female. Taking teachers as direct beneficiaries (of salaries and teacher education programmes) 68 per cent of total expenditure accrues to females.

Health sector

The demographic transition in Sri Lanka started with dramatic declines in mortality in the late 1940s and 1950s which were sustained by increased participation in preventive and promotive health programmes. The transition was moved further by declines in fertility in the past quarter century, brought about by delayed marriage thanks to longer schooling and acceptance of family planning. These socio-demographic changes have determined the age structure, marital status, and educational and labour force participation pattern of females. The demographic transition, together with urbanization, changes in lifestyles and other factors have given rise to an epidemiological transition.

Usage of the government western health system is slightly more by females (56 per cent) with one third of admissions being for obstetrics and gynaecology. Male admissions are higher for surgical, dental and psychiatric wards. Women appear to favour the larger hospitals where specialist care is available. In this sector too, while overall there is a predominance of women among health workers, senior managerial levels are dominated by men.

Agriculture sector

About 22 per cent of women are employed in agriculture, but agricultural service provision has continued to follow a traditional pattern which neglects their farming potential. The participation of women is low, both in the staff of the agriculture related departments and in the programmes they run. Within the Ministry of Agriculture itself, 36 per cent of the workforce are female, and they are concentrated in lower level jobs such as clerks or typists. Among professionals, about one third are females but this decreases to 9.5 per cent in senior management and zero in top management.

The propagation of modern methods of agriculture is through in-service and field training; but female participation in the institutional and field training conducted by the Departments is rather low. Of the Department's training courses, women are more interested in agricultural processing, horticulture, seed production, and water management than crop production, animal husbandry and organizational management and farmer nutrition. The proportion of female trainers in extension courses and in-service training institutions was also low (averaging 36 per cent) except in agriculture processing. Among extension workers, who provide the interface between the government agencies and the farming community, only 23 per cent are female.

Farmers' organizations are important means of increasing agricultural production and credit disbursement. The higher the percentage of female membership, the higher the credit utilization by women. In general, however, female membership in farmers' organizations is low. The proportion of women farmers in decision-making positions in these organizations is also very low, suggesting that they may be relegated to being passive onlookers.

Female participation in work under the World Food Programme is however high, in the eight districts where the programme is operating, ranging from 60 per cent in Hambantota to 85 per cent in Ratnapura, with the exception of Anuradhapura (42 per cent). The number of days worked per female participant in 1996 varied from 121 in Hambantota to 250 in Moneragala, suggesting that there is a considerable pool of female agricultural labour still available in some districts which could be trained to improve cultivation techniques; and that this programme was responding to a deeply felt need, particularly in 1996 when the country experienced a severe drought.

Industrial sector

The private sector has been the engine of growth of industrial activity. The Government has been withdrawing from regulatory and production activities and taken on the role of policy development and the provision of incentives. The Ministry promotes small-scale entrepreneurial development and handloom textile development through training, technology transfer, credit mobilization, etc. It also retains some residual regulatory functions with respect to the exploration and exploitation of minerals.

The Ministry facilitates the establishment of medium-scale industry through the development of industrial sites and services. The focus of government expenditure over the last few years has been the dispersal of industries into remote areas through the setting up of a chain of 25 industrial estates. The Industrial Park at Sitawaka, accounting for 70 per cent of the Ministry budget, combines planned facilities and utilities with the development of the surroundings as an industrial city. While the ownership of lots in these estates is mainly male, 80 per cent of the employees are female. Incentive packages provided by government encourage the adoption of more advanced technologies and increased employment opportunities at a higher skill level for men and women. Board of Investment incentives and guaranteed quotas for the 50 garment factories being set up in the South are expected to have a very favourable impact on reducing the high unemployment among women in these areas.

Direct beneficiary impact is mainly through training programmes in entrepreneurship development and technology transfer, but account for less than 10 per cent of the recurrent budget. Female participation in the courses of the National Institute of Business Management is around 30 per cent, in those of the Textile Training and Service Centre 44 per cent and in the Clothing Industry Training Institute 34 per cent. Specific programmes to develop women entrepreneurs have given rise to sustainable enterprises at village level, though on a small scale.

Social services

Social welfare expenditure focuses on maintaining the living standards of vulnerable groups, such as the very poor, invalids, those affected by floods and droughts, and the physically and socially handicapped. The expenditure for long term rehabilitation is as low as 5 per cent. The administration of these programmes shows an unusual and fairly equal gender ratio at managerial and staff levels (except in vocational training) but a predominance of males at the lower level. Overall, about 58 per cent of recurrent expenditure benefits females, as they tend to dominate as the beneficiaries of the programmes for the very poor and invalids, flood and drought relief. However, women seem to be neglected in vocational training for the physically and socially handicapped. The gender ratio for abandoned children and orphans in institutional care and with foster parents was fairly equal, but boys predominate in correctional facilities such as Certified Schools and Remand Houses.

Sex ratio in the public services employment

In the public services as a whole, only one third of employees are female. This proportion varies from 20 per cent in corporations, to 24 per cent in central government, and to 56 per cent in the provinces. Women predominate in the professional category (66 per cent) in the provinces and central government (as teachers and health professionals) and in the clerical category in semi-government institutions. At managerial level, however, women account for only 15 per cent of the cadre and 23 per cent of the technical category. There is hardly any discrepancy in earnings between men and women in the different occupational categories as they are on the same pay scales.

Overall, while economic growth has been expanding employment opportunities for both men and women, the quality of employment has also been improving. Many former unpaid family workers are now in paid employment. Women's share in public sector employment is increasing due to their strength in professional occupations which are expanding, and their increasing significance in managerial and technical occupations; on the other hand, there has been a decline in male employment, due to the restructuring and privatization of semi-government institutions where they were predominant.

Conclusions

While very little of the government budget is targeted specifically to women, the study found an equality of access and usage in the main service sectors; in education 48 per cent of recurrent expenditure benefited females, in health 56 per cent and in social services 57 per cent. In the production sectors, such as agriculture and industry, the support women receive is very low. There is evidently a need to devise programmes, delivery systems and sex-disaggregated impact assessments that will lead to equalizing opportunities for men and women. More resources should be given to technology transfer, organizational strengthening, training, extension services and communication systems so as to improve the participation of women. Inequalities in public sector employment also need to be addressed to allow women better access to managerial levels.

Each of the Ministries examined had distinct characteristics. The education sector, which has been a priority sector for the last century and continues to be a sensitive area, has already gone a long way towards disaggregating its recipients' data by sex on an ongoing basis. In the health sector, maternal and child health has been a focus since the 1930s. However, the participation of girls and women in other areas of health care has tended to be neglected and sex-disaggregated data is not collected on a routine basis at institutional or central level, except for epidemiological data. In the social welfare services, which are almost entirely devolved, there is no routine data collection at the central level, and no sex-disaggregated recipient data is collected by the provinces. In the agriculture and industrial sectors, no routine sex-disaggregated programme assessment had been undertaken; it was this study that highlighted for the first time the lack of female participation in training and other programmes.

The budgetary policies underlying the allocation of resources in these five Ministries are not deliberately discriminatory. However, the inadequacy of sex-disaggregated data and the lack of attention paid to the few existing sex-disaggregated data have perpetuated the programmes from which women derive low benefits, while new ones in the areas popular among women continued to be restricted. In order for the improved education of females to have an impact on productivity and incomes, the propagation of modern methods of agriculture, agro-processing and technology transfer are particularly important. For small-scale entrepreneurs, public sector programmes must respond to their needs for continuous advice on testing and quality control, and access to specialized research institutions. In this connection, the gender of the service provider can also play an important part and should be kept in the forefront of programme planning in all sectors.

Sociological research is necessary to ascertain the causal relationship and remedial measures that can be taken to improve female participation in the areas highlighted. New issues that are emerging, such as female migration for work abroad, also need to be carefully assessed. Current inequalities are likely to continue in the absence of a deliberate effort to change the systems in place and to monitor changes with adequate sex-disaggregated data. Therefore, the information generated in this study should be presented, by the respective work teams, to all the departments and agencies concerned to increase awareness of inequities in service usage with a view to remedying them when programmes are reviewed.

* * *

MAINSTREAMING GENDER IN THE BUDGETS OF LOCAL GOVERNMENTS

Ms. Maria Isabel T. Buenaobra
The Asia Foundation, Philippines

Background

The 1987 Philippine Constitution recognizes the role of women in nation building and ensures equality of men and women. Beginning in 1992, an environment for improved accountability and public participation emerged at the local government level under a new Local Government Code. The Code requires the inclusion of NGOs in decision-making at the local level and emphasizes the role of women in the decentralization process and people empowerment.

In this positive environment, NGOs have conducted policy researches and formulation, lobbying, and mass actions to bring about changes in laws and in public and institutional policies. Women's NGOs contributed by being in the forefront to the passage of landmark laws in the 1990s, including the Anti-Sexual Harassment Law (1995) and the Anti-Rape Law (1997).

The Women in Development and Nation Building Act requires allocating a given percentage of ODA for gender and women's concerns. In 1994, the National Economic and Development Authority (NEDA), DBM and NCRFW issued the Joint Memorandum Circular No. 94-1. This provided for the integration of GAD into the plans and budgets of government agencies in line with the Philippine Plan for Gender-Responsive Development 1995-2025. Every year since 1994, all national government agencies have been instructed to allocate at least 5 per cent of their budget to implement the GAD plan. In 1998, the Secretary of DILG issued a directive to local government units (LGUs) urging them to adopt the GAD budget policy in their planning and budget preparation.

The 5 per cent GAD budget is not expected to be an agency's total contribution to addressing gender issues. Rather, it is intended to direct specific allocations to promote the gender-responsiveness of all other areas of operation. Bodies such as NCRFW see the 5 per cent GAD budget policy as a tool of mainstreaming gender throughout each agency's budget.

The Asia Foundation:
gender and citizenship in budget advocacy

The Asia Foundation recently completed the Gender Budget Analysis and Advocacy (GBAA) Project, resulting in the publication of *The Gender Budget Trail: The Philippine Experience.*[33] The research was undertaken by partner NGOs for advocacy. The aim is to promote citizen participation in the budget process and to ensure transparency and accountability on the part of government officials. The project highlighted the need for civil society participation in gender budget initiatives as a vital element of democracy.

Budget analysis and advocacy has emerged as a powerful strategy for democratizing decisions on all aspects of the budget process, especially one of the most critical functions of the public sector – determining the use of public funds. While budgets are meant to distribute funds efficiently and fairly, in reality the ways funds are allocated are a function of the power balance between different groups. Entrenched, often male-dominated, interests channel funds to their priority interests, depleting public coffers. The majority of citizens, especially women and other marginalized groups, are frequently excluded from the budget process but bear the consequences of inefficient distribution of resources. If girls are entitled to education but inadequate allocations for teachers and schools resulted in limited student placements, boys often receive preference. Similarly, if there is inadequate funding for the justice system, women's grievances may never be adjudicated. GBAA complements economic and legal rights initiatives by directing attention to public expenditures as a focal point of exclusion and injustice on one hand, and transparency and accountability on the other. Budget projects can also highlight discrepancies between governmental commitments and allocations of public funds in reality.

GBAA projects challenge hidden gender biases in macroeconomic policies that appear gender neutral. Understanding of budget information and process for one sector or issue is transferable to other sectors and issues. Women can use GBAA to analyse and influence resource allocations at all levels of governments and in all sectors. They can also use gender budget projects to scrutinize macroeconomic policies for gender discrimination at one end of the spectrum, and how funds are distributed and used in their village on the other.

Aims of the project

The Asia Foundation and its partners took a citizen-led, problem-centred approach to budgets. The project started with identifying concrete problems that were the priorities of participating communities through attending to the often overlooked voices and interests in the policy process. A participatory approach was taken to analyse the identified problems and assess policies and budgets pertinent to them. In this integrated strategy, budget analysis was a tool rather than an end in itself: Strengthening citizenship was as important as making budgets more transparent and equitable. The project was not to make participants technical experts in budget issues but to improve citizens' ability to influence and work with local

---

[33] Debbie Budlender, Maria Isabel T. Buenaobra, Steven Rood and Marie Sol Sadorra, 2001. *The Gender Budget Trail: The Philippine Experience.* The Asia Foundation: Manila.

governments. It also aimed to provide a new gendered lens through which both governments and the civil society could assess policies and programmes, so that resources can be directed where they were needed most.

In addition the project's aim included:

- To promote equity, efficiency, and effectiveness in government policy and implementation;

- To promote accountability and transparency on the part of government and public representatives, and to minimize corruption;

- To inform and enhance citizen, particularly women's, participation and advocacy, by strengthening tools for policy implementation;

- To advance citizens' budget literacy and level of comfort at monitoring the money that was set aside or not for a policy commitment;

- To magnify the impact of decentralization through improved capacity of both government officials and community groups.

Important features of the Gender Budget Analysis and Advocacy Project

The important features of the GBAA Project were the following:

- Looked beyond the 5 per cent GAD. The aim of the 5 per cent GAD budget is to mainstream gender throughout all programmes and projects, and their related budgets. Unless we look at the other 95 per cent, we will not know how best to use the 5 per cent GAD budget.

- Citizen-led. The budget analysis is a process of citizen education that enables people to claim as citizens for public resources.

- Oriented to solving problems in an equitable and inclusive way. The project was to strengthen the capacity of local governments to address the needs of citizens, especially the marginalized, by combining technical expertise and practical experience.

- Use of gender as a tool for analysis and action, and as a way of identifying discrimination and promoting inclusive, equitable policies.

- Rights-based in a normative sense by endorsing the citizen's right to participate in public decision-making and emphasizing their rights to equitable access to public resources.

As NCRFW oversees national agencies, GBAA focused on local governments. There are about 1,700 LGUs and many barangays (smallest political unit), which should also be mainstreaming gender in their budgets. In addition, GBAA completed a set of research to give the national background for the local studies, summarizing the processes and directives at national level in respect of GAD budgets, describing how they related to local governments.

Three localities were chosen to conduct case studies:

- Angeles City in Pampanga is the site of a former United States airbase situated about 80 km from Metro Manila. There is a strong women's organization, the Ing Makababaying Aksyon (IMA) Foundation, which has been active in local politics. An IMA leader is presently the only woman on the city council. IMA's intervention made Angels the first city to have its own 5 per cent GAD budget ordinance. The ordinance created the GAD council, a mechanism for GO-NGO consultations to ensure GAD be integrated in the city's comprehensive development plan.

- Bacolod City, Negros Occidental in the Visayas, has the Development for Active Women Networking (DAWN) Foundation, a women's organization for the advancement of women's political participation and women's rights. DAWN's executive director was elected as a city councillor in 1995 and in this position, she has fought to ensure gender integration at both municipal and barangay levels.

- Surallah is in Mindanao. Unlike the other two case studies, Surallah is not a city but a first class municipality and the partner NGO here, Building Alternative Rural Resource Institutions and Organizing Services (BARRIOS), is a regional mixed-gender NGO based outside Surallah, with a strong link with the Institute for Politics and Governance (IPG) in Metro Manila. BARRIOS introduced the remarkably participatory barangay level planning in Surallah and a range of other LGUs.

Summary of research findings, challenges and recommendations

Lack of GAD plan and monitoring system

Although all the partner organizations emphasized the importance of a GAD plan to provide the framework and strategy for gender responsive local budgets, no local governments involved in the project had one. Their efforts on GAD were still at the level of conducting gender sensitivity training, policy formulation, funding for projects for women – sometimes as mundane as ballroom dancing – and the like. The lack of understanding of the GAD budget policy on the part of local government officials hinders the participation of women's NGOs in the budget process, particularly in crafting a GAD plan, preventing GAD from being a part of LGUs' development plans. This has implications in the absence of a system for monitoring budget expenditures and their impact on men and women.

None of the three local governments studied have a monitoring system. In fact, this statement is probably true of the overwhelming majority of local governments in the country. The Surallah municipality has asked barrios for assistance in developing a gender-responsive monitoring system. Monitoring is necessary because there is often a big difference between what is written in budgets and what happens in practice. Monitoring needs to ensure that allocated money is spent, to record on whom the money is spent, and to check whether the expenditure has made a difference in the lives of women and men, girls and boys in the community. The lack of evaluation standards has hampered the success of gender mainstreaming initiatives. Monitoring and evaluation standards must be crafted and installed by all agencies.

Role of civil society and importance of strategic alliance

The role of civil society groups in pushing for the integration of gender concerns in the budget process is important. The project partner NGOs in the case studies noted the successful lobbying by loose coalitions of NGOs, with strong local women's movements with dynamic NGO leaders, in realizing the GAD ordinance. The NGOs maintain good relations with the media as well as benefit from information support and capability-building assistance from national NGOs. However, they have minimal influence or participation in the budget process.

The project informed women and women's groups of the inside of the public funds allocation process. Because gender budget work relies on information from the government and legislators, strategic alliances between reformers within political structures and civil society advocates are essential. The experience women are gaining to influence budgetary decisions strengthens their ability to negotiate on other matters. In addition, the strategic alliances strengthen the constituency for broader changes to promote women's economic and legal rights.

The project partners have significantly increased their advocacy capacity as a key feature of GBAA. The models, strategies, and lessons from these groups will continue to be shared with their Philippine peers in this project in the following phase. Civil society participation in gender budget initiatives is important not only for sustainability, but also to ensure that women's real needs are known, to draw on expertise, and to increase democracy. NGOs, with expertise in participatory approaches to barangay development planning, can assist local governments in formulating sectoral development priorities, in identifying effective strategies and methods to integrate gender in their local budgeting process, in encouraging women's participation in local development plans, and in monitoring budget expenditures. GOs could reduce the demand for technical assistance through constructive collaboration with CSOs. The strategic combination of gender analysis, training, and citizen advocacy to make budgets more equitable and to increase accountability has the potential to have both an immediate impact on women's urgent needs by directing more resources to meet them as well as a long-term impact on establishing a gender-equitable economy.

Use of funds

The study found that in one case the city mayor used GAD funds for special projects. In another, some departments used them for GAD-related training, livelihood assistance, drug prevention, city beautification, etc. At the barangay level, big amounts are spent for honoraria of GAD focal persons. In the third case, GAD funds were used as "cookie jar" by the local budget officer who had complete control and discretion over their use. In sum, the project could not identify a gender focus in several of items that the local governments identified as part of GAD allocation. The GAD allocation might have been made as desperate efforts on the part of officials to complete the 5 per cent quota. Other cases might have reflected ignorance and inadequate understanding of gender analysis, gender mainstreaming, or gender-friendliness.

In this regard, the felt need for examples of good practice in GAD fund allocations that can truly help to promote gender equality has to be addressed. NCRFW published a list of "no-no's", the things that may *not* be counted as part of the 5 per cent GAD allocation, using examples drawn from real examples of GAD allocations in the past. Although illustrating that such funding as ballroom dancing for civil servants was a "no-no" was useful, more articulated and unequivocal categorization issued by NCRFW would help solving the current confusion among the officials in charge of budget allocation.

Political dynamics and shifts in leadership

The Angeles City GAD ordinance provided for the election of an NGO leader in the GAD council. However, the level of the NGO member's influence in the council fluctuated according to shifts of the majority there. In Bacolod City, NGO leaders were elected in the city council and served a critical and fiscalizing role in the city government. Relations between NGO leaders and government line agencies were stable. In Surallah, the municipal mayor changed from a traditional politician to a reform-oriented one, but the impact of this change was not yet known.

Progressive and reform-minded local government officials can help initiate and strengthen the task of mainstreaming GAD and women's participation in local governance. Government commitment to the initiative should include building a partnership with CSOs wherever possible. The utilization of the expertise and experience of women's NGOs, policy institutes, research institutions, and other agencies focusing on gender issues could supplement public resources and technical skills. It would also, over time, contribute to the building of the capability of the government officials and public representatives. Further, civil society participation will enhance the sustainability of gender budget initiatives.

Gap between policy and implementation

The Philippines is ahead of many countries in having a law on gender and the budget, as well as a government which is substantially decentralized under the Local Government Code (LGC, 1991). But this and other researches and NCRFW monitoring show that the law is being ignored or implemented in a half-hearted way. Even at the national level, only 133 of 334 agencies complied with the 5 per cent GAD directive. Overall, the allocation for the GAD budget stands at an average of 0.5 per cent of total general appropriations for each year of implementation.

Although there is no nationwide figure for the local government level, the absence of any GAD provision in the LGC seems to allow the continuing marginalization of gender issues. Further research on local level figures could provide insights on whether devolution of responsibilities to the local level, as mandated by the LGC, has made a difference in integrating GAD concerns in local development planning. The need to amend the LGC to provide for GAD concerns should be addressed.

Technical capability to integrate GAD

Budgeting is only one step in the government process of delivery to citizens. Before getting to the budget, government agencies need to conduct a comprehensive assessment of needs among women and men, girls and boys and draw up a plan to address those needs. Nonetheless, GAD budgeting is largely not integrated in general governmental planning and budgeting cycles, due largely to the lack of technical skills and political will.

NGOs with expertise in participatory local development planning, such as IPG, can assist in capability building among government officials to collect sex-disaggregated information, undertake gender-sensitive planning, and implement gender-sensitive monitoring and allocation of resources. All of these steps are building blocks in a coherent system needed for gender-sensitive government provision.

Common understanding of the GAD policy

The coordination among the oversight agencies, such as DBM and DILG, tasked to issue guidelines for implementation, should be strengthened. This includes clarification and definition of their roles, functions, and responsibilities. At present, conflicting interpretations of the 5 per cent GAD policy can be found: for instance, DBM Local Budget Memorandum No. 32 cites an amount of 5 per cent of all appropriations to be set aside for GAD-related projects, while DILG's Memorandum Circular No. 99-146 mentions the use of 5 per cent of the development fund (which is 20 per cent of the internal revenue allotment general grant from the national government) for GAD programmes. LGUs have difficulties in complying with the national budget policy when instructions from the national government agencies conflict among themselves.

The LGC should also be amended to explicitly include a gender budget provision. The local GAD budget should be sourced not only from the internal revenue allotment but also from all other sources of revenue. Local governments should create a mechanism to coordinate the local planning, implementation, monitoring, and evaluation of the GAD budget policy.

Gender mainstreaming: From local to national budgets and beyond "5 per cent"

Gender advocates in the Philippines are justly proud of their achievements in having institutionalized gender in budgets through the GAD budget provision. However, many are increasingly recognizing its limitations and the need to find ways to focus more clearly on the entire budget in order to use the 5 per cent GAD budget to address issues pertinent to the remaining 95 per cent. This research aimed to look at the entire budget instead of the 5 per cent GAD provision. However, the project team was faced with the difficulty to get government line agencies, officials, and NGOs to look beyond the 5 per cent GAD budget. Perhaps the GAD approach has made it hard for people to move outside the 5 per cent framework. The challenge is to ensure that the 5 per cent are used in a way that promotes the gender-responsiveness of the remaining 95 per cent.

While the Philippines is one of the leading countries with respect to gender budget work at the national level, relatively little work has been done at the local government level. NCRFW itself, with a very small staff, acknowledges that it cannot cope with the several hundred national agencies that need its assistance in drawing up gender-responsive budgets. NCRFW has thus actively supported research at the local level.

The Asia Foundation has supported women's organizations and others active in the local government sphere for years. LGU budget was a logical step in empowering women in local governance. GBAA project supported research and training of women's organizations in understanding the budget process so that women can monitor resource allocations and distributions from a gender perspective.

Building on the findings

The Asia Foundation is currently mobilizing resources to build on the initiatives and successes of the GBAA project to embark on the second phase of the project. It is a strategic time to link gender budget work at the national and local levels because the recent change in administration brought in a better national level environment for reforms. The Phase II would link the local to the national, to mainstream gender in sectoral analysis in the national-local nexus. Many national government departments are natural partners in this phase of the project, since their leaders are drawn from the civil society. These leaders, some at the Department Secretary level, had been very active in movements for governmental reform, promoting transparent budgets and citizen participation and movements for equality.

The Foundation recognizes that policy choices and budgets are shaped both by competing political agendas and by the level of technical capacity. Quality research and information, technical knowledge and effective advocacy are central to budget work. The proposed expanded GBAA project is designed to equip women's organizations with necessary tools and skills. It would strive for the informed participation of three interconnected sets of stakeholders: (1) reform-minded elected officials at the national and local levels; (2) functioning government institutions, staffed with responsive and technically qualified individuals; and (3) active, well-informed coalitions of women's and other CSOs capable of articulating demands based on felt material needs and basic human rights. The project will engage women's advocacy groups with other citizens' initiatives in:

- Defining a set of issues where budget advocacy is crucial;

- Carrying out research and analysis in two related sectors;

- Documenting case examples that illustrate how budgets develop;

- Developing advocacy and media strategies.

In addition to sectoral research and analysis, the project will examine the nature and constraints to citizen participation in budget work at the local level. Under public education, the Foundation will work closely with experienced popular media groups to produce a range of simplified budget materials for different audiences to be used in advocacy and public education.

All advocacy campaigns will link national agency budget preparation with local level implementation through civil society observance of DBM's internal budget hearings. DBM is instituting this reform for the fiscal year 2002 budget cycle, and technically sound analysis will increase the impact of such participation.

SESSION 5:

RESPONSIBILITIES AND ACCOUNTABILITIES FOR GENDER MAINSTREAMING

Moderated by

Ms. Patricia Licuanan

President, Miriam College

In the session on the responsibilities and accountabilities for gender mainstreaming, experience from within Government was provided from New Zealand by Ms. Wendy Moore, the Republic of Korea by Mr. Ji Kyu-Taek, the Philippines by Ms. Ermelita Valdeavilla and Tonga by Ms. Polotu 'A. F. Fakafanua. Experience on the role of NGOs in ensuring government accountability for policy commitments was presented from Sri Lanka by Ms. Swarna Jayaweera. At the symposium, Ms. Fakafanua's presentation was given in the case studies session. A summary of discussion based on the presentations is available in the Part II.

MAINSTREAMING GENDER ANALYSIS INTO GOVERNMENT POLICY DEVELOPMENT IN NEW ZEALAND

Ms. Wendy Moore

Ministry of Women's Affairs, New Zealand

New Zealand context, especially at the Cabinet policy process

The Ministry of Women's Affairs (MWA) is the key department responsible for ensuring the Mainstreaming of Gender Analysis in the policy development work of the core public sector through the preparation of Gender Implications Statements (GIS). The approach taken to mainstream gender analysis has four key elements:

(1) Commitment at the Cabinet level;

(2) Legitimizing the gender analysis framework;

(3) Supporting and encouraging key public sector agencies to incorporate gender analysis in all Social Equity Policies;

(4) Relationship building through collaboration across sectors.

The Cabinet Policy Process starts with a ministry preparing a Cabinet paper with recommendations. With the Minister's signature, the paper is submitted to the Cabinet Committee (Social Equity Committee). The Cabinet Committee may agree or disagree with the recommendations. The minutes of the Cabinet Committee are sent to Cabinet. The Cabinet confirms or amends the minutes submitted by the Cabinet Committee and issues directives to departments.

Gender Implications Statements (GIS)

The use of GIS in New Zealand is a method of integrating gender analysis into public policy development. For 12 months now, public service departments in New Zealand have been required to provide GIS in all Cabinet papers going to the Cabinet Social Equity Committee. The requirement for the GIS was prompted by the Government's concern over:

- The level of inequality in New Zealand society in the key areas of education, health, housing and employment;

- The poor quality of policy advice;

- The lack of a focus on how to reduce inequalities in society;

especially in terms of assessing the differential impact of policy on all women and men, and on Māori women and men in particular. In short, the hook for introducing the GIS was improving the quality of policy advice.

The GIS should report on whether gender analysis was undertaken as a part of policy development. Where gender analysis is not undertaken, the reason must be reported in the Cabinet paper. Where gender analysis is undertaken, the GIS must clearly explain the key analytical findings and the applicability of those findings to the policy proposal, including: the way and the extent in which a policy proposal affects women and men directly and indirectly; clarification of the desired outcomes, whether they are same or different for women and men; and ascertaining policy and operational options to address the identified issues. The department or agency responsible for the policy proposal prepares the GIS following consultation with interested parties. If the GIS state that there are no gender implications related to the policy, the department or agency that prepared the GIS is expected to state why this conclusion is reached. Departments and agencies are also expected to report barriers to completing the GIS, such as lack of access to disaggregated data. The GIS include monitoring the results by collecting the data pertaining to the outcomes by sex and ethnicity.

Roles and responsibilities in the implementation of GIS

MWA, Social Equity Officials Committee, Central agencies (State Services Commission, Treasury and the Department of the Prime Minister and Cabinet) and other public sector departments have roles, responsibilities and accountabilities in ensuring greater integration of gender analysis in public policy development.

MWA evaluates the effectiveness of the GIS. The evaluation focuses on whether gender analysis has been undertaken, the key findings and the key desired policy and operational outcomes for women and men where these are different or where the impact of the policy may be different. MWA also provides ongoing advice to other departments upon request or during the consultation phase of the policy development. MWA developed and provided a gender analysis check list, "key questions to ask", guidelines and frameworks for gender analysis and training and seminars. Following a pilot with departments, the training package is being updated to better reflect the individual needs of departments and agencies with an emphasis on how to apply gender analysis.

Officials' Committees are an important link between departments and agencies and the Cabinet Committees. They have generic responsibility for overall quality control of advice going to the Cabinet and specific responsibility for ensuring that gender analysis is carried out and that there is a GIS in Social Equity policy papers. The Committees respond to the Cabinet's requirements and provide high quality advice based on robust analysis, including consideration of gender implications. It is essential that the Committees have a clear understanding and commitment to that role.

Central agencies are responsible for articulating the Government's strategic direction for public service, and assuring that the public service has the policy capability to deliver outcomes relevant to the Government's strategic direction, and ensuring a "whole of Government" approach to implementing the Government policy. Departmental capability is an important aspect to an increased use and strength of gender analysis both in terms of the actual undertaking of the analysis and its quality. The State Services Commission believes that the new approach to public sector performance provides opportunities that complement the work of MWA. For example, it is envisaged that the departments in which improved outcomes for women are not achieved, due to the failure to adequately complete gender analysis, would improve their performance through discussions with MWA. The Treasury has worked with MWA to look at gender analysis of the budget processes.

Other Public Service Departments provide quality policy advice to the Government including gender analysis, preparing the GIS for relevant policy papers and responding to MWA's evaluation of the gender analysis and GIS. It has been observed that Departments are not routinely applying the "Key Questions to Ask in Gender Analysis". They are expected to consistently differentiate between men and women, and between all men and women and Māori men and women, Pacific women and men; and routinely use available data disaggregated by sex and ethnicity, which is critical in terms of producing quality advice that informs Ministers of the policy choices and probable outcomes for different population groups and a priority area in terms of analysis at the problem definition stage. They are also expected to consult with appropriate NGOs on a regular basis. These expectations are not always met. Some departments simply state that there are no gender implications without showing any evidence of having carried out the necessary analysis to make this assertion or stating that they relied on the administration exemption. Consequently the barriers to gender analysis and the differential impacts on men and women are not identified. It is extremely important that all departments develop the capacity and practice to include gender analysis in their policy development.

Constraints and challenges

Gender analysis is still seen as a "women only" approach. Lack of commitment and/ or capability in terms of people and funding continue to be major constraints across the core public service generally. Many agencies have neither the time nor the resources to produce quality gender analysis as well as focus on their own area of analytical expertise. These are key reasons why gender analysis is not routinely part of policy analysis per se. This finding suggests that accountability mechanisms being used may not necessarily achieve greater integration of gender analysis without being accompanied by sufficient resourcing and capability. MWA's evaluation of GIS indicates that departments are not using gender analysis at the problem definition stage and this creates difficulties for them when it comes to completing the GIS.

The next steps for New Zealand in the integration process

In order to overcome the barriers, such as the lack of human and financial resources and of the data disaggregated by sex and ethnicity and knowledge regarding the types of statistical information that are available, a strategy of the Government as a whole to address future and ongoing action on issues for women is necessary. A future oriented strategy and action plan which addresses the diverse lives of women and which has a strategic fit with the Government's long term priorities and provides a framework for Government action needs to be developed. The strategy and action plan should confirm and advance the goals for women of: equity, opportunity and choice, full and active participation, adequate resources, no discrimination, a society that values the contribution of women but also ensures that the use of gender analysis is relevant to both genders and not just for women.

The full development and implementation of an Action Plan for Women is an essential step forward as it will provide a context within which the integration of gender analysis can be driven. Emphases will be given to the usefulness of gender analysis when applied to different population groups to enable comparative analysis and to the need for disaggregated data. Having a framework within which relevant departments can work is likely to assist the integration of gender analysis across the public sector while integrating gender analysis across all Cabinet Committees is likely to increase impact on all policies and agencies. Full commitment from central agencies and officials committees is essential because this is where the capability work (central agencies) and quality control work is done. Finally, the need to develop effective accountability approaches to measure the effectiveness of key public sector agencies in developing policy and budget allocations from a gender perspective has to be highlighted.

* * *

GENDER MAINSTREAMING AND NON-GOVERNMENTAL ORGANIZATIONS: THE SRI LANKA EXPERIENCE

Ms. Swarna Jayaweera

Centre for Women's Research (CENWOR)

In Sri Lanka, the national machinery for the advancement of women began with the establishment of the Women's Bureau in 1978. In 1983, a Cabinet Ministry was assigned to include women's affairs among its functions, which evolved into an independent ministry, the Ministry of Women's Affairs in 1994 and the National Committee on Women in 1993. Alongside, attempts of gender mainstreaming were made through the formulation and adoption of a Women's Charter in 1993 and the preparation of a National Plan of Action (1995-1996). An exercise was undertaken to engender the National Budget in 1998-1999. Regrettably, however, the impact of these gender mainstreaming measures has been minimal. The inadequate resources and power given to the national machinery has prevented it from effectively participating in the national planning and monitoring process. As a result, women's concerns have been kept dichotomously separated from national development plans and kept in peripheral women specific projects. The acceptance of the Women's Charter and the ratification of CEDAW in 1981 as a state policy prompted little interest in incorporating their provisions in national legislation. The National Plan of Action developed in the months after the Fourth World Conference on Women (FWCW) never got off the ground and is now being updated.

Collective actions by NGOs

NGOs, particularly women's NGOs, were concerned with the relative marginalization of gender issues in national development programmes. The originally low key and disparate NGO efforts have developed into sporadic but collective actions on the national scene in the 1990s. The collective actions have four levels:

1. Participation in the formulation of the Women's Charter (1993) and the National Plan of Action (1995-1996) and its revision (2000-2001);

2. Participation in the CEDAW process through the preparation of the Shadow Report and its presentation to the CEDAW Committee;

3. Advocacy for gender issues to all political parties before the general elections in 1994, 2000 and 2001. An NGO, the Women's Political Forum, took an initiative to organize the participation of twelve women's organizations in developing, publishing and disseminating the *Women's Manifesto* for the general elections in the last two elections. The two major political parties incorporated some of the issues in the *Women's Manifesto* into their parties manifestos;

4. Establishment of an NGO Forum for women on the eve of FWCW in 1994. The Forum, comprised of 15 national women's organizations, works with a large number of other NGOs and CBOs throughout the country. The Forum specifically engaged, through the national media, in an advocacy programme to project some of the critical areas of concern in the Beijing Platform for Action, such as women's political participation, work and reproductive health and violence against women.

Centre for Women's Research

Since its inception in 1984, CENWOR has focused on the absence of gender mainstreaming in national development programme and subsequently intensified efforts through multi-pronged approaches to incorporate gender concerns in programmes at all levels of the polity and to monitor their impact. CENWOR has eight approaches to promote gender mainstreaming:

Regular review of women's situation in 10 areas of concern

In order to articulate issues for national discussion on the eve of the Nairobi World Conference in 1985, CENWOR evaluated the extent to which women's concerns had been incorporated in the national development programme in Sri Lanka.[34] It conducted subsequent reviews of women's situations on the occasions of FWCW and its five year review (1995 and 2000),[35] and of the fifty year anniversary of the political independence in 1998. The reviews have given visibility to the marginalization of gender concerns and the needs for mainstreaming.

Policy oriented research and evaluation

CENWOR has continuously explored issues of "missing women", or the relegation of women to the margins of the national development process, especially in large programmes such as the Accelerated Mahaweli Development Programme and the Integrated Rural Development Planning. The researches revealed the social exclusion of women in low income families and the incorporation of women as low cost labour as a consequence of macroeconomic reforms and structural adjustment programmes (SAP).

Programme monitoring and gender audit

Continuous monitoring of state programmes is a strategy to promote gender mainstreaming. Evaluations of specific programmes, such as of the assistance for women and children victims of armed conflicts and domestic violence and of vocational training,

---

[34] CENWOR, 1985. *United Nations Decade for women progress and achievements of women in Sri Lanka.* Colombo.

[35] CENWOR, 1995. *Facets of Change, Women in Sri Lanka 1986-1995.* Colombo.
CENWOR, 2000, *Post Beijing reflection: Women in Sri Lanka 1995-2000.* Colombo.

have been fedback to policy deliberations. Gender auditing of planning and monitoring institutions at national, provincial and district levels found that there were no mechanisms and only minimal awareness and skills to mainstream gender issues.[36] Vitarana found that the mandatory Environment Impact Assessment missed gender issues.[37] A gender audit of relevant ILO Conventions is in progress, while preparation for gender auditing of selected state institutions and of the implementation of the Women's Charter and CEDAW is under way. CENWOR also assisted the Department of National Planning to publish its study on engendering the national budget.[38]

Policy dialogues and inputs at the national level for legislative reform and planning

A series of policy dialogues and advocacy sessions with high level policy makers and administrators was useful to inform them of the needs to integrate gender issues in national plans and programmes in the agriculture, industry and services sectors, and was contributory to criminalization of gender based violence in the revised Penal Code. A dialogue with key personnel responsible for the Census in 2001 was fruitful to integrate the full spectrum of women's work in reporting the labour force participation. This was complemented by a media programme on the eve of the Census to sensitize women to the need "to be counted". More dialogues are being conducted for further legislative reforms, such as to amend land laws that ignore women's rights and to remove barriers for women to enter vocational training. Underscoring the recognition of gender as a cross cutting issue, CENWOR members are also on the policy level committees of the Ministry of Women's Affairs, the Foreign Employment Bureau, Vocational Training Authorities, as well as the SAARC Convention on Trafficking in Women and Children, the SAARC Social Charter, and the UNDAF of Sri Lanka.

Production and dissemination of print and electronic materials for use by state and non-state agencies for sensitization in various areas of concerns

CENWOR produces materials designed to engender national programmes, policies and practices. Examples are motivational materials focusing on diverse careers used by state vocational training authorities; the Gender Resource Book for teachers and national teacher education institutions; functional literacy materials with a gender perspective used in non-formal education programmes; and proposed inputs to the Police Training School curriculum. Further, a set of legal literacy materials is being used widely to integrate women in the legal and political processes.

---

[36] Jayaweera, Swarna 2000. *Gender Audit: planning and monitoring institutions and organizations*, CENWOR: Colombo.

[37] Vitrana, Kamini 2000. *Environmental assessment studies-A gender perspective*, CENWOR: Colombo.

[38] Department of National Planning 2000. *Engendering the national budget*, CENWOR: Colombo.

Sensitization of policy makers and administrators at all levels

In order to surmount the perceived lack of awareness of the need for gender mainstreaming in the administration, CENWOR conducts face-to-face sensitization programmes with officials of key state agencies.

Provision of information through database and ICT

CENWOR is developing a database of sex-disaggregated data pertaining to employment, education, health and political participation as well as using modern technologies, such as creating a web site and establishing tele-centers in rural locations to promote gender mainstreaming.

Networking with state and other non-state agencies and organizations

CENWOR's efforts at gender mainstreaming and monitoring are facilitated by networking.

Contributions of other NGOs

CENWOR is not alone in gender mainstreaming efforts. In addition to the contributions already described in the above, the following are some of effective approaches taken by other NGOs:

(i)   Research and advocacy by the Muslim Women's Research and Action Front for reform of Muslim personal laws to remove barriers to gender equality in the legislative process;

(ii)   Development of draft for domestic violence legislation by the Women and Media Collective;

(iii)   Advocacy for a uniform minimum age of marriage by the Lawyers for Human Rights and Development;

(iv)   A campaign to ensure the right of migrant workers to vote at general elections by the Migrant Services Centre;

(v)   Development of a media policy by the Women's Education and Research Centre;

(vi)   Training of police officers by the Women's Development Centre;

(vii)   Promotion of entrepreneurship and organization of Annual Trade Fairs for women entrepreneurs by Agromart.

Conclusion

This overview of NGO activities promoting gender mainstreaming in national policies and programmes indicates that NGOs use different approaches and tools such as research, evaluation, advocacy and sensitization, production of policy instruments and programme materials, and ICTs. It also reflects the commitment of NGOs to developing new initiatives. The needs for regional technical assistance has to be emphasized in equipping personnel in

State agencies and research institutions with skills of gender analysis, developing gender sensitive indicators and gender impact assessment techniques as tools to move forward the process of gender mainstreaming. For NGOs, an opportunity to participate in regular regional reviews to exchange and learn from country, regional and international experiences is useful. Finally it is salutary to underscore a caveat that gender mainstreaming is not gender "male streaming" or incorporating women in national development programmes that perpetuate gender inequalities. The conceptual framework for gender mainstreaming has to be the recognition of women's rights as human rights, the equitable gender division of labour, the promotion of equal access of women and men to assets, resources and services and the control of these resources to ensure the empowerment of women.

* * *

MINISTRY OF GENDER EQUALITY AND MAJOR POLICIES IN THE REPUBLIC OF KOREA

Mr. Ji Kyu-Taek

Ministry of Gender Equality, Republic of Korea[39]

Ministry of Gender Equality (MOGE)

In the Republic of Korea, the Ministry of Gender Equality was established in January 2001. Its major role and function is consolidating and coordinating women's policies among relevant ministries in achieving gender mainstreaming. The Ministry has one office and three bureaus. They are: The Planning and Policy Coordination Office, Gender Equality Promotion Bureau, Women's Human Rights Promotion Bureau, and Cooperation and Liaison Bureau. There are 11 divisions under the Minister. The total number of staff of MOGE, including the Minister, is 102. The ratio between male and female staff is 35 to 65 per cent.

Key laws

The Ministry deals with five major laws related to gender issues. They are:

(1) Women's Development Act (1995): The basic act describing the idea of gender equality and promoting women's status. Under this act, the Ministry has established a five-year basic plan for women's policies.

(2) Gender Discrimination Prevention and Relief Act (1999): The act mandates the ministry to operate the Committee on Gender Equality Promotion. This Committee can receive complaints of gender discrimination or sexual harassment cases and investigate the cases and advise the violator to correct his or her wrongdoings.

---

[39] Summarized from transcript of presentation.

(3) ***Prevention of Domestic Violence and Victim Protection Act*** (1997):   According to this act, the government supports the operation of counselling centres and shelters for the victims of sexual and domestic violence.

(4) ***Prevention of Prostitution Act*** (1962):   This act prohibits the selling and buying of sex and provides penalty for violation.

(5) ***Military Sexual Slavery Livelihood Protection Act*** (1993):   The act provides support for the comfort women who were used as sexual slaves by the Japanese army during the Second World War.

Policy goals and direction

The Goal of MOGE is the realization of a gender equal, democratic and welfare state in which respect for human rights is guaranteed.   For the achievement of this goal the Ministry has two directions: one is the development of women's human resources, which will help to enhance the global competitiveness of the Republic of Korea; the other is protecting women's rights and improving the quality of their lives.   MOGE promotes gender mainstreaming through making de jure policies concerning women de facto reality as a part of everyday life.

Development of women's human resources

MOGE develops and facilitates women's human resources through three main strategies.   They are:

1.   Expansion of women's participation in public sector

In expanding women's participation in the public sector, MOGE has introduced a quota system for political parties and recommended that at least 30 per cent of their Proportional Representation Candidates be female.   Also, in ministerial committees, the participation of women has increased from 23.6 per cent in 2000 to 28 per cent in 2001. MOGE hopes to raise this percentage to at least 30 per cent by 2002.   As for affirmative action for advancing female civil servants, MOGE has implemented a guideline of appointing at least one female director or chief in each government ministry or bureau.   In 2000, the female public officers ratio in the 5th level and above[40] was around 4 per cent.   To increase this figure, MOGE has set a target of 10 per cent of 5th level and 20 per cent of 6th level female by the year 2005.

2.   Assistance for women's economic activities

In assisting women's economic activities as one of the means of developing women's human resources, MOGE is operating 46 Women's Resources Development Centres nation wide.   The centres provide women with education programmes, counselling, training and job information.   The centres enable women to find jobs more easily.   MOGE is also working to build infant and childcare facilities to alleviate concerns of working women with children. Maternity leave has been extended from 60 to 90 days through revising related laws.

---

[40]   Government official status levels with 9 the lowest and 1 the highest.

3. Building women's capacity in ICT

MOGE is striving to build women's capacities in the area of ICT. With the support of universities and Women's Resources Development Centres, women now have more opportunities for professional training in E-biz, web design, etc., and therefore have a better chance in finding and maintaining their jobs. Around 600 women have received such training up to the year 2001. MOGE is also constructing a web site for women, named "Women-net", which will begin its operation early in 2002. It is expected to play a central role in communication among women.

Protecting women's rights

Protecting women's rights is another main direction to which MOGE tries to accord the necessary means and measures:

1. Immediate and fair relief in gender discrimination cases

As mentioned above, MOGE operates the Committee on Gender Equality Promotion, consisting of 10 members. It receives reports of cases of gender discrimination and investigates them. This committee is invested with the authority to decide whether the case is gender-discriminatory. If necessary, the committee can publicize relevant facts to the media.

2. Systemization of prevention policies to counter sexual harassment

As a preventive measure for sexual harassment, MOGE conducts various kinds of education and publishes education materials. MOGE also runs an "Instructor Pool", consisting of more than 300 professional instructors for education on sexual harassment.

3. Prevention of violence against women and protection for the victims

To provide support for the victims of domestic and sexual violence, MOGE operates an emergency "hot line 1366". This line connects women with relevant organizations such as medical, judicial facilities and the police. MOGE also manages 141 domestic violence counselling centres and 91 sexual violence counselling centres, which can provide victims with legal and medical support. In addition, MOGE runs 30 shelters for victims of domestic violence to provide them with a place to turn to at times of crucial need.

4. Efforts to making "gender-equal culture" a part of everyday life

In contriving to make gender-equal culture a part of everyday life, MOGE holds a "Women's Week" on the First week of July every year. In addition, MOGE holds campaigns and monitors the mass media throughout the year for gender-discriminatory acts or statements.

Constraints in gender mainstreaming

Two main constraints in gender mainstreaming in society in the Republic of Korea are the pervasive traditional customs and habits and the shortage of childcare facilities.

1. *Pervasion of traditional customs and habits, stemming from the doctrine of Confucianism*

With the male oriented thinking and practices of Confucianism doctrines prevailing in most parts of society, women are faced with distinctively set gender roles that work to their disadvantage.

2. *Shortage of childcare facilities*

The shortage of childcare facilities poses as an obstacle for women's participation in economic activities, and is the main reason that the participation of highly educated women in economic and social activities in the Republic of Korea is so low. MOGE allocates as much resources as possible in assisting working women.

MOGE proposed budget for the fiscal year 2002

MOGE's budget for FY 2002 is 42.7 billion won (W 1300 = US$ 1). The budget increase of 10.9 per cent from 31.8 billion won last year is the highest among all government ministries of the Republic of Korea.

Major programmes of MOGE for FY 2002:

- Assistance for the victims of sexual violence: W 17.4b. (US$ 13m.)

- Women Development Fund: W 10b. (US$ 8m.)

- Operation of "Women Resources Development Centre": W 7.5b. (US$ 6m.)

- Co-project with women's NGOs: W 2b. (US$ 1.5m.)

- Construction of "Women-Network": W 1.1b. (US$ 1m.)

- Others: W 4.7b. (US$ 3.5m.)

The characteristics of the proposed budget can be summarized: First it aims to expand assistance for marginalized women, especially victims of sexual violence, domestic violence and sexual trafficking. It plans to strengthen medical assistance for the victims of sexual violence by providing the expenses for medical treatment. It also intends to boost preventive activities such as education programmes. It will also provide assistance for comfort women, or the women used as sexual slaves by the Japanese army during the Second World War. Secondly, the budget intends to promote efficient policy through cooperation with women's NGOs, in such forms as co-project with women's NGOs. Finally the proposed budget provides for promoting and building women's capacity in ICT.

* * *

RESPONSIBILITIES AND ACCOUNTABILITIES FOR GENDER MAINSTREAMING

Ms. Ermelita V. Valdeavilla
Executive Director
National Commission on the Role of Filipino Women

The National Commission on the Role of Filipino Women (NCRFW) is the national focal point for women in the Philippines. During the first decade of its existence (1975-1985), NCRFW was regarded as the principal agency for carrying out policies and programmes for the advancement of women. However, new perspectives emerged after the United Nations Decade for Women (1975-1985) and the top level revamp during the term of President Corazon Aquino helped shift the concentration of responsibilities and expectations from the NCRFW to key agencies of government. The Aquino government declared that responding to the concerns of women was everybody's business. The role of NCRFW was redefined as to catalyze, coordinate, and provide leadership and technical assistance to government agencies.

This paper attempts to capture a snapshot of the NCRFW's insights in redistributing responsibilities and accountabilities for gender mainstreaming among government agencies and its partners. It defines what "responsibility and accountability" meant to the NCRFW, presents the mandates and how gender mainstreaming responsibilities are distributed, and describes some accountability mechanisms set up for gender mainstreaming.

Accountability and responsibility: What do they mean to us?

The concept of accountability and responsibility may be clarified by asking the following five questions: *Who* should be blamed? *by whom? about what? when?,* and *so what?* It is about an agreement between the duty-holder and claimholder to deliver what types of results, when, how, and at what cost. It may be illustrated by the following formula:

$$\frac{\begin{array}{l} \text{Responsibility} \\ +\ \text{Power} \\ +\ \text{Resources} \\ +\ \text{Action} \end{array}}{\text{Results/Time}} = \text{Reward or Sanction}$$

Mandate

Gender mainstreaming consists of numerous complex responsibilities that must be clearly and systematically assigned, and synergistically accomplished by multiple agents to deliver the desired impacts. It is not enough to say that gender mainstreaming is a responsibility of everybody. The specific responsibilities should be fleshed out, their relationship with one another should be established, and the proper party should be selected to deliver such responsibilities. This being so, a system of responsibility allocation must be clarified, negotiated, and supported by policies or laws.

Cognizant of these, the Philippine Government adopted policies and laws that delineate responsibilities on gender mainstreaming. The following are some examples of them:

- *Women in Development and Nation Building Act* (RA 7192): This law provides that all agencies of government should submit a semi-annual gender report to the Congress and the Office of the President, copy furnished to the national women's machinery. This is one of the bases of NCRFW's monitoring role in relation to the gender plans and activities of government agencies and their instrumentalities;

- Executive Order No. 273: This provides, among others, that agencies shall include the implementation of the *Philippine Plan for Gender-Responsive Development* (the 30 year gender plan) into their plans, budgets and monitoring and evaluation systems. It also provides that gender shall be part of the key result areas of agencies;

- GAD Budget provision in the Annual General Appropriations Act: This mandates the national women's machinery to review the GAD plans and reports of government agencies.

Distribution of Responsibilities

Under a project assisted by the Canadian International Development Agency (CIDA), a study of the planning cycle and their mechanisms was conducted which pointed out the agencies with mandates that are critical to gender mainstreaming.

Roles and Responsibilities

NCRFW		COLLABORATING AGENCIES
Information and Training services and referral		Oversight Agencies: Standard setting and coordination
Policy analysis and development	$\longrightarrow$	Statistical Agencies: Gender-responsive statistics
Project development and implementation		Line Agencies/Sub-national bodies: Modelling best practices in gender mainstreaming
Monitoring and evaluation		Academic/Training institutions: Gender training and development of materials

The above diagram shows the relationship of the national women's machinery (NCRFW) with the rest of the bureaucracy in terms of promoting gender mainstreaming. It shows the NCRFW as the lead agency principally responsible for advocacy and promoting information, providing training services and referral, policy analysis and development, implementation of projects that develop systems, tools and skills for gender mainstreaming, and monitoring and evaluation of government actions on women's and gender concerns.

The NCRFW works with four types of government agencies. Oversight agencies are those that are principally mandated to oversee the work of other government agencies. Among them are the National Economic and Development Authority (NEDA), Department of Budget and Management (DBM), Department of Interior and Local Government (DILG), and the Civil Service Commission. Partnerships have been built with these agencies in order that they may integrate gender in their standard setting and coordination functions.

Three statistical agencies of government also work closely with NCRFW. These are the National Statistical Coordination Board, the National Statistics Office and the Statistical Research and Training Centre. They are concerned with mainstreaming gender in national statistics, developing and conducting gender training for statisticians and local planners, and undertaking special studies to obtain data that are significant to gender assessment and analysis.

The mandate for implementation rests in the line agencies and local government units (LGUs). Thus, they are mandated to consider gender in their planning, programming and budgeting, implementation and monitoring and implementation. They are also mandated and encouraged to set up gender focal points or local commissions on women, to adopt gender and development code and to link with women among their constituents and partners. They are also encouraged to try out innovative strategies on gender mainstreaming and to document them for sharing with others.

State colleges and universities are also covered by government policies on gender and are encouraged to set up GAD Resource Centres from where LGUs and agencies could access technical resources and information on gender planning and budgeting.

Negotiating roles and responsibilities

To get the roles and responsibilities negotiated, both at the technical and managerial levels before pertinent policies are issued, would ensures ownership, assist building of consensus over contentious issues, and minimize potential problems in the implementation process. Such negotiated roles and responsibility would help even more than a policy or legal instrument.

The negotiation of roles and responsibilities in development planning begins at the technical level. Technical staff of concerned agencies meet and clarify the stages and processes involved in development planning. Then, in each of these stages and processes, the needed interventions on gender mainstreaming are identified. It is important that these two topics are first discussed objectively before they are delineated to ensure that they are exhaustively tackled. Then, they identify which agency is responsible for each intervention on the basis of their germane mandates. The capacity building needs (to carry out the assigned interventions) are identified and corresponding actions are taken.

The process moves on to the higher level on which the recommendations of the technical team are discussed and approved. This process requires sponsorship of the highest officials of NCRFW and of the concerned agencies. Normally, the executing policy is approved at this level.

Accountability mechanisms

1.   **Women** – To follow up government action on the Beijing Platform for Action, a group known as Philippine Beijing Score Board was set up by women NGOs. This group maintains a scorecard on relevant indicators and works with the Committee on Women of the Houses of Representative and Senate to create a forum where government agencies are tasked to report on their performance on gender mainstreaming. This is usually done in partnership with the NCRFW.

2.   **Department of Interior and Local Government** – This is the government's arm for monitoring the work of LGUs. DILG uses a set of indicators, called Local Productivity Performance Measures, to assess the performance of government agencies in various aspects. Gender indicators are being incorporated in this instrument.

There is also a competition for the Galing Pook Award, an award of excellence in local administration. Its selection criteria includes gender concerns. It is also ensured that the pre-screening committees have members who are gender-sensitive. A special citation on gender is also one of the awards added to the categories.

LGUs submit GAD reports to the local offices of DILG. Some of them do so through NEDA. Both agencies provide NCRFW with a copy of the reports, although it is desired that such reports are processed and synthesized by both agencies before furnishing NCRFW with a copy.

Presently, there is a campaign to have a State of the Women report by LGUs.

3.   **NCRFW** – NCRFW reviews and synthesizes the accomplishment report of agencies and produces a report on their performance. The report is presented during budget hearings, both in the Senate and in the House of Representatives. NCRFW also provides legislators with questions that they could ask the heads of various government agencies when they present their annual budget proposals.

The gender budget policy has made NCRFW a welcome member of the technical budget hearings, where questions are raised on agencies' performance on the utilization of the GAD budget and technical advices on their upcoming plans are provided.

As a signatory to CEDAW, NCRFW undertakes an assessment and reporting process every four years. This is a mechanism for reflecting on the country's performance on a mid term basis. The process is participatory, involving both government and NGOs, as well as members of the academe.

4.   **Department of Budget and Management** – DBM looks into the accomplishment reports of agencies and their budget proposals. In the process, DBM checks on the claims for gender budget. DBM also makes room for NCRFW participation in budget hearings. More training, particularly in gender planning and budgeting for its middle level staff and field personnel, to strengthen its capacities would benefit DBM in implementing its role.

5. Congress – The Committees on Women in both chambers of Congress are still among the most powerful allies of NCRFW in ensuring that accountabilities and responsibilities are complied with. The budgeting process continues to be a strategic avenue for monitoring performance on gender mainstreaming. In addition, special hearings are occasionally conducted to monitor government agencies' work on gender mainstreaming.

6. President – President Aquino instituted a bi-annual en-banc meeting with NCRFW Board of Commissioners to keep the President updated on the developments on gender and get her support on matters that require Cabinet action. The mechanism was improved under President Ramos' administration in which he instituted a quarterly meeting with NCRFW Board of Commissioners and occasional meeting with the Cabinet where NCRFW presented a report on the agencies' performance on gender mainstreaming. Unfortunately this mechanism died during the administration of President Estrada and efforts are underway to get it back into place under the current government.

Conclusion

Responsibilities and accountabilities are important in sustaining gender mainstreaming. A framework for delineating responsibilities and accountabilities has to be developed, taking into consideration the mandates of critical agencies, the interventions needed, the system of procedural and substantive coordination, and the desired outcome.

The active participation of gender activists in government, both at the technical and highest levels is essential. The most important, however, is the role of the women's movement in serving as a "gender-watch" because this is the factor that will keep government in constant action. An effective scheme of rewards and sanctions are also essential in fostering performance on gender mainstreaming.

* * *

GOVERNMENT OF TONGA:
STRATEGIES FOR GENDER MAINSTREAMING[41]

Ms. Polotu 'A. F. Fakafanua
Women and Development Centre, Prime Minister's Office, Tonga

Background

Tonga is a constitutional monarchy and has 171 islands, of which only 36 are inhabited, with 670 square kilometres of total land area in the South Central Pacific. According to the 1995 census, the population is 97,784, of which 49.3 per cent are female, and main sources of incomes are agriculture, government services, remittances and aid with

---

[41] The presentation is based on the following documents published by the Government of Tonga: *Annual Report of the Prime Minister's Office for the Year 2000* (2000); Kingdom of Tonga, *National Policy on Gender and Development* (2001); and with UNIFEM Pacific, *Tonga Progress Report Beijing+5*, Suva (1999).

per capita GDP US$ 1,973. Tonga attains high scores on the Human Development Index, including longevity, with average life expectancy of 69 years, and high adult literacy rate of 98.5 per cent. The Government maintains priority to the social sector – in its recurrent budgets for the past five years, expenditure on health has risen by 30.5 per cent and in education by 27.6 per cent.

Tongan women have been privileged in the Tongan society, culture and traditions, compared with men. The *fahu* system entitles the sisters of a man and all the sisters' children precedence over his resources and valuables. The entitlement includes the fruit of the brother's harvests and a privileged position in celebration and traditional ceremonies such as weddings, birthdays and funerals. The privileged status of women currently, however, is being compromised and limited mostly to traditional and cultural functions, due to changing social values influenced by a cash economy.

Government's commitment to women and development

The Government of Tonga has committed to women and development, as reflected in its commitments made at global conferences and their five year reviews, such as FWCW (Beijing), ICPD (Cairo), the World Summit for Social Development (Copenhagen) as well as the Pacific Platform for Action on Women's Development (1994) and the Commonwealth Plan of Action of Gender and Development (1995).

The Government has endeavoured to develop and institutionalize effective mechanisms for gender mainstreaming in Tonga, through the Women and Development Centre (WDC) and the Langafonua National Council of Women. The Centre was originally established as the Women Affairs Unit through a series of Cabinet Decisions on women and development issued in 1993, and redesignated the Women and Development Centre (WDC) as the national focal point for women's development in 1996. Another Cabinet Decision in 1993 recognized the Langafonua National Council of Women as the NGO focal point for women's development towards the development of women's work at the community level. The Cabinet also decided in 1993 that the Prime Minister's Office should coordinate women's issues in Tonga, to develop a National Policy on Women and Development, and a National Advisory Committee on Women, which was in 2000 designated as the National Advisory Committee on Gender and Development (NACGAD).

WDC was established with the following long term objectives:

- To integrate women into the mainstream of the development of the country;

- To provides assistance and consultancy to women so as to enhance their economic productiveness and their role in the economy;

- To consolidate with women's groups and organizations, in developing and implementing programmes for women in the fields of education, health, agriculture, fisheries, commerce and industries, nutrition, home management, income generating activities and communication.

The re-establishment of *Langafonua 'a Fafine Tonga,* or the National Women's Council, has expedited the growth of women's groups and improved interaction between Government and NGO women. It also contributed to better understanding and coordination of women's activities and resources in Tonga.

Government's strategies

Tonga has a policy framework in place to integrate gender concerns into the national development process A National Policy on Gender and Development was developed through broad discussions among the Government, NGOs and donor agencies present in Tonga and was approved by the Government in August 2001. NACGAD in operation since April 2000 is tasked with the implementation of the Policy.

Infrastructure for institutionalizing women's activities and a mechanism to integrate gender dimension into the formulation, appraisal, and approval of all development assistance projects were established. On the government side, WDC provides timely quality policy advice on gender equity issues to government ministries, other development agencies and NGOs. On the NGO side, *Langafonua* National Council of Women, which had been established in 1953 by the late Queen Salote, was recognized as the counterpart of WDC to work for the empowerment of women, income-generation, handicraft creation, and environment affairs. It should be highlighted that in the Tongan process of gender mainstreaming and the project implementation, NGOs have been officially included. The above mentioned National Policy on GAD and NACGAD are a few examples that influential sectors in the society have been strategically involved with, including for National Council of Women, NGOs, community groups, church groups, the private sector and other members of the civil society in addition to Government ministries and departments.

The Prime Minister is the Minister responsible for Women's Affairs, which lends WDC policy influence, a position with power and priority over other sectors. Gender Focal Points have been assigned in each of the line Ministries and received gender training. Gender sensitization of and strengthened networks of Gender Focal Points committed to the inclusion of gender equity is a desired characteristic in the Vision of the Government of Tonga Strategic Development Plan 7 for 2001-2003. A core group of trained policy makers and officials in line ministries and NGO representatives advocating for and supporting GAD Policy implementation and the capacity of key Government ministries and NGOs, particularly the WDC, line ministries and *Langafonua,* are evidencing that the mechanism to facilitate the WDC Policy implementation has been strengthened.

Donor interventions to support government's efforts

There have been two major projects by international donors that have contributed to gender issues in Tonga. The first one was a project sponsored by the UNIFEM Pacific Subregional office on "Institutional Strengthening and Capacity-Building", which started in 1996. The project first assisted the national machinery for women (WDC) and its NGO counterpart, the *Langafonua* National Council of Women's Council, to develop their work programmes for 1996-1999. Then assistance was provided for capacity building training for senior officials in WDC and the *Langafonua* as well as Central Planning Department,

Ministry for Finance and Ministry of Agriculture. The project, together with NZODA,[42] assisted the development of the 1998 Gender and Development Policy (GAD Policy), with the designation of a Gender Focal Point to coordinate consultation on the GAD Policy in the following year. In addition, the project addressed women in politics by providing training for women voters and women candidates running for the parliament as well as provided other technical assistance.

Another major international intervention was the UNDP Gender Support Facility (GSF) project, which was launched in 1997 and implemented from 1999 to 2001 with the total budget of US$ 143,000. This and the above UNIFEM project were complementary to each other. The project was initially designed to fulfil UNDP's commitment to allocate 25 per cent of programme funds directly towards improving gender equity and to facilitate the Government of Tonga's efforts towards gender mainstreaming and the development of women and the family. The UNDP project provided assistance to strengthen the capacity of government agencies and NGOs to address gender concerns, increase women's NGO outreach, and integrate gender across UNDP's other projects in Tonga.

The project has the following objectives:

- To promote a development approach that recognizes and invests in the potential contribution of all sectors of society and ultimately result in fair and equal distribution of resources and services for all men and women and their families in Tonga;

- To strengthen the institutional capacity of the Women and Development Centre, Prime Minister's Office and the *Langafonua*, to ensure that women's concerns are addressed in the national development process.

For these objectives, GSF supported a broad based bottom up consultative process to develop a national policy on Gender and Development. Funding through GSF to WDC and *Langafonua* contributed to strengthening coordination between women's groups and improved interaction between Government and NGO personnel. The establishment of the *Langafonua* National Women's Council expedited the growth of women's groups. GSF enabled *Langafonua* to conduct a major organizational review involving extensive consultation with rural organizations throughout the country. The feedback of this review resulted in a significantly new role for *Langafonua* and the development of the organization's first Constitution. The Constitution provides the organization with a legal framework and a clear direction for the future. This consultative process used in developing the *Langafonua* Constitution and a strategic plan itself contributed to greater public awareness about gender issues and a more unified commitment to achieving gender equity, as it involved numerous government departments, NGOs, private sector representatives and villagers. The document was translated into local vernaculars and a simplified version was developed for training purposes. Overall, this has resulted in better understanding and coordination of women's activities and resources throughout the country.

---

[42] NZODA, New Zealand Official Development Assistance, has been replaced in 2002 with NZAID, or New Zealand Agency for International Development.

In addition to formulating policy and enhancing relationships between people at all levels, an added benefit was that through the consultations people became more comfortable with gender terminology. Controversial areas have been identified and further consultations are planned to provide stakeholders with an opportunity to resolve contentious issues before the finalization of the gender policy and submission of the gender policy to Cabinet.

GSF funded several staff members of WDC and other government departments, *Langafonua* and NGOs to participate in gender related training programmes. These experiences have increased the staff confidence and commitment to gender work. Further, *Langafonua*'s institutional capacity was enhanced through the placement of a national United Nations Volunteer (UNV) funded by GSF. In addition UNIFEM provided important technical support in strategic and operational planning for *Langafonua* and the WDC.

The Facility is highly valued for the accessible and flexible support that it provided to the WDC and *Langafonua* in carrying out planned activities. GSF in coordination with other donors ensured adequate levels of technical and financial assistance. Stakeholders believe that GSF has expedited policy and programme development in Tonga and has reinforced the usefulness of effective consultation at all levels. The Pacific Islands Forum Secretariat cited it as a good practice from the Pacific in 2000.[43]

GSF was also helpful in attracting resources from other donors to carry out planned activities. For instance, UNIFEM provided funds for a Gender Focal Point at *Langafonua*, who was primarily responsible for coordinating the consultative process. In addition, NZODA and UNESCO provided financial and technical support for complementary activities, which addressed a constraint of lack of human resources. In 1998, NZODA also funded a report titled "A Statistical Profile of Men and Women in the Kingdom of Tonga". As a follow-up to the recommendations in this study, GSF supported the establishment of a gender statistical database housed at WDC to facilitate the production of accurate statistical data on gender equity issues and has enhanced policy and programme development.

Where to now?

The National Policy on Gender and Development was developed through the consultations which started in 1999 and coordinated by a UNIFEM funded Gender Focal Point. The review of the policy through national workshops and consultations were supported by GSF and has now been approved by Cabinet in August 2001. The Policy framework is linked to the National Development Vision and is integrated into the national strategic development planning process. The National Policy on Gender and Development has a vision and strategy and 10 policy areas:

- Vision: Gender Equity by 2025: That men, women, children and the family as a whole achieve equal access to economic, social, political and religious opportunities and benefits.

---

[43] Pacific Islands Forum Secretariat. 2000. *Gender and Development: Good Practices from the Pacific 2000.*

- Strategy: Promoting universal and free participation and partnership of men and women in all spheres of life – religion, society, politics, economics and culture.

- The 10 policy areas: Gender and the Family; Religion; Culture; Health; Education; Politics; Economy; Regional and Rural Development; the Public Sector; and the Private Sector.

Tonga must build, based on the vision and strategy, a society that allows equal participation of males and females, young and old. Such a society will respect the uniqueness of each individual and will ensure that opportunities are fair and that each person may plan a role in society according to his or her abilities and ambitions. Striving for a realization of such a society requires rethinking of the rigidly defined roles of men and women. This can be achieved by providing the opportunities and support for women to develop their abilities to maximize their participation and benefits from society.

The process for the Cabinet to approve the National Policy on Gender and Development also expedited the process to make the National Advisory Committee for Gender and Development (NACGAD) operational: it had the first meeting in April 2000. NACGAD plays an instrumental role in ensuring that matters concerning the conditions that affect women, men and families are appropriately integrated into government policies and plans. In addition, the multisectoral NACGAD based on the direction provided by the National Policy on Gender and Development coordinates between Government, NGOs and local groups.

In this regard, GSF sponsored by UNDP played an important background role in supporting the formation of institutional mechanisms and in establishing a national framework for implementation of the National Policy on Gender and Development.

Conclusion

The review of the Government's commitments to and its strategies for gender equity, and how international donors have supported the efforts gave some lessons: collaboration and networking is crucial for effective implementation with commitment of all stakeholders. Although the priority agendas of different stakeholders would affect their respective commitment to gender issues, a wide consultation process will create ownership and commitment to gender mainstreaming. In addition, although the lack of human resources is a major constraint, collaboration and networking also can mitigate the lack to some extent. All stakeholders have to acknowledge that progress takes time, and sometime plans and time frames cannot be met during implementation.

The infrastructure for gender mainstreaming has been established in Tonga. We are committed to continue mainstreaming gender into the development. We call on development partners for further interventions to support Tonga's initiatives.

SESSION 6:

STRATEGIES FOR GENDER MAINSTREAMING

Moderated by Ms. Rosa Linda Miranda

Case studies on development of strategies for implementing gender mainstreaming were presented from a number of sectors – education (Ms. Redya Betty Doloksaribu, Indonesia), human rights (Ms. Shanti Dairiam, IWRAW), forestry (Ms. Kanchan Lama, FAO/Nepal), development assistance (Ms. Rosemary Cassidy, AusAID, Australia), census (Ms. Suman Prashar, India), national reconstruction (Ms. Joana Vitor, Timor Leste), and political participation (Ms. Shalini Bijlani, PRIA). This session also includes the country reports of Azerbaijan and Thailand, which were distributed at the symposium. The summary of discussion based on the presentations is available in the report in Part II.

ENGENDERED HILLS LEASEHOLD FORESTRY AND FODDER DEVELOPMENT PROJECT (HLFFDP). AND EMANCIPATED WOMEN

Ms. Kanchan Lama

Former National Consultant, Technical Assistance Part
Hills Leasehold Forestry and Fodder Development Project[44]

Project context

The right to property inheritance provides the basic position to a Nepalese to become a citizen who enjoys important rights to participate in development of the self and the country. Nepalese women have been fighting to obtain an equal property inheritance right on par with men. The economic and social condition of Nepalese women is no better than women in other South Asian countries. The gender relationships in Nepal vary according to traditional practices and social biases of different ethnic, cultural and linguistic groups. In general, however, women live under the control of other elderly women and male members of the family in areas related to mobility, decision-making and participation in public life. Therefore, unless a development project addresses gender issues in a proactive way from the very beginning, women's participation as agents of change remains unfulfilled.

---

[44] Review and comments provided by Ms. Revathi Balakrishnan, FAO Regional Office for Asia and the Pacific and Mr. W. Rudder FAO Nepal are acknowledged with thanks.

At the national level, the National Development Plans, especially the Ninth National Development Plan and the Agriculture Perspective Plan of Nepal, provide greater scope for promoting gender issues in various development programmes. Currently a number of gender mainstreaming programmes are being implemented by the United Nations and other international agencies, which promote a conducive environment for promoting gender equality. In this context, the Hills Leasehold Forestry and Fodder Development Project (HLFFDP) proved to be one of the most successful projects in Nepal for promoting gender equality in access to resources and social mobilization. The project design and implementation demonstrated an effective model for community based natural resource management for poverty alleviation with gender equality.

The project

In January 1990, His Majesty's Government of Nepal and the International Fund for Agricultural Development (IFAD) signed the Loan of Agreement for HLFFDP. The Government of Netherlands funded an FAO project to provide technical assistance (TA) and technical backstopping support in implementation of HLFFDP. Four Government Line agencies were involved in HLFFDP, each with a specific role and task. The lead agency coordinating the project was the Department of Forest (DoF) and three collaborating agencies that extended their technical support in their concerned areas were the Department of Livestock Services (DLS), the Agricultural Development Bank of Nepal and the Nepal Agricultural Research Centre.

HLFFDP had the dual objectives to (1) eliminate extreme poverty with increased incomes through diversifying livelihood options and reducing dependency on land, which was common with traditional production methods; and (2) improve the degraded land on the hills by changing production methods. It operated in 10 of the 75 districts of Nepal. The project implementation effectively started in 1993. It should be noted that the gender component was promoted by the donor agency.

The dual objectives were achieved through leasing blocks of degraded forestland to groups of poor households. The vegetative cover of the leased land was regenerated, mainly as a result of improved management, such as controlled livestock grazing and fire, and enrichment planting of grasses and trees. This management secured a resource base for the poorest households that were given land lease and the exclusive use of the land. With assured access to additional fodder production from the leased land, families strived to increase their income from livestock production and other activities. This was reinforced through increasing production on private land and other income-generating activities.

HLFFDP emphasis on gender integration

The project included specific objectives in the design for gender integration through the Technical Assistance Phase 2 as:

- Integrate gender and disadvantaged (ethnic) group issues and considerations in the leasehold forestry and fodder development approach and implementation.

The Technical Assistance document also contained gender as an immediate objective as:

- Development of appropriate and gender-sensitive technical models for the rehabilitation of degraded forest lands in association with improved livestock management.

Livestock management is the most common activity for rural women in Nepal and provides a stream of income controlled by women. The HLFFDP design was responsive to the multitasking responsibilities of women in local production system and recognizes the constraints for women's participation.[45] Nepalese rural women climb the steep hills to collect fodder and fuel, which results in long strenuous days. The task consumes much of their time with little left for leisure or family care. HLFFDP created a viable option to collect fodder and fuel closer to homesteads. The social processes that were adopted to create access to production resources are: (1) group mobilization for land management and credit and savings, and (2) long-term (40 years) land lease, ensuring land tenure to motivate farmers to adopt sustainable land management strategies.

Gender equality considerations were integrated through hiring women Group Promoters to (i) organize women's and women integrated groups and (ii) train rural men and women in gender awareness at the grass-roots levels. The livelihood outcome was that income from the livestock sale, most often an income under women's control, provided for family needs. The most crucial benefit to women as individuals was the time saved by collecting fodder and fuel close to homesteads. Since time was the basic resource under the direct control of rural women, it can be used for expanding income and social options. Hence, the project directly benefited women as individuals. The design was such that there was a good fit between gender roles at the household level and the project interventions.[46]

Review results on gender considerations in HLFFDP

A gender analysis was carried out in July-August 1999, by holding five workshops with the field staff and male and female farmers in order to assess the situation. The review found that:

- As of 1992/93-1997/98, out of 1,200 leasehold forestry groups, women's groups constituted 12 per cent, while 44 per cent were men's and 44 per cent were mixed groups.

- The sex ratio of the chairpersonship of leasehold groups was 16 per cent for women and 84 per cent for men.

---

[45] Sterk. A. 2000. *Leasing degraded forestland: an innovative way to integrate forest livestock development in Nepal*. FAO/RAP.

[46] Balakrishnan, Revathi 2000. "Widening gaps in technology development and technology transfer to support rural women". Human Resources in Agricultural and Rural Development Journal, FAO.

- In animal health training, participants' ratio of women and men was 19 and 81 per cent. Illiteracy and extensive household workload among women were major constraints preventing their participation in various activities launched by the District offices.

- Women perform 90 per cent of the forestry activities. However for nursery management training, often men were counted as participants because of their easy mobility and access to information. This was also true for many other project activities aimed to benefit farmers of both sexes, such as exposure visits, credit, livestock services and group formation.

- The most important issue was that delivery of information to female farmers required extra efforts that would not be necessary to deliver the same to male farmers.

- This constraint was also related to the staffing pattern of the Project Coordination Unit (PCU), of which women consisted 10 per cent and men 90 per cent.

- In the TA part, at the time of the review, women and men staff at the central level was 50:50. All the 46 Group Promoters at the community level recruited by the PCU with support from TA part were women. The TA part remained very active in hiring women staff while the government hiring system was neutral on this.

Gender mainstreaming in HLFFDP

Based on the review outcomes, new strategies were adopted to improve the gender situation in HLFFDP: (1) Promoting gender-sensitive organizational culture at the central and district levels; (2) Capacity building among the project staff and the Group Promoters; and (3) Establishing communication and networking to produce a synergetic effect. In implementing these strategies, professionals at three levels were targeted; (i) Planners and policy makers level, (ii) District implementation level, and (iii) Grass-roots farmers level.

Interventions

(i) Policy makers level

At the policy makers level, a working culture on gender and development was developed. Intervention was made to promote dialogue on gender and organizational culture in as many forums as possible within the project programmes, such as meetings, workshops, interviews, and interaction programmes. The project policy directive was operationalized by:

- Identifying gender specific outputs and related activities to implement project objective

- Identifying specific cross-cutting outputs and related activities in other project objectives

- Directing resources for mobilizing rural women to participate in leasehold groups through project funded promoters

- Monitoring women's participation in leasehold activities and access to credit and project inputs

(ii) District level

To implement new gender-responsive strategies at the District level, Gender Focal Points (GFPs) among the line agencies staff in the project delivery level were identified. The staff serving at the grass-roots level and the staff in partnering line agencies were given capacity building to raise gender concerns and technical skills. Network among GFPs and other partner agencies and organizations in the 10 project Districts was developed. CEDAW awareness raising among the technical people (GFPs) was also conducted.

(iii) Grass-roots level

A cadre of 46 local women Group Promoters were employed and given CEDAW awareness raising to work as change agents. They mobilized women to actively participate in project and other activities to make a visible presence in all kinds of local development programmes. The DLS joined in by employing another 10 women livestock promoters on the same line as Group Promoters. Magazines were developed to facilitate information exchange among GFPs in the technical agencies at the District level and the Group Promoters serving at the grass-roots level. Solidarity building among the grass-roots motivators engaged in all the natural resource management projects under DoF was also conducted. In addition, gender sensitivity training for both men and women farmers was given, while efforts were made to link with adult education programmes to improve citizenship awareness.

Impacts

These project efforts resulted in active and expanded participation of rural women in leasehold groups and developing a cadre of Group Promoters. The rural women gained expertise both in the social process of participation for shared benefit and in managing ecologically fragile environment. The monetary returns through livestock assets and fodder is an incentive for participation. Women could save time through access to fodder close to their homesteads. With easier access, men volunteered to collect fodders and thus extended hands in household work sharing. Since women are busy in community meetings, men can see the importance of sharing household workload such as cooking and childcare.

The major driving force in the whole effort was capacity building among the field staff of the line agencies and the Group Promoters through intensive gender training programme given every six month. They provided continuous gender awareness programmes to the farmers. The project supported cross learning from other projects and programmes, such as study tours for women and district level workers to learn from examples of gender integration and extension within Nepal. The GFPs of line ministries were the catalyst with their active interest in promoting gender considerations in the field work.

Women's participation ratio increased to 50 per cent at all meetings, training and study tours. Women-managed saving and credit groups became very effective and qualified to access formal credit. They were found to make better use of the leased land by producing quality fodder and raising healthy livestock. This has changed the living status of the leasehold families. The Group Promoters have established relationship with other line agencies such as, District Education Office, District Agricultural Office, and Cottage Industry Office, from which they obtained resources and opportunities for their communities. In fact they proved to be the backbone of the project planning, monitoring and training. Their role was also recognized through their inclusion in all the officials meetings of District level line agencies. Women have been the most influential participants in the village development councils in their respective communities. The two magazines published by the Group Promoters and the GFPs helped them to gain respect as resource persons for social mobilization in natural resource management. Thus through a systematic effort, the project intervention remained successful in promoting a working culture at the staff level and also in fostering capacities among women to participate effectively.

Current status

The Project phased out in July 2001 and currently the Government has incorporated leasehold forestry in its general forestry development programme in 26 districts. The collaboration among the four technical line agencies initiated by the project ceased to be functional within the national framework. However the leasehold farmers, especially the women, who have become used to getting services from the four line agencies, still access the agencies for relevant services. Some of the Group Promoters have registered their own institutions as NGOs and attract District line agencies and other development agencies to mobilize resources for their own community development. They are very confident about their capacity and the importance of working for development of women farmers.

Lessons learnt from HLFFDP on gender

The impact of the project can be seen as sustaining at the grass-roots institutions level although the process no longer exists at the national level. The project should have been continued at least for four more years to enable the leasehold farmers, especially disadvantaged women, to organize themselves as active associations, which was the vision of the project. Nonetheless like-minded development professionals could benefit from the lessons learnt in the project.

Certain factors hampered sustaining the project driven gains and prevented effective mobilization for ensuring continued momentum for gender mainstreaming and gender equality. Two major hindrances were (1) that women do not have the right to immovable property and (2) that women very often do not have the citizenship and the citizenship paper, which was required to participate as members in leasehold groups and cooperatives, consequently depriving women without citizenship papers of land lease rights.

Weak institutional arrangement at the national level was a hindering factor. This was aggravated by the lack of harmonization on gender related policies and actions between national and local level institutions. For example, the field offices of the line agencies were not provided with adequate guidance and implementation instruments to operationalize national and institutional policies. Rather, there was a prevailing perception among line agencies that emerging people's organizations for credit and decentralized administration may not be accountable to gender mainstreaming policy commitments made at the national level. They were not sure either if they could enforce gender equality norms to local membership organizations. Field level operation suffered from inadequate commitment and lack of expertise to support policies addressing gender concerns.

The confusion among the governmental offices did not help clarifying ones at the grass-roots level. Grass-roots level organizations were dissociated from accountability to uphold national policies and international commitments for gender equality and central institutional directives. The membership organizations and its leadership were not adequately informed of national policies, failing to give commitments to gender equality. At the bottom, individual men and women suffer from the uncertainty about guaranteed lease rights on the long term basis. Uncertainty of the long-term benefit sharing modalities among the participants in forest resource related project and programmes was another factor hindering the project impact.

Uneven understanding of national policies on gender equality and advancement of women among project national and international partners needs to be addressed. Efforts with resources for gender mainstreaming and integration of women continued to be donor driven with inadequate budgetary support from the government.

For a conclusion, several suggestions can be extracted from the lessons learned:

- Project design from its formulation stage should be informed of the empirical findings of gender role analysis.

- Strategic gender intervention should be made at all levels of agencies implementing the project.

- A gender-sensitive culture should be promoted within the organization in order to better facilitate gender intervention.

- Technical experts in the government should be given opportunities to develop and improve their gender-responsive capacity through effective training, coaching, guidance and follow up.

- The role and responsibilities of GFPs should be clearly defined and the definition be understood by all parties. GFPs should also be given exposure to extended gender concerned discussions with professionals working on gender issues, such as advocates for CEDAW and women's rights, economists, or lawyers.

- The management level should be open and supportive to the innovative ideas and suggestions made by the gender experts.

- Gender programmes should be separately budgeted.

- The importance of communication for gender promotion to increase and improve understanding and motivation to work on gender related issues should be underscored.

Finally, working at the farmers' level, the following two lessons should be fully utilized:

- Successful outcomes of gender training could be obtained when both husband and wife participate in it. However precaution should be taken not to underestimate the existing biases related to the presence of women in front of the men.

- Grass-roots motivators (promoters) are the best catalytic agents for bringing changes into the discriminatory behaviours towards women and also for effective handling of gender related issues at the community as well as the District level.

* * *

MAINSTREAMING WOMEN'S HUMAN RIGHTS IN DEVELOPMENT WORK[47]

Ms. Shanti Dairiam

Director
International Women's Rights Action Watch (IWRAW)

Mainstreaming of women's human rights is twofold: First, it can be seen within the United Nations framework. The protection and promotion of human rights was the subject of the World Conference on Human Rights in Vienna in 1993. The conference recommended that efforts to mainstream human rights must include the interests of women. The second issue, which I would like to highlight in this presentation, is the development of human rights concepts. We have to talk about *women's* rights because the concept of human rights has been insufficient to protect and promote the rights of women.

The gross violations of human rights committed in the Second World War shocked the world, calling for an urgent action to protect and promote human rights. The needs for and the importance of protecting human rights in the United Nations framework were very clear. However, as such needs and importance were seen as a consequence of the war, the most important human right in this context was the right to live. Violations of this right during the Second World War were seen as the experiences of men, as victims of extra judicial killings, mass executions, torture or political imprisonment that had taken place in the public sphere. The violated rights were seen as *men's* rights, concerns with *women's* rights were not there.

Women's experiences and life circumstances tended to be different from men's. As a result, women's experiences and life circumstances were not taken into consideration at the end of the Second World War, when the United Nations was established. This had led to the

---

[47] A summary based on a recording of the presentation.

situation where the human rights theory and practice used in the United Nations system did not match women's needs. Women's experiences and life circumstances are different from men's, but the human rights theory and practice has been consistently developed with an almost exclusive focus on men's experience and interests.

For example, domestic violence was seen as a tragedy but not as a violation of the right to live. It was because, in the traditional theory and practice of human rights, only the state was considered to be the agent that could commit violation of human rights, not private persons. In the traditional view, the violation of human rights would take place within the "state versus citizens (who were men)" scenario.

The inadequacy of the traditional view of human rights has to be addressed, so that women's perspectives and experiences can be integrated into the whole theory and practice of human rights – especially at the global level in the United Nations framework. This includes the work of various institutions within the United Nations system: the treaty bodies, the Special Rapporteurs and working groups. An inter-agency cooperation is coordinated by DAW and OHCHR to ensure that these institutions integrate women's perspectives in their work.

There are five treaty bodies that are tasked to incorporate women's rights issues: CEDAW Committee; Committee of Civil and Political Rights; Committee of Economic, Social and Cultural Rights; Committee of Racial Discrimination; and Committee of Torture. The treaty bodies play a very critical role in ensuring integration of women's rights through the meetings of their chairs that are regularly held to exchange views and understandings among the committees of the United Nations.

Mainstreaming women's rights in development work

The framework for mainstreaming women's rights in development work is CEDAW, which is the source of the standards being used to mainstream women's rights.

The CEDAW framework provides two critical principles: namely, the *Principle of Non-Discrimination* and *the Principle of Equality*.

The Principle of Non-Discrimination. This is a negative injunction. It contains actions and obligations that should *not* be done, that are prohibited. But this is not enough, positive elements and fulfilment are missing.

The Principle of Equality. The equality dimension brings in the positive obligations of what has to be done. The obligations to bring about equality in gender mainstreaming will contain the following elements:

(a) Protection (e.g., regulating role of the state in times of globalization)

Women's rights have to be respected by state agents as well as by non-state agents. And the state has the duty to protect women's rights from violations of non-state agents.

(b)   Promotion and fulfilment of equality

CEDAW provides a "Model of Equality", containing the *equality of opportunity*, the *equality of access to the opportunity* and the *equality of results*. The *equality of opportunity* is a formal kind of equality, which requires all laws to have provisions of gender equality. But this formal equality is not enough for the fulfilment of equality in practice. The *equality of access to the opportunity* means that positive actions have to be taken by the states to provide conditions that actually enable women to exercise and enjoy their rights to equal opportunity. Although there is hardly any intentional attempt to deny women's human rights, there might be actions that have the *effect* of doing so. Article 1 of CEDAW states these actions as discrimination against women. It is also important to consider the different attributes that women have, such as lower level of education and literacy level than men. These disadvantages of women are the consequences of past discrimination, which require positive actions to be taken by the states to overcome to attain equality. The *equality of results* means that there must be de facto results and achievements in addition to efforts to bring them about.

* * *

WOMEN AND GIRLS' EDUCATION AND GENDER EQUALITY IN BASIC EDUCATION IN INDONESIA

Ms. Redya Betty Doloksaribu

Assistant Director for Women Education,
Directorate of Community Education, Indonesia

Background

Indonesia is the largest archipelago in the world, situated between two continents, Asia and Australia, and two oceans, the Pacific and the Indian oceans. About 6,000 of the 13,667 islands and islets are inhabited by the population of 210 million, of which 50.7 per cent are female. There is a significant difference in the number of women compared to men in many positions in government, private organizations and politics.

The education system in Indonesia consists of formal, non-formal and informal systems. Basic education is conducted through the formal system of six-year primary and three-year junior secondary schools and through the non-formal system with Package A and Package B; Package A is similar to primary school and Package B is similar to junior secondary school. The non-formal system is both for school age children who cannot go to formal school and for adults who did not go to school.

In 1984, the six-year compulsory education was introduced to promote the importance of basic schooling. After 10 years of implementation, in 1994 the Government of Indonesia increased the length of compulsory education to nine years. It was planned that the target of compulsory education would be reached to be ready for the AFTA free market in 2003 and APEC free trade era in 2010. But owing to the economic crisis in the late 1990s, the target was not reached and extended to 2008/2009.

The development of national education was carried out on the basis of four main strategies: (1) expansion and equalization of educational opportunities, (2) improvement of the quality of education, (3) improvement of the relevancy of education to the development needs, and (4) efficiency in educational management.

At the initial stage of the second long-term development plan, which started in 1994/1995, an emphasis was given to human resources development in all sectors and sub-sectors of the national development. The development of national education cannot be separated from elements that affect development, such as (1) the importance of value-added orientation, (2) changes in the social structure, and (3) effect of the globalization process. Based on that, emphases have been given to teaching and using science and technology in education.

Women and Girls' Education[48]

Since the nine-year basic compulsory education was introduced in 1994, all efforts were focused to increase participation rate and improve quality of primary and junior secondary education. Data of the Ministry of National Education show that the large gender gap which existed at primary and junior secondary schools in the mid 1980s was narrowed to only 1-2 per cent in the 1990s. Once enrolled in primary schools girls performed better, resulting in higher progression rate. Data in 1999 showed that in urban areas 28.2 per cent of girls and 25.6 per cent of boys finished primary school, while in the rural areas the percentage of girls was 34.8 and of boys was 37.7. Both in urban and rural areas the percentage of girls who are not sent to school and not finishing primary school is higher than boys.

The percentage of girls who graduated from junior secondary schools is lower than boys in both urban and rural areas. This may be due to the traditional belief that as girls are going to become housewives who take care of children, they do not need higher education. In addition, efforts for gender equal education encounter more mundane problems, such as low budget allocation by the government for education, with lack of community participation to promote Education for All (EFA). Consequently, there are not enough teachers with the necessary qualifications nor educational facilities, especially in the rural areas.

---

[48] Ministry of Education and Culture, 1994. *The Development of Education System in Indonesia, Country Report*; Ministry of National Education, 2001. "Universal Basic Education: The Roles of Distance Education and Policy Implications", presented at the E9-Ministerial Review Meeting in Beijing, 21-23 August 2001; State Ministry of Women's Empowerment, 2001. *Gender Analysis in Education Development* (in Bahasa Indonesia), Jakarta.

The inadequate government education budget often forced parents to pay for the facilities and operational cost, but the economic crisis made it difficult for the parents to pay. This caused a larger percentage of dropouts and more school-age children not going to school. Geographic and demographic conditions give additional difficulty for equality and quality of education.

Examples of the strategies to overcome the problems:

1. Schools to implement community-based management in order to empower the community to take responsibility in the management of the school.

2. Raise gender awareness and provide orientation for preschool, primary school and junior secondary school teachers.

3. Encourage the establishment of Community Learning Centres (CLCs) especially in the rural areas.

4. The Government to facilitate implementation of Package A and Package B for dropouts and illiterate adults, especially for women. Besides the academic programme, training in employable and saleable skills should be given.

Gender analysis

Gender analysis was carried out for the development of education programmes by the National Development Planning Agency assisted by the Women's Support Project II, sponsored by CIDA.[49] Four main programmes were the foci of analysis: Basic Education and Preschool Programme, Secondary Education Programme, Higher Education Programme, and Out of School Education Development Programme. The tool used for the analysis was Gender Analysis Pathway, developed by the National Development Planning Agency. This study was specifically looking into three issues of gender inequity: (1) access to all types and levels of education, (2) quality and efficiency in education, and (3) selection of study programmes at higher education.

Gender inequity is affected by four basic factors: (1) access, (2) participation, (3) control, and (4) benefit. Several gender problems in educational development need to be given further attention and actions have to be taken to overcome those problems, particularly:

1. Very obvious gender inequity at Vocational Secondary schools and higher education because of the social values of the Indonesian people.

2. Gender bias in school books for language and social studies.

3. Inefficiencies in teaching and learning process due to the low participation rate of girls.

---

[49] National Planning Agency (Bappenas) and WSP II-CIDA, 2001. *Gender Analysis in Educational Development* (in Bahasa Indonesia); State Ministry of Women's Empowerment and Women Support Project II-CIDA, 2001. *Gender Mainstreaming, a Strategy in Development* (in Bahasa Indonesia), Jakarta.

4. Institutionalization of gender inequity due to the scarcity of women in positions of decision-making.

5. Persistent gender segregation in the selection of study programmes at higher education, causing gender discrimination in the work place.

The analysis also found that girls drop out at a higher rate than boys at all levels of education. The results of the gender analysis shows a need to reformulate education policy to be gender-responsive.

National policy and programmes

In the year 2000, the President issued a Presidential Instruction (Inpres No. 9/2000) on Gender Mainstreaming in National Development, with its Implementation Guidelines issued in 2001.[50] With the guidelines, the Ministry of National Education started to familiarize gender mainstreaming to all Ministry officials. Several workshops were held to incorporate gender mainstreaming in existing programmes and in planning of new programmes.

The National Education Programme 2000 (Propenas 2000) stated that education policies should be reformulated to become gender-responsive, including:

1. Expand and equalize education opportunities.

2. Develop quality human resources through various activities conducted by all components of the nation.

3. Upgrade academic competencies and professionalism of teachers and their prosperity.

4. Improve the education system, including diversification of curriculum to meet the different needs of students.

5. Improve the education system also based on the decentralization principle, autonomy of science and management .

6. Improve the quality of public and private educational institutions.

7. Empower all educational institutions so that values, attitude and competencies become their institutional culture.

To implement the policies several development programmes for the education sector were established: (1) Preschool and Basic Education programme, (2) Secondary Education programme, (3) Higher Education programme, (4) Out of School Education programme, (5) Synchronization and Coordination of Education Development programmes, (6) Research and Capacity Building programme, (7) Development of Resources for Science and Technology programme, and (8) Improvement of Independence and Excellence in Science and Technology.

---

[50] State Ministry of Women's Empowerment, 2001. Implementation Guidelines for Inpres No. 9/2000 on Gender Mainstreaming in National Development (in Bahasa Indonesia).

Preparation of the National Education for All (EFA) Plan

A National Team on EFA was established and the Director General of Out of School Education and Youth was appointed the National Coordinator of EFA. In August 2001 the Team held a national consultative meeting to discuss the National Action Plan on EFA.[51] The results were going to be used in all sub-sectors of Education. They agreed to prioritize and design educational services for people in remote areas and/or with low income, street children, boat people, the disabled and nomads.

The Directorate General of Primary and Secondary Education has the following strategies:

1. Improve the delivery quality of primary education through the Science Education Quality Improvement Programme (SEQIP) and World Bank and ADB projects.

2. Rehabilitate primary school buildings.

3. Improve open junior secondary schools (SLTP Terbuka) by distance education.

4. Improve life skills education at all school levels.

5. Involve the community in education quality improvement and develop school based management.

The Directorate General of Out of School Education and Youth has the strategies to reach the children who could not enrol in formal school:

1. Provide early educational opportunities for children not yet in kindergarten or playgroups.

2. Increase access to education through the Mobile Library and Community Library in each district and village.

3. Optimize Madrasah and CLCs and develop contract schools for isolated areas, conflict areas, plantations, and suburban areas.

4. Improve quality and relevance of junior secondary schools by adding skill training.

5. Improve educational efficiency.

National level coordination

EFA is coordinated by the Ministry of National Education with other ministries such as the Ministry of Religious Affairs and the Ministry of Internal Affairs. At the school level, EFA is coordinated among schools, pondok pesantren, NGOs and CLCs.

---

[51] EFA Working Group. 2001. Education for All National Action Plan 2001-2015. National Consultative Meeting, 29 August – 1 September 2001 (in Bahasa Indonesia).

Gender mainstreaming is coordinated by the State Ministry of Women's Empowerment. The Ministry of National Education initiated the establishment of the Consortium for Women Education (KoPPI), which is expected to be the partner of the Government to propose strategies for EFA and increased participation of women in education.

International cooperation

Several international organizations, such as UNFPA and UNICEF, have contributed to dissemination and education on gender mainstreaming and gender analysis. UNICEF participated in the development of the National Action Plan for EFA. International assistance for gender mainstreaming is being sought.

Conclusion

Gender equality in basic education is being pursued in the EFA programme and still in progress. Delays in action was due to the economic crisis in 1997, from which the country is not yet fully recovered. With the Government's commitment to provide a larger portion of the national state budget for education and to reach all school age children in the basic compulsory education programme, gender equality is also expected to be realized in the formal education sector. In the out of school education, functional literacy education programmes, especially for women, will be delivered through CLCs.

* * *

GENDER PERSPECTIVE IN CENSUS OF INDIA, 2001[52]

Ms. Suman Prashar
Office of Registrar General and Census Commissioner, India

Introduction

India has a history of continuous census-taking since 1872. The first synchronous census was conducted in 1881, and since then it has been conducted every ten year without break. The Census of India 2001 is the fourteenth in this continuous series and the sixth since India obtained its independence in 1947. The Census Act 1948 forms the legal basis for the conduct of the census in independent India. Though population census is a union subject, it is executed through the state administrative machinery.

---

[52] Detailed Census Data and other related information including the provisional results of 2001 Census are available at the web site of the Office of Registrar General & Census Commissioner: http://www.censusindia.net.

India consists of 35 states and union territories consisting of 593 districts, 5,564 sub districts and 5,161 towns and over half a million villages. As per provisional population results, its population stands at 1,027 million, of which 531 million are males and 496 million are females. The magnitude and sheer size of population and its growing divergence has made the Indian census one of the most challenging single administrative exercise in the world. It involved the participation of two million enumerators and supervisors counting more than a billion people in about 220 million households. The enumeration was held between 9 and 28 February 2001 with the revision round from 1 and 5 March 2001.

The Indian Census has the tradition of collecting and presenting data separately by sex on various sociocultural, economic and demographic aspects. In fact it is the only source that provides the basic counts of males and females, right up to the village level for the rural areas and the ward level for the urban areas, which are the lowest administrative units. The Census thus provides invaluable and interesting insights into the existing imbalances in the society between men and women. This information forms a vital input for policy and planning both at the national and sub-national levels.

Problems and magnitude

The pronounced sex differentials in many variables have remained under the constant focus of data users and planners. In the earlier censuses the fact that women were missed out in counting had been debated upon. It has also been argued that women's economic pursuits are not recorded/reported adequately in certain parts of the country, resulting in low female work participation rate (FWPR). This problem is further perpetuated by rigid mind set about gender roles. Economic activities that women intermittently undertake and domestic chores are not treated as "work", as sometimes it is difficult to isolate non-economic activity from economic activity. Ignorance about definition of work also leads to non-reporting. For instance in the 1991 Census, Punjab had an inordinately low 4.4 FWPR. The enumerators did not to probe the respondents, mainly men, to find details of women's contribution in economic activities, especially their unpaid work in family enterprises or agricultural activities. The declining female sex ratio and low FWPR in certain parts of the country are perhaps due to general apathy and social and cultural insensitivity on gender issues.

Theoretically the census has always emphasized on individual characteristics, with questionnaire and instructions that are not marked by the male bias and are by and large gender neutral. Against the normal social practices, instructions clearly spells out that each question has to be individually asked. To ensure that women's individuality is not compromised or conditioned by male bias, it was also reiterated that women can also be head of the household, speak a different mother tongue, and profess different religion etc.

In response to the interest generated about women issues and more particularly economic contribution in the unpaid and informal sector, the definition of "worker" was amplified in the 1991 Census to include unpaid work on family farms or family enterprises. A publicity campaign was undertaken to sensitize the public about this aspect. However, the 1991 Census results showed regional disparities in gender statistics, which remained under constant attention of researchers and policy planners.

Efforts in 2001

In the 2001 Census, adequate attention for gender sensitization was undertaken in earnest. Possible causes for gender bias to creep up in the data collection and dissemination was explored. A special cell was established to oversee gender issues and sensitize census functionaries at different levels involved in supervision and conduct of the 2001 Census.

The gender sensitization primarily focused on three aspects:

- Sensitizing the Directors of Census Operations and other senior functionaries of the Directorates and the State Governments at every opportunity through discussions in depth on sex ratio, age, literacy and female work participation of their own state, which enabled them to understand and appreciate the problem in its proper perspective.

- To impart thorough and appropriate training to all census functionaries right up to the enumerators with the help of special modules and data sets relating to gender issues.

- To undertake adequate steps to build up public awareness through a wide spread publicity campaign specially focusing on the contribution of women in various economic activities.

One of the major steps taken was to significantly improve the Instruction Manual for enumerators and the Household Schedule. In the Instruction Manual, special efforts were made to draw the enumerators' and supervisors' attention to the basic count of population, especially to better net the elderly and the unmarried woman as well as the girl child in the household. Instructions were given to record the names of members in a particular sequence so that no female member in the household is missed even inadvertently.

Under reporting female work was identified as a major grey area. All efforts were made not to miss her economic activity. During the training, the cultural bias of the respondents or proxy respondents or of the enumerators against recognizing and reporting the economic contribution women intermittently pursue and domestic chores was pragmatically addressed. In order to properly capture the part time work done by women,

the enumerators were encouraged to ask probing questions. Further, to raise awareness that a number of different economic activities in which women are engaged as paid or unpaid workers are "work", they were depicted in 32 illustrative sketches. These sketches present women working on a formal or informal basis within the precincts of the household or outside by lending helping hands to their male counterparts. They were part of the Instruction Manual published in 16 major regional languages and available to all the field functionaries right up to enumerators. In addition, emphasis was also laid on activities generally performed by women in particular areas or regions.

The definition of work was further amplified at the 2001 Census, whereby production of milk (milching) even for solely self/domestic consumption was treated as "work". This was expected to net women's contribution in animal husbandry widely prevalent in many parts of the country. This was in addition to unpaid work on the family farm and enterprises already included at the 1991 Census.

The next step was to make the format of the household schedule, the questionnaire canvassed at the population enumeration, more gender sensitive. For instance a question on fertility specifically sought information by sex of the child (daughter and son) instead of children so that information on female children are not left out even inadvertently.

The office of the Registrar General of India held several consultative sessions with Government Departments and NGOs to address the gender issues in the census more pragmatically and systematically. A special field study was conducted to explore methodology for an improved recording of female work participation at the 2001 Census, rendering recommendations adopted to improve the methodology for training of enumerators.

Census Advisors

In order to achieve the objective of complete and accurate coverage of women and their participation in economic activities, vigorous campaigns and focused attention were launched in districts that yielded very low female sex ratio, literacy and work participation rate at the 1991 Census. 237 districts were identified based on the 1991 data, which had either FWPR of less than 20 per cent or a deficiency of more than 50 females per thousand males. They also included districts with significantly lower female literacy rate than male. These were treated as critical districts, which required additional efforts in terms of sensitization, training and publicity. With help from United Nations agencies, special Census Advisors were engaged in almost all the critical districts to train and help the field functionaries on gender issues. Census Advisors also helped Master trainers in gender specific questions with local examples to facilitate better comprehension. The training was also supplemented by audio and video cassettes in regional languages eliciting probing questions on gender related issues.

Some Directorates held special thematic sessions where women officials were specially invited to undertake training on gender issues. Special efforts were made to engage as many women enumerators and supervisors as possible to undertake the fieldwork.

Wherever possible Anganwadi workers (local women officials involved in the child and nutrition programme) were trained to work as census enumerator. These efforts helped in establishing better rapport with the respondents, particularly encouraging women respondents to come forward in giving information.

Publicity

For the success of such a huge exercise as the 2001 Census, India, adequate publicity was necessary to create awareness. An important component of a publicity campaign was to sensitize and create awareness among the general public on gender related issues, with extensive display of posters and banners illustrating female work, including the unpaid work done by women. A number of audio and video spots appealing women to come forward and report their economic activities were produced and relayed through radio and television networks. A number of articles dedicated to women issues and their basic enumeration, disability, age, among others, were published in English and vernacular languages. A special census postage stamp was also released using the census logo adopted for the Census of India, 2001. The logo represented both phases of census of house-listing and population enumeration. The four figures, two males and two females, signify ideal family size and its sex composition. The two children stand for the replacement level of fertility, representing the national goal of population stabilization. This gender sensitive logo was extensively used in official stationery and publicity material.

The provisional results – 2001 Census

The provisional population results of 2001 show an increase in female sex ratio (females per 1,000 males) from 927 in 1991 to 933 in 2001 at the national level, with increase in sex ratio in 27 states/union territories. 445 districts accounting for 77 per cent of the total districts showed increase in the sex ratio. This was the second time in the hundred years of the history of the Census that sex ratios in both rural and as urban areas showed an increasing trend. This increase is pronounced in the seven plus age group. This perhaps suggests better enumeration of women at the Census of India, 2001.

Child sex ratio

Despite the increase in the adult sex ratio there has been decline in the child sex ratio in the age group 0-6 in the majority of the states and districts. This shows a grim picture of the status of the girl child in certain parts of the country. Decline in the child sex ratio from 945 in 1991 to 927 in 2001 has activated the socio, political, legal, administrative setups of the country. Child sex ratio in the age group 0-6 at the national level for rural and urban areas is presented below. Compared to the previous census the child sex ratio has shown declines at the subnational level and in the majority of the districts. Some districts across the country present inordinately low child sex ratio in the age group 0-6 of less than 850 girls per 1,000 boys and put a question mark on the future of the girl child.

Table 1. Sex ratio (1901-2001)[53] rural-urban					Table 2. Child sex ratio in the age group 0-6 (1981 to 2001)			
Decade	*Rural*	*Urban*	*Total*		*Decade*	*Rural*	*Urban*	*Total*
1901	979	910	972					
1911	975	872	964					
1921	970	846	955					
1931	966	838	950					
1941	965	831	945					
1951	965	860	946					
1961	963	845	941					
1971	949	858	930					
1981	951	879	934		**1981**	963	931	962
1991	938	893	927		**1991**	948	935	945
2001	946	901	933		**2001**	934	903	927

Literacy status

The literate is a person of seven years or above in age who can read and write with understanding in a language. Literacy is one of the important indicator for women's empowerment relating to their health, hygiene affecting child birth, childcare practices and overall socio-economic uplifts. The Census provides information on literacy level by sex right up to the village level. The information is provided also for historically marginalized social groups of scheduled castes and scheduled tribes separately. Besides, information

Table 3. Literacy rate in India 1951-2001[54]

Census year	*Persons*	*Males*	*Females*	*Male-female gap in literacy rate*
1951	18.3	27.2	8.9	18.3
1961	28.3	40.4	15.4	25.1
1971	34.5	46.0	22.0	24.0
1981	43.6	56.4	29.8	26.6
1991	52.2	64.1	39.3	24.8
2001	65.4	75.9	54.2	21.7

---

[53] Based on interpolated population of Jammu and Kashmir in 1991 and for Assam in 1981.

[54] (a) Literacy rates for 1951, 1961 and 1971 Census relate to population aged five years and above. The rates for the 1981, 1991 and 2001 Census relate to the population aged seven years and above.

(b) The 1981 Literacy rates and WPR exclude Assam where the 1981 Census could not be conducted. The 1991 Census Literacy rates and WPR exclude Jammu and Kashmir where the 1991 Census could not be conducted.

about gender gaps in literacy and school attendance among the school age groups brings out cultural bias against the girl child. The above table presents nationwide literacy rate since 1951 and highlights the gender gaps in basic literacy rates.

Work participation rate[55]

Work is defined as participation in any economically productive activity with or without compensation, wages or profit. Such participation may be physical and/or mental in nature. Work involves not only actual work but also includes effective supervision and direction of work. It also includes part time help or unpaid work on farm, family enterprise or in any other economic activities. All persons engaged in "work" as defined above are workers. Persons who are engaged in cultivation or milk production even solely for domestic consumption are also treated as workers. Among the workers defined in this manner, "Main Workers" are workers who had worked for the major part of the reference period (6 months or more), while "Marginal Workers" are workers who had not worked for the major point of the reference period (less than 6 months).

As detailed in the above, FWPR was very low in certain states in the 1991 census. It is a matter of great satisfaction and encouragement that the concerted efforts and vigorous campaign brought an upward trend in FWPR. For instance in Punjab, which had the lowest FWPR in the country with FWPR of 4.4 per cent in 1991, has an increased FWPR of 18.7 per cent as per preliminary results of 2001. A preliminary result shows increases in FWPR both in rural and urban areas (table 4). Table 5 presents FWPR in some of the states with a large number of critical districts at the 1991 and 2001 Census. There has been a perceptible increase in the female work participation in the north Indian States of Punjab and Haryana, where female work participation rate were very low in the earlier censuses. In the other eastern and central Indian States of West Bengal, Bihar and Uttar Pradesh also there have been significant gains in the females marginal workers suggesting better netting of women's economic activities (table 6).

Table 4. Work participation rate by sex in India
(1981 to 2001)

	1981		1991		2001 (Provisional)	
	Male	*Female*	*Male*	*Female*	*Male*	*Female*
Total	52.6	19.7	51.6	22.3	51.9	25.7
Rural	53.8	23.1	52.6	26.8	52.4	31.0
Urban	49.1	8.3	48.9	9.2	50.9	11.6

---

[55] Reference period for determining a person as worker and non-worker is one year preceding the date of enumeration.

Table 5. FWPR in India and selected States			
State (Number of critical districts in 1991)		1991	2001 Provisional
India		22.3	25.7
Punjab	(17)	4.4	18.7
Haryana	(19)	10.8	27.3
West Bengal	(9)	11.2	18.1
Uttar Pradesh	(43)	12.3	16.8
Bihar	(15)	14.9	20.7

Table 6. Female marginal workers in India and selected States		
State	1991	2001 Provisional
India	6.3	11
Punjab	1.3	6.8
Haryana	4.7	13.9
West Bengal	3.3	9.2
Uttar Pradesh	4.9	10.2
Bihar	4.9	11.2

Special tables

In the Census 2001, apart from traditional sex-disaggregated data based on individuals, household tables and special tables with emphasis on women and girl children are being produced for the first time to assess the status of women with respect to literacy. The following tables along with other sets of tables will provide interesting insight into the sociocultural and economic dynamics operating at the household level with reference to gender mainstreaming.

❏ Table on the households by number of female literates among female members of the household aged seven and above in the households.

❏ Households with at least one member aged 15 years and above with or without matriculation by size of the households.

❏ Number of households with at least one female matriculate.

❏ Number of households with at least one female graduate.

❏ Households by marital status, sex and age of the head of the household.

❏ Households having female children in the age group 5-14 years by number of school attending female children.

❏ Households by size and number of female members seeking/available for work.

❏ Households by number of disabled females.

* * *

129

GENDER MAINSTREAMING IN POLITICS:
USING *PANCHAYATS* IN INDIA AS A CASE STUDY

Ms. Shalini Bijlani

Programme Officer
Participatory Research in Asia (PRIA), New Delhi

Women in the Indian Context

Almost 70 per cent of the Indian population resides in rural areas wherein the social structure with core values, promote male domination over females. Prohibitive social conditions encompass women's lives. Other additional factors have also aggravated life conditions such as poor nutrition and heavy labour that is linked to high mortality rates of women in childbearing age, and less access to education particularly after puberty, which limit opportunities for women.

The long hours women spend on work at home or in the field are unaccounted in the national statistics due to limited interface with the market. As regards to control and access over resources, decision-making, ownership to assets and even earning respect as human being, men are privileged. Women are not consulted in anything save a few domestic matters. To ensure women do not attract strangers' attention, their mobility and voicing opinions is restricted, with their faces covered under a veil. Women are victims of social, economic and cultural conditions. Any accomplishment and failure in efforts to promote equal rights needs to be understood against this backdrop.

Women in politics

Men have represented women with a pretext that women were not interested in politics. The voting pattern of women from the first *lok sabha (*Lower House of the Indian Parliament) to the 1999 general election shows otherwise – that there is a remarkable growth in women's participation. At the national level, prominent women leaders amply exemplify women's interest in politics and freedom struggle. Their presence was lost after the Independence, however. The Constitution of India proclaims equality as a fundamental right and yet reserved seats for women have not been adopted.[56] Women's representation has marginally increased from 4.4 per cent five decades ago, to 8.1 per cent in the current term at the national level. This pattern is applicable also to the State Assemblies (*Vidhan Sabha* in local parlance – Legislative Assembly of the State or Province).

At the grass-roots level, *Panchayats* seek to increase women's representation and leadership by reserving a third of total seats among the membership as well as Chairpersonship at three levels of *panchayats* (district, block and village level) for women. *Panchayats* existed in pre-British period but without any appreciable participation of

---

[56] Reservation was however adopted for Schedule Castes and Schedule Tribes in higher level representative bodies – Lok Sabha and Vidhan Sabha.

women and lost their significance after the Independence. *Panchayats* were revived as Constitutional bodies through the 73rd Constitutional Amendment Act (CAA) in 1992. The 73rd CAA is significant as an empowering agent for rural women, opening "the door" to the public arena and ushering nearly 0.8 million women to different level *panchayats* offices in different states.[57]

States and gender mainstreaming in the context of *Panchayats*

The present case study deals with the experiences of PRIA's intervention in Haryana, one of the economically progressive states among the 28 States in India. Haryana has the second highest GDP in the country, yet fares poorly on social indicators such as the Human Development Index (HDI). While the introduction of *panchayats* is a positive factor for women's leadership, impediments exist in the State Conformity Act of some States, including Haryana. In Haryana only persons who meet the two-children norm criteria are eligible to contest in elections. The condition is perceived as undemocratic as it is oblivious to the fertility rate of 4.2 in Haryana, preventing many potential candidates from contesting. This shows no consideration for the rights of women who have completed childbearing age or have virtually no decision-making power with respect to childbearing.

In contrast, the Madhya Pradesh (province) Government appreciated women-headed *panchayats* which have significant achievements to the credit of women heads by acknowledging them as "Model *Panchayats*". Civil Society Organizations (CSOs) reach out to people in orienting them to their basic rights, complementing the efforts of the State, which has limited outreach and resources to make an impact.

CSOs interventions to mainstream gender in *Panchayats*

The influx of women political leaders through the 73rd CAA led to the dawn of a new reality in politics. *Panchayats* as an institution give women much required space and is a liberating and enabling mechanism. On the other hand, the social structure is embedded in traditional patriarchal values that set restrictive conditions on women. Both the systems viz. *Panchayats* as institution and the social structure have placed conflicting demands on women leaders. The 73rd CAA as a top down policy fails to address this reality. It was a challenge for CSOs to facilitate women in taking advantage of *Panchayats*, a process that could transform the social structure and power relations. The other challenge for CSOs is to make the institutional mechanisms supportive of women's political participation. This is the framework to analyse the effect of PRIA's work.

PRIA's intervention

In a vacuum, political parties or interested family members fielded dummy (who cannot play the role) women candidates for reserved seats. Introducing genuine women leaders required manifold tasks: capacity building, awareness generation and sensitization,

---

[57] PRIA, 2000. A Balance Sheet. PRI: New Delhi. This figure does not include members from Bihar, Jammu, Kashmir, Lakshadweep and Pondicherry.

mass scale mobilization, networking, and information dissemination at various levels. A training policy and a supportive environment had to be developed. PRIA, like many other CSOs, scaled up its interventions to orient people across the country. As a quick and wide scale orientation was needed within a stipulated time period, a Campaign Mode was therefore adopted.

1. Pre-Election Voter Awareness Campaign (PEVAC)

As the first step to orient women to election process and *panchayats*, PRIA launched PEVAC. Women were oriented to the rights to contest (represent) and to vote in governance without giving in to any influence. PEVAC had four major components:

- **Sharing voters' list:** To make the voters' list inclusive, PRIA shared the list with the women electorate and found that many young girls had been left out. To counter this omission, PRIA approached girls in colleges and at home and held group discussions with their family members. They were said to follow the tradition to put women's names in the list only after marriage, for reasons such as to avoid changes of residence or name. To have one's name included in the voters' list is the foundation to exercise one's rights to vote and to contest. After the discussion, some managed to put their names on the list. Many, however, decided to wait until they got married.

- **Setting up information booths:** To facilitate women candidates to fill in the nomination form correctly, PRIA installed information booths with women volunteers to lend support. PRIA cooperated with the media to help women access information and enable them to make informed decisions.

- **Facilitating campaign for women candidates:** To support women candidature in rural areas where campaigning for women was uncommon, PRIA mobilized Community-Based Organizations (CBOs) such as Self-Help Groups, Youth Groups etc. With support from other women in the community, women candidates gained more resources and confidence to campaign with hand made posters, slogans, rallies, meetings and home visits.

- **Orienting women polling agents:** To help women overcome their hesitation to cast the votes in men's presence, women volunteers served as women polling agents. The women polling agents identified women behind the veil and helped them in the polling booths. The women-friendly polling booths increased the number of women electorate who cast their votes.

2. Post-Election: Awareness and skill based programmes

With no precedence or role models, women who were elected to political seats for the first time needed skills and capacities to govern. To prevent these women from behaving as mere token representatives guided only by family members, PRIA organized several programmes.

2-A. Capacity and knowledge building programmes

Knowledge building programmes to disseminate information on *panchayats* and **capacity building programmes** to develop leadership, communication and problem-solving skills were organized exclusively for the elected women and their male relatives. To enable women who showed hesitance to attend programmes alone, PRIA allowed male relatives to accompany them and attend capacity building programmes. This addressed the male relatives' apprehensions, built an environment of trust and secured their support for such programmes. In addition, the programme oriented the male relatives to their new roles and responsibilities in supporting women.

Methods used included introduction games and simulations to encourage women to overcome social restrictions and be assertive leaders of the *panchayats* especially in the presence of men. Introduction games required men and women to sit in pairs and introduce each other, while simulations made women and men contact with each other to break the divide. Women acknowledged that such programmes helped to build rapport with men and boost their confidence to sit and interact with men. The programmes got them to feel and articulate as leaders and to be seated in front unlike in villages where they are relegated to sit at the back.

Based on needs assessment of women leaders, PRIA also conducted capacity building programmes exclusively for women and train them to confidently participate in planning meetings. Programmes addressed women's need for leadership, articulation, collective analysis and building a sense of solidarity amongst them. It also helped women in recognizing their needs as special and crystallize issues for *Gram Sabha*[58] *meeting*.

2-B. Facilitating mobilization, demand for accountability in **Gram Sabha**

Gram Sabha (village council) had erstwhile been men's council with their large presence and voices dominating the meetings. To break with this, PRIA organized campaigns involving street plays, wall writings, slogans, posters and small group meetings with men and women to help them deliberate and prioritize issues for council's meetings. The campaigns taught people about the council meetings and the importance of women attending them.

PRIA enthused women to collectively analyse the reasons for their exclusion from such forum and strive for inclusion. Men were sensitized to women's concerns and in the process their support was secured. PRIA facilitated Women's Groups in selecting informal women leaders for representing their concerns in *Gram Sabha* and demand accountability from leaders of *panchayats*. PRIA assisted women leaders, especially the ward-wise leaders who were not clear on their roles in the community development, to fulfil their responsibility to represent the ward on issues of health, education and sanitation.

Through these programmes, some women have positively enhanced their positions in the meetings. However there are instances which still remain a challenge wherein women experienced disrespect from men like *Panchayats* Secretaries. They discouraged women from speaking and lowered women's confidence, despite orientation given to *Panchayats* Secretaries.

---

[58] Village Council undertaking planning for people's need.

3. Networking for learning exchange programmes

Given the gamut of problems impinging on women's representation and leadership, the value of ongoing support to women cannot be over emphasized. The need to regularly meet, communicate and learn from experiences of women leaders is well recognized.

- **Women's convention:** As articulated by women, "Strength is in numbers": The convention encourages women to *collectively* reflect on common issues and seek answers through open discussion. For instance, prior to second round of elections, it encouraged women to draw lessons from the first political term. They agreed to contest in elections not only on reserved but also unreserved seats to increase women's representation. The convention has had various positive impacts, including raising women's self-perception that promotes collective action on issues. On International Women's Day, it provided women with an opportunity to interface with Government officials. Women accessed pertinent information on issues and demanded accountability from them. Information need is greatly pronounced especially within women leaders because timely information is crucial to governance.

- **Exposure visits:** PRIA organizes two types of exposure visits for women. The first type is to take women to governmental administrative offices to instil confidence to communicate with government officials, and access information. To go one step further which is to travel and meet with these officials independently, however, still remains a challenge for women. The second type is the exposure visit to other parts of the State (Province) to interact with other women leaders. Interaction with diverse sources has motivated the women leaders' to take initiatives. A women chairperson in Kosli village, who was elected on the unreserved seat, demonstrated creative leadership to generate income for the village development. She served as a role model for many women leaders to explore creative means to augment resources for development. Through the exposure visit, another woman leader in a far off village in Panchkula district (of the same State) was inspired and encouraged to mobilize resources for a community hospital.

4. Participatory planning, monitoring and evaluation

As *Gram Sabha*s have only a limited scope for village development planning, PRIA initiated "microplanning" or a bottom-up planning process to include all sections in the same and exploring diverse resources to translate the plan into action. Microplanning has clearly evinced a potential to address women's limited participation, and orientation to vital planning skills has prompted women to participate in planning meetings and negotiate for inclusion of their needs in the overall plan. Women's needs for toilets and water taps have been recognized as important in microplanning.

The microplanning exercise prompted the use of participatory approaches in other areas also. For example, Uttar Pradesh (another province), a partner NGO of PRIA, oriented women's Self-Help Groups to monitor the developmental activities of the village. Women were trained to use simple techniques of Participatory Monitoring to evaluate developmental programmes and government functionaries.

5. *Research, advocacy and information dissemination*

The factors that impinge on women's public roles and responsibilities in the governance had to be identified through research. A study on women's leadership investigated both enabling and inhibiting factors at the end of the first term to address the issues and concerns related to women's leadership. Advocacy efforts followed researches. Findings endorsed and pointed to the increased need for information in supporting women leaders. With the help of *panchayats* and the community, PRIA established Village Information Centres, an evolving mechanism to adequately provide timely and accurate information to the village. Timely Information has aided women particularly to monitor the village development and to hold officials and leaders accountable for their decisions and actions.

6. *PRIA's organizational efforts within*

The conduct of the personnel of an organization working in the field needs to be gender sensitive for their interventions to have positive influence. PRIA established the Committee for Gender Awareness and Mainstreaming Programme (CGAMP) to orient its personnel on gender issues and incorporate gender sensitivity in the organizational culture. PRIA also paid attention to the composition of its field teams. A local team of PRIA consists of a man and woman social animators to intervene at the field sites. A woman animator working alongside a man animator provides a role model for community women to emulate besides helping in reaching out to women constituencies. The presence of women animators proved beneficial in helping women to assert themselves.

Ways forward

Many forces against women's leadership remain. Access to information necessary to govern is still a problem. Respect that should be accorded to women as elected leaders has not been paid, reducing women's confidence to govern. In addition, social restrictions curtail their voice, mobility and rights to decision-making. Enabling mechanisms have to be developed to fortify women's position as leaders and reduce negative forces.

- **Functional literacy:** A major limitation that keeps women in a weaker position may be traced to the lack of functional literacy. Women leaders often sign on documents without reading and understanding the consequence. As a result, illegal and false court cases have been levelled against them. In this context, a literacy programme that concentrates on reading skills is most desirable in its first phase.

- **State training policy:** Regular and ongoing training programmes which address the needs of the elected leaders especially women are necessary. The programme should employ innovative methodologies, strive for a wide outreach, and be gender-sensitive, with a scope to evolve on the basis of feedback. It is envisioned that through such training programmes women understand their rights and obtain skills to voice and assert their concerns, make informed decisions, and demand accountability.

- **Supportive measures for women's leadership:** Women who have not had opportunities to participate in local-self governance need time to understand and function as representatives. In this regard, the Government machinery must be sensitised to build supportive relationships with women leaders. For example, women need more than five years to become effective as chairpersons, but the chairpersonship reserved for women rotates every five years. While the principle of rotation is desirable, there needs to be some other ways to accommodate and support the needs of newly elected women leaders.

- **Active coordination among stakeholders:** To strengthen women's leadership at the grass-roots level, all stakeholders, such as the Central and State governments, the media, academics, NGOs and community based organizations, need to clearly define their roles and coordinate with one another to comprehensively mainstream gender into development.

* * *

VIETNAM-AUSTRALIA FIVE TOWNS PROVINCIAL WATER SUPPLY PROJECT

Ms. Rosemary Cassidy
Gender Analyst
Gender, Health and Education Group, AusAID

The project

The Vietnam-Australia Five Towns Provincial Water Supply Project (VPWSP) commenced in 1995 and was completed in June 2000. The A$71 million project was jointly funded by the Government of Australia and the Government of Viet Nam and administered through AusAID in close consultation with the Vietnamese Ministry of Construction (MOC). The main aims of the project were to improve access to and utilization of safe, sustainable, continuous water supply and to contribute to environmental sanitation conditions in Bac Giang and Bac Ninh in the north, Ha Tinh in the centre and Tra Vinh and Vinh Long in the south of the country. The project involved three main integrated components of construction, institutional strengthening and community development. VPWSP was implemented by an Australian consortium of companies, in cooperation with MOC and the Project Management Boards in each of the five towns.

VPWSP brought economic and social benefits to more than 400,000 people in the five towns through providing new and improved water supply systems. Through the community programmes and in cooperation with the local people, the project developed community awareness activities focusing on the value of clean water and environmental sanitation. It led to a strong interest in the community in participating in local environmental improvements.

The community development component of the project, which was aimed at preparing people for the introduction of clean, potable water to their towns, included:

- Public Health Awareness campaigns in the provincial towns based on clean water, health and sanitation;

- Micro-activities such as paved laneways and drainage;

- The Primary School Health Education Support Programme introducing participatory methodology both within and outside class activities focusing on clean water, sanitation, hygiene and environment.

VPWSP approached the provision of piped water supply with the integration of community development and institutional strengthening. Although implementation of gender strategies was delayed, positive outcomes were achieved. For example, in the last two years of the project five women were promoted or transferred to Water Supply Company (WSC) management positions and a number of women in Bac Giang were placed in positions of responsibility in the WSC's ward offices. Women's involvement in community development work and their contribution was crucial to successful micro-activities. VPWSP supported them through gender training, sharing of lessons learned and evaluating key gender and community benefits of the project. Women were instrumental to the success of the project, particularly the community development component.

Policy context

The Australian Government is committed to the promotion of equal opportunities for women and men as participants and beneficiaries of development and requires that a gender perspective be incorporated in all AusAID activities. The Government of Viet Nam is similarly committed to gender equality and the advancement of women. The rights of women are enshrined in the Vietnamese Constitution. Viet Nam signed CEDAW in 1980 and ratified it in 1982. The National Plan of Action for the Advancement of Women in Viet Nam by the Year 2000 was issued in 1997. This Plan defines the roles and responsibilities of each Ministry to set targets and take actions to improve the gender balance in Vietnamese institutions at all levels of government.

Gender advisory input[59]

The project identified women as forming a significant portion of project beneficiaries due to their domestic responsibilities and the role water use plays in the conduct of their day-to-day work. At the beginning of the project there was input from a Gender Adviser focusing on:

- Women as employees in the Design and WSC and Construction companies

- Women as primary users of water in the areas served by the project

- Women as primary teachers of sanitation, hygiene and disease prevention practices in the community.

---

[59] Report of the GAD Adviser. September 18, 1995.

137

The Gender Adviser's report identified potential strengths and obstacles relating to women's and men's participation in the project. Various strategies were recommended including how to effectively integrate men in discussions relating to priorities given to household water spending. The importance of working with the Vietnam Women's Union (VWU) was highlighted, especially in relation to the environmental health and micro-activities programmes and in the public health education and schools campaigns. The Adviser also emphasized the importance of consulting with both men and women to ensure that decision-making was informed by both women's and men's views.

Despite the initial Gender Adviser's input, implementation of gender strategies was delayed. The project initially focused on major technical challenges in implementing the construction and engineering components of the project. The institutional strengthening phase was also delayed initially. Despite this, the project later succeeded in incorporating a gender perspective into project activities.

Monitoring implementation of
gender issues – a shared responsibility

Responsibility for monitoring implementation of VPWSP was undertaken by the posted officer in Viet Nam with backup from AusAID officers in Canberra, and the Technical Advisory Group (TAG consisting of technical experts), which visited the project on a regular basis. Prompted by AusAID the TAG of 1998 included a gender expert. The subsequent gender analysis revealed that the community development programmes had not sufficiently targeted women. For example, lower success rates in implementing micro-activities were found to occur when women did not play a key role.

	Bac Giang		Bac Ninh		Ha Tinh		Tra Vinh		Vinh Long	
	men	women	men	women	men	women	men	women	men	women
Supervisors	2	16	23	10	18	1	13	13	10	12
Environmental health monitors	103	105	57	61	63	23	71	27	61	33
No. of micro-activities	1368		650		83		31		169	

The above table illustrates that in towns where numbers of women involved were equal or close to men more micro-activities were built, yielding more money contributed by the householders. Other contributing factors include timing (Bac Giang and Bac Ninh started earlier), proximity (Bac Giang and Bac Ninh were in close proximity to the project offices), wealth, disparity and regional differences in lifestyle, attitudes and commitment to local cadres.

TAG recommendations in 1998 led to the development of a gender strategy[60] which analysed key gender issues and included a time frame for implementation. The strategy emphasized the importance of gender awareness training at all levels of the project. Following the 1998 TAG visit, gender training was conducted for all members of the Project team (including the team leader, the construction advisers, engineers, the finance officer and the institutional strengthening officers), MOC staff and WSC managers, followed by training for all WSC staff in each of the five towns.

The purpose of the initial gender training course were (1) to strengthen the gender sensitivity and gender analysis skills of project personnel; (2) to identify opportunities and constraints to gender equality within the project; and (3) to develop strategies to enhance the gender responsiveness of the project. The course focused on gender analysis skills and methodologies to better address gender issues in the project, and provided an opportunity to discuss elements of the gender strategy.

The initial gender training course also included role-playing in relation to the project and a SWOT (strengths, weaknesses, opportunities and threats) analysis of gender issues. Particular recognition was given to the dynamic and successful Vietnamese female project officers. One of the strengths of the project was the positive impact of good role models, which had a further positive impact on how counterparts and beneficiaries viewed the capabilities of women. The initial training course gave a recommendation that the training be outsourced to qualified Vietnamese trainers. This recommendation was implemented and the main presenters of subsequent gender training were representatives of VWU and the Vietnamese Youth Union.[61] The training was considered highly successful and contributed to the renewed focus on gender issues in the project.

Sharing experiences and lessons learned – the conference[62]

Towards the end of the project a National Community Development Conference was held in Hanoi in 2000. In the preceding year, a study evaluating women's involvement in the project was undertaken to inform the Conference with its findings. An Australian Youth Ambassador who worked closely with the project's community development and the female Vietnamese project officers undertook the study to gain insight into whether community women in the five towns had benefited from the project, and if so, in what ways. It also sought to identify lessons learned which could be applied to future work and projects.

Questionnaire interviews were conducted based on various references including the AusAID Guide to Gender and Development,[63] the Project Implementation Document and references on water supply, sanitation and women. Interviews with community members

---

[60] AusAID 1999. "Development of a gender strategy".

[61] Fischer, Rosal M. 2000. "A study of key women and community benefit in the Vietnam-Australia Provincial Water Supplies Project". Hanoi.

[62] AusAID, 1999. "Lessons learned during implementation of project".

[63] AusAID, 1997. *Guide to Gender and Development*. http://www.ausaid.gov.au/keyaid/gender.cfm

were organized by the town-based project staff to give a representative sample of the community. Interviews took place in all five towns: 37 people were interviewed, 3 men and 34 women. In addition, 12 community feedback forms from 9 men and 3 women were received.

The study found that women benefited from the community development component by living in a cleaner environment. More and better access to water resulted in women having the means to maintain cleanliness, and consequently, less disease meant less time caring for sick family members. Other benefits included increased income and social contacts within their community. Women reported that relationships within the community had strengthened, through having met, planned and worked together despite difficulties at the outset.

The evaluation study also highlighted the following project outcomes:

- Through improved pathways and drainage systems, routine chores such as cleaning and maintenance of pathways, rubbish disposal, household cleaning, washing and cooking were alleviated. Access to clean potable water increased substantially along with education in sanitation and hygiene needs and practices.

- Alleviating cleaning and maintenance and water collection duties provided women with more time for their children, families and businesses. Older people have more time to relax and enjoy their surrounding environment.

The National Community Development Conference in 2000 brought together Australian and Vietnamese participants from VPWSP, an ADB provincial towns water project, WSCs, community development motivators, the five towns involved in the project as well as from other provincial towns, other donors and various government ministries.[64] It provided an opportunity to share lessons to improve project sustainability and resource management; facilitated the exchange of key community development lessons; identified good practices in integrating the building of town water supply systems with environmental sanitation health improvements and community health awareness programmes; and provided an opportunity to highlight the key role played by women in the community development activities.

Conference participants agreed that the project had resulted in, among other things:

- Reduction of water borne and hygiene related disease through the provision of clean water and sanitation facilities.

- Improvement in attitudes, understanding and behaviour in relation to sanitation through the health education programmes and the physical works.

- Improved control of wastewater through the inclusion of commune level sanitation and environmental facilities, the paving of pathways and the development of sewerage and drainage master plans.

---

[64] "Community development in the Vietnam-Australia Provincial Water Supply Project". Conference Report, 12-13 January 2000, Hanoi.

Project outcomes – gender specific

Strategies	*Outcomes*
Gender training to increase awareness and sensitivity to gender issues.	Gender training was provided for project staff and staff from water supply companies. VWU gender and community health training at commune level and educational activities were also undertaken.
Specifically targeting of women for full participation in project boards and committees.	VWU representatives were placed on each Water, Sanitation and Health Sub-Committee.
Active involvement of VWU in the development of community participation.	VWU was actively involved in the development of community participation through Public Health Awareness campaigns. The project designated VWU chairs as Supervisors.
Encouragement of gender balance in the selection of Supervisors and Environmental Health Motivators.	Gender balance was encouraged primarily by utilizing VWU as a key organization with contacts at all levels. Both male and female EHMs were found to be important – women as primary users and controllers of money and men in their support for women's decision-making.
Specific targeting of women in the delivery of health messages and in the collection and monitoring of information on community conditions.	Women were specifically targeted through their employment as Supervisors and EHMs. Health posts and teachers at the primary schools and working with VWU were fundamental to the delivery of information and education.

Lessons learned[65]

Gender specific lessons

Implementing gender considerations into the project earlier would most likely have made the Community Development component more effective sooner. It took some time to recognize that VWU members with their mandate and training for community outreach, were effective community Environment Health Motivators (EHMs). The project also recognized the vital role that Vietnamese women played at all levels, in their roles such as Project Officers, as consultants, or teachers who participated in the primary school programme and as motivators. It was also important to ensure that both women and men were involved at every level of the process in community related activities in order to successfully motivate communities.

---

[65] AusAID. 2000. Project completion report. Vietnam-Australia Provincial Water Supply Project.

In order to identify gender issues and recommend strategies to address barriers for women and men to participate in projects, gender specialist's advice is necessary. To implement these gender considerations in a non-traditional sector project further requires early analysis, training input and monitoring. The project learned that trying to teach people to consider how their work might affect men and women differently and to take action accordingly does not result from just one round of introductory gender training. Reinforcement through advocacy, role models and advanced level training is needed. In addition, it should be noted that successful implementation of gender strategies requires support at all levels, from the team leader, project staff, the recipient government and the donor agency.

The importance of monitoring mechanisms has to be highlighted. Incorporating gender expertise into project monitoring mechanisms is vital. Major projects like VPWSP should include gender expertise in TAGs or equivalent monitoring mechanisms which are designed to provide independent advice on project implementation.

Lessons in general

Integrating community activities into mainstream Town People's Committee activities and budgeting is critical for sustainability. Linking this with Provincial plans and budgeting would enhance the impact. For this and other purposes, community representatives need to be involved in the project from planning, implementation, monitoring through evaluation and participate in decision-making, as well as representatives from VWU, the Youth Union, WSC, the Urban Environment Company and health and education authorities. Especially, initial and ongoing participation of WSCs at all stages of community development is important. For micro-activities, it is important to simplify policies and procedures to get micro-activities going. In implementing community education campaigns it is important to find the right channels of communication for different provinces or towns.

* * *

EAST TIMOR GENDER MAINSTREAMING PROJECT

Ms. Joana M.D. Vitor

Senior Gender Advisor, Office for the Promotion of Equality
UNTAET Headquarters, Dili[66]

Background

Timor Leste has moved from being administered by the United Nations to independence in May 2002, through two transitional stages in which its nationals have taken on increasingly greater roles in the administration.

---

[66] Summarized from transcript of presentation.

In the first transitional administration, a Gender Affairs Unit (GAU) was created. It was situated in the National Planning and Development Agency. In the second transitional administration, the Unit has been placed under a National Advisor and is now known as the Office for the Promotion of Equality. It has an even more unique and powerful position now because it is attached to the Office of the Chief Minister, where the Advisor on the Promotion of Equality provides advice directly to the Chief Minister.

Objectives

In 2000, while under the first transitional administration, GAU submitted to AusAID a proposal for a Gender Mainstreaming Project. The Project commenced early in 2001 with objectives:

(1) To enhance the capacity of GAU (now the Office for the Promotion of Equality) by developing generic gender mainstreaming guidelines as a tool to mainstream gender within policy development processes, procedures and programmes;

(2) To build the capacity of national counterparts within GAU as well as the capacity of officials in selected departments to understand and use the guidelines.

Under this project, the focus is on the efforts at the national level, although the importance of developing guidelines for district level operations is regarded also important.

The project was divided into six stages of short term inputs, ranging from two to eight weeks. The first stage was to review existing gender mainstreaming guidelines; the second stage was to undertake a situational analysis; the third stage was to develop the new guidelines; the fourth stage was to introduce the guidelines; the fifth and current stage is to consolidate the guidelines and the sixth stage will be to evaluate the use of the guidelines. A consultant was contracted to develop the guidelines. During the first three stages, she was assisted by a "Young Professional", who was developing her professional career through this mentoring approach supported by AusAID.

Implementation

Stage 1: A review of available guidelines revealed that many of them were complex and sophisticated.

Stage 2: Data for the situational analysis of the work of the administration and gender issues within the administration and in wider society was gathered. At the same time the consultants lobbied with the heads of departments for their support for staff involvement in gender mainstreaming workshops and the use of the guidelines in the future.

Stage 3: Development of draft generic guidelines. The main approaches to the guidelines were:

- To explain the reasons for doing what was suggested, including the benefits in terms of effectiveness and efficiency

- To encourage government officials to question their thinking and procedures

- To use a 6 processes model of decision making within an administration to develop relevant questions to encourage gender sensitivity in developing and implementing policy, programmes, regulations etc. (figure 1)

- To explain the term "gender" and raise gender awareness

- To provide local examples as illustrations

- To use as little technical language as possible

- To include a section for a plan of action to be developed and filled in by the respective departments

- To include a monitoring and evaluation framework which could be used for monitoring by the self as well as monitoring by GAU (the Office for the Promotion of Equality).

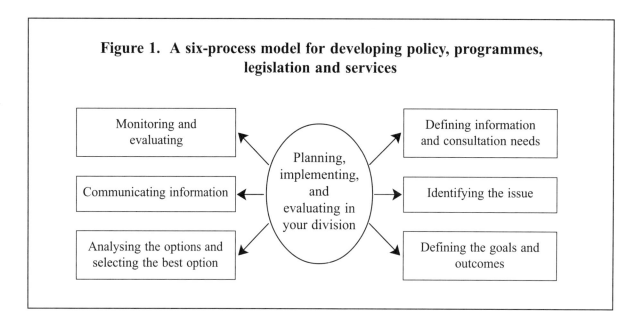

Figure 1. A six-process model for developing policy, programmes, legislation and services

Stage 4: Two one and a half day workshops (an original and a repeat) were held. Participants were from the Divisions of Agriculture, Water Supply and Sanitation, Commerce Industry and Tourism, Labour and Social Services, Border Services, Civil Servants and Public Employees and the Office of District Affairs. The Divisions of Health and Education, where there was no support from the heads of the divisions nor from the Minister at that time, had low participation. The guidelines were provided to participants a week before the workshop for them to become familiar with the document. Each division was asked to supply four participants, including both women and men. The total number of participants was 32. One third of the participants were men.

Participatory approaches and group work were stressed. On the first day, participants discussed gender and how it related to their personal lives. The sections of the guidelines concerned with bureaucratic decision-making were introduced and discussed in the afternoon. The division groups were then asked to complete a small project during the week, before the second round of the half day workshop. They were asked to apply an aspect of the guidelines to their work (such as, data collection, monitoring, communication strategy, or biases and preconceptions). During the week, the consultants met with the participants from each division to encourage them and to help overcome any problems. The following week, a half day workshop was held at which the divisions presented how they had applied the guidelines to their work. They were asked to provide further ideas for improvements to the guidelines. In the divisions, each group also developed a plan of action for introducing the guidelines to their colleagues who had not attended the workshop. The monitoring and evaluation framework for the guide was introduced.

The participants were enthusiastic about the workshops but would have liked more time. There were requests for more workshops. Participants requested GAU to send a memo to the heads of divisions to set aside a specific time for them to discuss the workshop and guidelines with their colleagues. Before departing at the end of Stage 4, the consultants visited each division to discuss any problems participants were having and any suggestions they had for improving the draft guidelines.

Stage 5 (current stage): The four national staff members of the Office for the Promotion of Equality,[67] including the three recruited after Stage 4, have familiarized themselves with the Indonesian language version of the guidelines and made suggestions for improvements.

The consultant has followed up with six of the seven divisions which had participated fully in the workshops. One division was subsumed in the administration restructuring and the participants could not be located. Ongoing work includes mini workshops with divisions to discuss gender issues in their work and the application of the guidelines, the development of sectoral guidelines and a gender awareness raising module, and meetings with Ministers appointed under the new administration to gain their support for the application of the guidelines.

The National Advisor for the Office for the Promotion of Equality intends to obtain the Chief Minister's endorsement of the guidelines and to discuss the guidelines with the Cabinet members. This is a crucial step for the institutionalization of the guidelines.

Stage 6: Evaluation.

Achievements

The workshops increased gender awareness and interest, especially amongst workshop participants, who filtered them in various degrees to those staff who did not attend. Meetings were held by staff themselves to discuss gender issues and the use of the guidelines in four of the six departments contacted. Gender groups and contact points established in the departments to monitor and take action on gender issues and

---

[67] Between Stage 4 and 5, the administration was restructured and GAU was renamed the Office for the Promotion of Equality and located strategically within the office of the Chief Minister.

mainstreaming gender in the development and implementation of policies and programmes. The departments[68] have requested for further meetings to discuss gender issues and the application of the guidelines. Sectoral guidelines for Water Supply and Sanitation and Agriculture were requested. On staff recruitment, the Division of Water Supply and Sanitation, where there had been few women, recruited two women, one in a senior position. Increased emphasis is placed on recruitment of women in two other departments.

The guidelines have had impacts at the personal level as well, through informal spread of understanding and interest in gender issues and gender sensitivity. For example the father of one GAU national staff read the guidelines and told his son to do more work in the house because it would be fair to his sister; the wife of one of the workshop participants who is in a senior position in the Department of Education became interested in the guidelines and discussed gender issues with her husband.

Lessons learned and conclusion

This is the first time that gender mainstreaming has been attempted in the process of establishing a new government. In order for this initial work to be consolidated, the next phase will be essential. This second phase should focus on capacity building, the introduction and application of the guidelines, and on monitoring and evaluation of the gender mainstreaming process.

In some ways the development of the generic gender mainstreaming guidelines seems to have been premature. Although it is advantageous to introduce such guidelines when an administration is in its formative stages, the state of flux and impermanence of the administration was a hindrance. The conditions relating to the post conflict reconstruction and the changing structure and impermanent nature of the transitional administrations pose challenges. The conditions were further complicated by the lack of established and codified procedures for decision-making on, among other things, policies, programmes and regulations in the administration.

The freeze on recruitment of national staff at GAU and other divisions meant that some national staff were not in place when the workshops were held. In the case of GAU, for example, there was only one national staff at that time. The shortage of staff meant the existing staff was charged with too heavy a workload to build their capacity with regard to the guidelines in a timely manner. Adding to the lack of time due to the shortage of the staff, the complexity of the guidelines itself posed another time constraints to the staff. Despite the efforts to develop simple guidelines, they are still a complex document, which demand considerable time from the staff to understanding and introduce to others. The location of GAU in the first transitional administration was not strategic, which was addressed in the second transitional administration and the Office for the Promotion of Equality is now located in the Office of the Chief Minister.

---

[68] Governmental Divisions in the first transitional administration were restructured into Departments.

The lack of gender awareness raising prior to the workshops meant that the workshops could not focus sufficiently on the guidelines. Gender awareness raising needs to precede the guidelines so that people can more quickly and better understand them. The introduction of the guidelines needed to be preceded by preparation of participating divisions with gender awareness raising workshops. An international staff in the Office for the Promotion of Equality is currently preparing a gender awareness raising module which could support the guidelines.

The importance of the support from the Heads of the Divisions has to be highlighted over and again. Regrettably, two divisions, Health and Education, did not have the support from the head and the staff could not participate despite the interest of the individuals. Efforts to make up for this lost opportunity and to introduce the guidelines to departments which did not participate are necessary. Also, for those divisions which participated in the workshops, there is a need for continuing follow up and consolidation.

* * *

REPORT ON THE SITUATION IN THE FIELD OF GENDER MAINSTREAMING IN AZERBAIJAN

Ms. Farah Adjalova

Department of Human Rights
Democratization and Humanitarian Problems
Ministry for Foreign Affairs, Azerbaijan

After regaining its independence, Azerbaijan joined in major international instruments on the protection of women's rights. Azerbaijan signed the United Nations Convention on the Political Rights of Women in August 1992 and became a party to CEDAW in 1995.

The Government of Azerbaijan has made several achievements in the sphere of gender policy. The State Committee on Women's Issues was established by a Presidential Decree[69] in 1998 to implement the state policy on gender. This fact highlights that gender issues are considered at the highest state level in Azerbaijan. The main objectives and purposes of the Committee are to protect the rights of women and to increase women's participation in the social and political life of the country. It is remarkable that the State Committee on Women's Issues of the Republic of Azerbaijan is the only state structure in the South Caucasus in the field of gender policy.

---

[69] "On establishing of the State Committee for Women's Issues of the Republic of Azerbaijan", 14 January 1998.

In March 2000 the President signed a Decree, "On Implementation of the National Gender Policy in the Republic of Azerbaijan". The decree was given to provide "in practice equality between women and men and particularly for their representation in the system of public administration on a proper level". It envisages to ensure equal representation of women and men on the supervisory level in all state structures and preparation of a statistical information up to international standards on women's status in Azerbaijan.

Further, it charges the Cabinet of Ministers to:

Assure in practice, in the network of implemented economical reforms, creation of equal opportunities for women, on a par with men, guided by the requirements of a gender policy, with a view to provide employment for female refugees and internally displaced persons to prepare and implement the employment programme; with a view to enforce women's rights protection and submit certain amendments and annexes in the legislation of the Republic of Azerbaijan, to analyse the acting legislation and to make suggestions on that.

It ordains the Cabinet to submit the report on the course of implementation of this Decree annually up to the 1st of March. In order to launch the practical implementation of the Decree, gender focal points were appointed in the governmental structures. According to the Decree women should be appointed as one of the Deputy Heads of the Executive Power in all regions of Azerbaijan, which has already been implemented in a large number of regions.

In June 2000 the Cabinet of Ministers adopted the "National Plan of Action on Women Issues for 2000-2005". The Plan was elaborated based on the Beijing Platform for Action and the national priorities. It covers political, social, economic, cultural, educational, and health spheres as well as the problems of refugees and internally displaced women. It envisages to elaborate the State Programme on women and power and to implement the relevant measures aimed at ensuring more active participation of women in political and public life and decision-making process. The National Plan of Action includes the participation of both the state structures and NGOs. An interagency group was established in order to implement the provisions of the National Plan of Action.

On gender policy, the Government of Azerbaijan cooperates closely with international organizations such as United Nations agencies and the Office for Democratic Institutions and Human Rights of the Organization for Security and Cooperation in Europe (OSCE/ ODIHR). Various projects in the field of women's political participation and their involvement in policy-making and decision-making are being implemented in Baku and other regions of Azerbaijan.

The status of Azerbaijani women, however, remains complex. Progress is mainly going on in the capital and some of the big cities. In the rural area, the difficult social-economic circumstances restricts women's right to self-development, making their lives more difficult.

The hardships of the period of transition and the consequences of the Nagorno-Karabakh conflict between Armenia and Azerbaijan are the main reasons of serious economic and social damages.[70] The conflict caused more than one million refugees and internally displaced persons, of which 54 per cent are women. At present 95 per cent of them are deprived of necessary livelihood. Only 20 per cent of employable women have jobs.

Another reason for the low participation of women in social, political and public life is the existing traditional stereotypes of the image of woman in society, whose role is limited within the boundaries of family.

This situation demands a new approach to the building of the national gender strategy. At the moment we are in the process of building the national machinery to develop gender mainstreaming strategies and incorporate the gender component in practical activities within the Government. In this respect, the working group comprising gender focal points in the ministries under the State Committee for Women's Issues is important. The working group meets every month to elaborate a new gender policy within each ministry and to discuss what has been done in this field.

As a young independent state, Azerbaijan does not have much experience in building its own state gender strategy. We need the assistance and support of countries with rich experience in the field of gender mainstreaming, countries that are successfully implementing diverse projects and strategies. We need also the strong assistance of international organizations in providing necessary technical support and implementing a wider range of projects in Azerbaijan. We stress our needs to participate in meetings and conferences to exchange views with the countries that have similar problems, obstacles and approaches to the building of national gender strategy.

Foremost we need not only official meetings and adoption of documents but also to apply international experiences both at bilateral and multilateral levels concerning national gender policy practices. We need to incorporate gender mainstreaming strategy at all levels, conduct trainings for intergovernmental focal points, and elaborate special gender-sensitive legislation. In this regard further collaboration is called for with international organizations for new approaches and ideas embracing all necessary stages of the process of gender mainstreaming in Azerbaijan.

* * *

---

[70] Information about the conflict, including the history and situation of women caught there, especially refugees and internally displaced persons, is available at the web site of the President of Azerbaijan, http://www.president.az/azerbaijan/az8.htm, or, http:/president.gov.az/azerbaijan/nk/index.htm

STRATEGIES FOR GENDER MAINSTREAMING: THE CASE OF THAILAND

Ms. Maytinee Bhongsvej

Executive Director
Association for the Promotion of the Status of Thai Women

and

Ms. Supatra Putananusorn

Chief, Women's Information Centre
Office of Thai National Commission on Women's Affairs (TNCWA), Thailand

Thai women and their economic and social status

In the past two decades the government, NGOs and women's movements have made considerable efforts to advance the status of women and to strengthen their roles in order to reduce gender inequalities. As a result, in present day Thailand, women play an integral role in all aspects of national development.

Thai women participate actively in the labour force, constituting nearly half of the economically employed population. Women, whose potential and capabilities have been recognized, now have much better access to job opportunities. During the late 1980s and the early 1990s, women formed the majority of workers in the export and tourism industries, which brought in the highest foreign exchange earnings. However, the economic crisis in 1997 has taken its toll and women have been hit harder.

Sustained national economic growth in the pre-crisis years brought about social development in many aspects in Thailand. Women's health has improved and literacy rate has increased significantly to 91 per cent. However, while women's conditions have improved in some areas, inequality still persists in others.

The promulgation of the People's Constitution in 1997 was the most significant positive change which has moved and will move the Thai society closer to the goal of gender equality. The Constitution explicitly guarantees equal rights between men and women and requires that the state promote gender equality. This is the context of the more intensified advocacy for gender mainstreaming in recent years to ensure that women's voices are better heard and the needs for the equitable sustainable development of the country are responded to. To attain the goal involves multi-pronged strategies, two of which are discussed here: empowerment of women and mainstreaming gender perspectives in the national policy and planning processes.

Empowerment of women: Making women more visible

Although Thai women play active roles in all spheres of national development, traditional values and customs have ascribed a subordinate position to them in social hierarchies. Empowerment of women through increased representation at all governance levels is thus an important means for women's voices to be heard.

150

In politics and administration, women's representation is still negligible. At the national level, women senators and members of parliament form less than 10 per cent of the total. At the local administration level, propelled by TNCWA, the national machinery for the advancement of women, and NGOs, women form around 10 per cent, an increase from 6.4 per cent in 1997. In the government service, about 85 per cent of top executive posts are occupied by men. Women are also underrepresented in ad hoc committees where the directions of development and national policies are decided.

The efforts to increase women's representation have been directed by both women themselves and through the changes in institutional power structure. Within the government services, recently the Office of the Civil Service Commission, the governmental central personnel agency, circulated guidelines recommending all governmental departments to take the proportion of female and male officials into consideration in personnel administration practices. The targeted practices include promotion, particularly to the executive level, and provision of conducive career advancement opportunities including provision of scholarships for education and training or work assignments. The guidelines principally advocate that one sex should not exceed two thirds in number.

Setting a quota for female representation in the political arena has also been advocated by women's movements. One of the few achievements is the constitutional requirement of having a minimum of one third female members of any special parliamentary committee set up to deliberate on legislature related to women's affairs.

The most significant achievement in recent years is that the proposal for the Village Fund Committee to have equal participation of men and women won the Prime Minister's approval. The One Million Baht Fund is one of the current government's policies to bridge the gap between the rich and the poor by enlarging economic opportunities at the grass-roots level through the Village Fund allocated to all 80,000 villages and urban communities in the country. The persistent advocacy and solidarity of GOs and NGOs working for women made visible the significance of women's involvement for the effective implementation of the Fund.

Mainstreaming gender perspectives in national development

To ensure sustainable and equitable development, it is necessary to mainstream gender perspectives in the national policy and planning process. Within the government service, TNCWA has launched a two-year pilot project to build its capacity as groundwork for gender mainstreaming in nine selected departments. This is to ensure that gender perspectives are reflected in development policies and processes. The targeted agencies are those in charge of planning, budget, statistic, public relations, civil service, local administration, community development, industrial promotion, and curriculum and instruction development.

The project's key components include organizational development and personnel development. Regarding organizational development, TNCWA held a workshop to review its vision, mission and strategic plan in order to fully perform its functions in promoting gender equality and accelerating gender mainstreaming. Coordination mechanism between the Office of TNCWA and the participating departments were set up with the aim of strengthening the linkages. Gender indicators, a powerful tool for monitoring and evaluation of gender-related changes in government policies and activities over time, have been reviewed to cover emerging issues. The computer and information system is being developed to provide easy access to database and effective transfer of sex-disaggregated data and gender information among relevant agencies. The time use survey, an effective tool to measure women's invisible work, is being carried out by the National Statistical Office. The survey results will fill the gap of unavailability of data to a certain extent. Further in the administrative reform of the government currently in progress, the status of TNCWA will be upgraded and attached to a newly established Ministry of Social Development and Human Security. The restructuring is expected to contribute to the integration of gender perspectives within government processes.

On personnel development, the staff of TNCWA received skills training in gender mainstreaming and gender advocacy to firmly understand the goals and objectives of gender equality and gender mainstreaming. As the national policy and advocacy coordinating body, it is essential that the staff has adequate knowledge and skills in policy analysis and be able to provide technical assistance to facilitate the implementation of the targeted agencies. Training of Trainers and Training on Gender Mainstreaming were held for five middle-level officers of each participating department. They are now conducting a trial training prior to the inclusion of such training in the regular training programme of each department. International experience in gender mainstreaming has also been drawn for the maximum benefit of the project.

For capacity development across the system, TNCWA has restructured its organization to extensively and more effectively perform its function as the key policy coordinating and advocacy body. Seminars are planned for woman parliamentarians and men counter-parts to meet with woman experts in different fields. The purpose of the seminars is to share experience and concerns on women's status and impact of development programmes on women and men. Women's role in policy making and administration at both national and local levels will be highlighted. This is to generate strong political understanding and commitment to gender equality and gender mainstreaming. The plan regarding legal framework to support and enforce gender responsive governance is now under review.

Realizing the essence of wider gender mainstreaming in national development, the government has recently approved the institutionalization of gender mainstreaming in all ministries and departments. Chief Gender Executive Officers (CGEOs) will be appointed in all government agencies at both ministry and department levels. The major task of CGEOs is to oversee gender integration in policy and planning processes including delivery of services to the public in his or her respective government departments. The Gender Mainstreaming Focal Points (GMFPs) at different levels will also be appointed as a coordinator for gender mainstreaming in the organization. Both CGEOs and GMFPs will be trained to fully understand the significance of equality and gender mainstreaming. Heading and being supported by a team of trained focal points, and gender trainers and advocates, CGEOs are expected to be instrumental to effective gender mainstreaming in the government service.

In accelerating a long-term process of change, a workplan to promote gender mainstreaming has been developed. The plan includes: (1) training of CGEOs, GMFPs and line ministries and departments, local governments and grass-roots women's organizations; (2) technical assistance for all agencies, both GOs and NGOs, covering the production of core training manuals or documents for related training and consultation; (3) research and dissemination of gender indicators and information; (4) policy advice necessary to promote women's welfare, protect women's rights and analysis of gender impact of key policies and programmes; and (5) monitoring and evaluation of the progress, results and outcomes of the policies. For the realization of gender mainstreaming in government service, partnership with all stakeholders is required. This includes the experience and expertise of NGOs.

Beyond the boundary of the bureaucracy and in a larger context of the society as a whole, NGOs have made a meaningful contribution to gender mainstreaming in the Thai society, either by itself or through NGO networks or in partnership with the national machinery. The Women Constitution Network, Women in Politics Institute, Gender and Development Research Institute and female labour union movements are some of the prominent ones. In fact, in the context of the gender mainstreaming approach, NGOs have launched different institutional mechanisms and many gender-sensitive activities. Their initiatives have resulted in many gains, such as the emergence of the government's clear policies for women and legislative changes. The annual award to outstanding women heightens public awareness on the contribution and changing roles of women. Importantly they contributed to a larger pool of trained women leaders through training to reshape the development agenda at the national and local levels.

To broaden the reach of TNCWA it is essential to go beyond the confines of government. TNCWA is working to build networks with media professionals and grass-roots women's organizations nationwide. TNCWA will hold national workshops for advocates in selected sectors within the civil society to identify appropriate gender mainstreaming strategies, approaches and action plan of each sector. Cooperation among and across sectors will also be discussed. The selected sectors include those working as transformers of images and perceptions, intellectuals, profit-makers and advocacy groups.

SESSION 7:

GENDER MAINSTREAMING IN INTERGOVERNMENTAL PROCESSES

Moderated by
Ms. Thelma Kay

To highlight the importance of incorporating gender perspectives in inter-governmental processes, the experiences of ASEAN (paper prepared by Ms. Moe Thuzar and delivered by Ms. Vilayvanh Dilaphanh), ADB (Ms. Anita Kelles-Viitanen), Forum Secretariat (Ms. Patricia Sachs-Cornish) and of support to member countries in SAARC (Mr. S.K. Guha, UNIFEM South Asia) were presented. Ms. Thelma Kay (ESCAP) moderated the discussions.

GENDER MAINSTREAMING IN ASEAN: THE INTERGOVERNMENTAL PROCESS

Prepared by
Ms. Moe Thuzar
Senior Officer, The ASEAN Secretariat

and

Delivered by
Ms. Vilayvanh Dilaphanh
Lao Women's Union

As part of the larger ESCAP community, ASEAN countries have learned much from the rich and diverse experiences of other member states in their endeavours in bringing women's issues and concerns to the forefront of national agendas. ASEAN as an organization itself has also benefited from these shared experiences and has been able to translate this into concrete activities to further promote existing cooperation among its Member Countries.

ASEAN Cooperation in Women's Affairs: the regional mandate

ASEAN cooperation regarding women's affairs was brought into a formal context when the ASEAN Women's Programme (AWP) was established by its first meeting from 7 to 10 June 1976, in the Philippines. AWP had as its terms of reference:

1. To promote and implement the suitable and effective participation of women whenever possible in all fields and at various levels of political, economic, social and cultural life of society at the national, regional and international levels;

2. To enable women in the region to undertake their important role as active agents and beneficiaries of national and regional development particularly in promoting regional understanding and cooperation and in building more just and peaceful societies;

3. To integrate in national plans the specific concerns of women and their roles as active agents in and beneficiaries of development, specifically considering their role as a productive force to attain the full development of the human personality;

4. To design and promote programmes involving the participation of the community and non-governmental women organizations towards strengthening the national and regional resilience;

5. To strengthen solidarity in the region and international women's forums by promoting harmonization of views and positions.

Since the inception of AWP, however, accomplishments in the major issues concerning women in development did not gain as rapid a momentum as desired, despite subsequent cooperation activities at the regional level. This was a point recognized at the 4th Asia and Pacific Ministerial Conference on Social Welfare and Social Development organized by ESCAP in October 1991 in Manila. Among others, the Conference brought to the attention of this region that there had been slow progress in incorporating women's concerns in national development plans; women's contribution to agriculture and food production had not been fully recognized; and in the modern economy, women's participation rate was much lower than that of men. Indeed, gender inequality seemed to be the norm at the outset of the 1990s.

Despite obstacles encountered, significant inroads have been made to raise the profile of women in national development processes. At the decision-making level, gender issues have gained more recognition and consideration. A milestone for women in ASEAN was the signing of the Declaration on the Advancement of Women in the ASEAN Region by ASEAN Foreign Ministers in July 1988. The Declaration is a concrete testimony to the recognition of the multiple roles women play in the development process, and the many difficulties in the realization of their full potential and aspirations. The First Regional Report on the Advancement of Women in the ASEAN region (1996) informs that women's participation in decision-making had improved since the signing of the Declaration; all ASEAN Member Countries expressed commitment to ensure equality between men and women in their societies and had followed up the commitment with the necessary legal measures to integrate women's concerns into the national development plans. These measures are also supported in some Member Countries with projects for the advancement of women. Gender sensitivity programmes for government officials are also conducted regularly in at least four Member Countries. Collaboration among various women's organizations at both national and regional levels is carried out by national networks and the ASEAN Sub-Committee on Women.

At the Fourth ASEAN Summit held in Singapore in 1992, ASEAN leaders echoed the commitment in the 1988 Declaration, in calling for the greater involvement and increased participation of women in the development process of ASEAN Member Countries. At the Fifth ASEAN Summit in 1995, the leaders agreed to work towards the equitable and effective participation of women. This commitment has been reiterated in the ASEAN Vision 2020 adopted by ASEAN leaders at their 2nd Informal Summit held in Kuala Lumpur in 1997.

The Hanoi Plan of Action adopted at the Sixth ASEAN Summit in 1998 as a blueprint of action to implement Vision 2020 calls for the following with regard to women's concerns, under its priority areas on social and human resource development:

4.9 Work towards the full implementation of the Convention on the Rights of the Child and the Convention on the Elimination of all Forms of Discrimination against Women and other international instruments concerning women and children.

5.7 Intensify efforts of the ASEAN Network for Women in Skills Training to enhance the capacity of disadvantaged women to enter the work force.

Gender Mainstreaming in ASEAN: the Intergovernmental Process

The ASEAN Women's Programme (AWP) was renamed the ASEAN Sub-Committee on Women (ASW) at the request of the 15th Meeting of the AWP in 1996. The ASW has now been elevated to a senior-officials level body, with the name ASEAN Committee on Women (ACW) to provide a new depth to ongoing policy coordination for addressing the needs and concerns of women in ASEAN. The ACW meets on a regular basis annually. The ACW holds the mandate to monitor implementation of the 1988 Declaration on the Advancement of Women, and is responsible to prepare and publish a status report every three years. The ASW at its 16th Meeting agreed to continue to issue publications of a like nature on a regular basis, in order to monitor the progress of implementation of the Declaration on the Advancement of Women in the ASEAN Region. The Second Regional Report is now in preparation to present a regional profile of women's participation in the political, economic and social life of their countries, and collaboration at the regional level.[71]

---

[71] At time of writing. The Second Regional Report was published in early 2002.

This reporting process is governed by a mechanism formulated and adopted in 1995. A two-day training workshop, titled "Development of a Monitoring and Reporting System on the Implementation of the Declaration on the Advancement of Women in the ASEAN Region", was convened in September 1995 with UNDP support. The training workshop was designed to equip participants from ASEAN countries with a framework for monitoring and reporting based on the indicators already in use by member countries and consolidating inter-country reports on the status of women, so that this framework could be used as a continuous monitoring and reporting mechanism. Two participants from each ASEAN country involved in statistical data gathering, planning and/or monitoring of national plans and programmes for women produced a set of guidelines for country-level inputs and an integrated regional report.

Elements of the monitoring and reporting mechanism finalized at the training workshop include data and information on the profile of women's participation in political, social, economic and cultural lives of their respective countries; promotion of women's participation through community and NGOs; integration of women's concerns into national plans and programmes;[72] and promotion of women's solidarity in the region. This mechanism guided the First Regional Report published in 1996 and will also serve as a guide for future Reports. The ASEAN Secretariat, in consultation with the focal points of ACW, coordinates the gathering and compilation of the reports.

Gender mainstreaming in ASEAN is thus carried out through the collaborative mechanism of ACW. ACW is currently working towards the convening of an ASEAN workshop on gender mainstreaming in 2002, coordinated by the Philippines and with support from the UNDP Asia Pacific Gender Equality Programme. This workshop will bring together all the ten ASEAN countries to share experiences and strategies – including those that worked as well as lessons learned – and to make existing dialogue among countries in this area further enriched and more dynamic. With a long-term goal to develop capacity region-wide for gender mainstreaming at policy and programme levels, the project will also attempt to identify an ASEAN-wide mechanism to assist countries in implementing effective gender mainstreaming strategies, especially those which are "new in the business" of gender mainstreaming.

Another ASEAN project, ASEAN Network for Women in Skills Training, was implemented from 1996 to 1998. The participants in the regional seminar in Thailand agreed that the benefits brought to the women trainees and policy makers alike warranted the continuation of the project into an expanded second phase. The second phase focused on developing a set of strategies to address the lack of access by women to opportunities for employment and training. With UNDP support, ASEAN Member Countries developed and operationalized a regional work programme in mid-2000. Thus, ASEAN today has a set of

---

[72] This includes expressions of international commitment to women's advancement; statements of mandate and specific policy provisions; development programmes and projects in all sectors; and mainstreaming efforts undertaken by Governments.

strategies, in the form of a regional work programme for ASEAN women in skills training, to address skills training needs of women in the region, the need to anticipate and prepare for changes arising from economic downturns and the changing nature of the labour market and the implications for women in many different roles.

Implementation of the projects in the work programme commenced with the recent workshop on sharing best practices and expanding new skills training for disadvantaged women held in Chiang Mai. Mainstreaming the needs and concerns of women in the ASEAN region, particularly in terms of their employability and income-generation skills, has become an important consideration for national governments at a time when the threat of yet another economic downturn is looming on the horizon. Empowering women with necessary skills and knowledge is important in helping them fulfil their multiple roles in society.

In June 2001, the ASEAN Secretariat and the World Bank embarked on a joint initiative entitled "Meeting the Challenge of Development in the ASEAN Region in the 21st Century: Social Development in the National Development Agenda". Under this initiative, a series of video-conferences are being conducted, focusing on mainstreaming social concerns such as rural development and poverty reduction, gender, labour and employment, and social protection into the development agendas of ASEAN countries. A video conference session on gender mainstreaming was conducted in July 2001 drawing together inputs and contributions from participating ASEAN countries. Case studies and best practice examples from the participating countries highlighting innovative approaches to gender mainstreaming were shared and discussed during the three-hour session.[73]

The road ahead

ASEAN leaders have recognized and reaffirmed the importance of women and their participation in the development of their respective countries. The cross-cutting nature of gender issues requires a sustained commitment of our leaders to keep gender concerns incorporated in the national plans and policies in all areas of development. The reporting and monitoring mechanism for implementation of the Declaration of the Advancement of Women in ASEAN ensures that mainstreaming of women's concerns into national development policies and programmes will be sustained.

The fact that the 1998 Hanoi Plan of Action calls specifically for strengthened collaboration in working towards the full implementation of CEDAW and other relevant international instruments signals commitment at the highest level to address the needs and concerns of women, ensuring that gender mainstreaming will continue to remain high on ASEAN agenda.

---

[73] The presentations and discussions at the video conference session are available on the joint ASEAN-World Bank web site at www.worldbank.org/gdln/dl.htm, under the hyperlink entitled "Social Development in the National Development Agenda: ASEAN".

Declaration of the Advancement of Women in the ASEAN Region

Bangkok, 5 July 1988

The Minister for Foreign Affairs of Brunei Darussalam, the Minister of Foreign Affairs of the Republic of Indonesia, the Minister of Foreign Affairs of Malaysia, the Secretary of Foreign Affairs of the Republic of the Philippines, the Minister for Foreign Affairs of the Republic of Singapore, and the Minister of Foreign Affairs of the Kingdom of Thailand:

Desiring to further intensify the aims and purposes of the Bangkok Declaration of 1967, the Declaration of ASEAN Concord of 1976, and the Manila Declaration of 1987;

Recognizing the importance of active participation and integration of women in the region in sharing the future development and progress of ASEAN and the necessity of meeting the needs and aspiration of women in the ASEAN Member Countries;

Aware that women constitute half of the total population of the ASEAN region; and

Taking cognizance of the multiple roles of women in the family, in society and in the nation and the need to give full support and provide facilities and opportunities to enable them to undertake these tasks effectively.

Do hereby declare that:

In the context of strengthening regional cooperation, collaboration and coordination for the purpose of advancing the role and contribution of women in the progress of the region, each MEMBER COUNTRY, either individually or collectively, in ASEAN shall endeavour:

1. To promote and implement the equitable and effective participation of women whenever possible in all fields and at various levels of the political, economic, social and cultural life of society at the national, regional and international levels.

2. To enable women in the region to undertake their important role as active agents and beneficiaries of national and regional development, particularly in promoting regional understanding and cooperation and in building more just and peaceful societies.

3. To integrate in national plans the specific concerns of women and their roles as active agents in and beneficiaries of development, specifically considering their role as a productive force to attain the full development of the human personality.

4. To design and promote programmes involving the participation of the community and non governmental women organizations towards strengthening national and regional resilience.

5. To strengthen solidarity in the region and international women forum by promoting harmonization of views and of positions.

* * *

ADB'S WORK AND PLANS ON GENDER MAINSTREAMING

Ms. Anita Kelles-Viitanen

Manager, Social Development, Asian Development Bank

In 1998 the Asian Development Bank (ADB) adopted a new Policy on Gender and Development, recognizing the importance of addressing gender concerns in sustainable development. We also realized that the Policy alone would not be sufficient unless carefully operationalized. For this reason, the Bank's Policy also included a commitment to prepare a Gender Action Plan. A Gender Action Plan has been prepared for the years 2000-2003 in close consultation with individual Departments in terms of their concrete commitments made on the sectoral activities and on future loan and Technical Assistance Programmes. The Plan will help to address glaring gender disparities in the countries and in the sectors. The Plan covers both our programme and project work. For example, several country reviews have been carried: in Indonesia, the Lao People's Democratic Republic, Cambodia, China, Nepal, Pakistan, Sri Lanka, Thailand and Viet Nam. We are also preparing and publishing country briefing papers on a regular basis. Gender mainstreaming in our projects is done through a process that starts with a mandatory Initial Social Assessment that scopes and identifies all major social dimensions and challenges including those relating to gender. When major gender concerns are found, a careful gender analysis needs to be carried out.

We will also closely integrate gender concerns into the ADB's Poverty Assessments. We have prepared and published various sectoral gender checklists including those on education, health, water supply and sanitation, urban development and housing, and agriculture. Checklists for forestry, environment, resettlement, governance and transport are also planned.

An External Forum on Gender and Development with high-level experts and advisors (both from the government and NGOs) was established in 2001 to advise and guide the Bank and to maintain dialogue on latest trends and challenges relating to gender in the region.

Planning, coordination and conducting training on GAD for ADB staff and executing agencies will also constitute an important element in the GAD work programme. These will be given mainly on a sectoral basis. We have already provided training in three sectors: forestry, water supply and sanitation, and on urban development. GAD in-country training for executing and implementing agencies will also strengthen mainstreaming of gender concerns into our loans and technical assistance projects. Such training has already been provided to the Local Government Engineering Department in Bangladesh, the Department of Irrigation in Nepal and the Ministry of Agriculture and Development in Vietnam. A training of trainers programme on social development including gender has also been established for India.

There are many other activities, all of which cannot be mentioned in this short time. But one more area, nevertheless, deserves to be highlighted: that is, addressing emerging regional problems such as trafficking of women and children, and HIV/AIDS. ADB as a regional financing institution with its subregional programmes such as the Mekong Programme provides a good opportunity not only to address such issues but also to work closely with other development partners. It is important that we build upon our complementarities and comparative advantages.

* * *

GENDER MAINSTREAMING EXPERIENCES FROM SOUTH ASIA

Mr. S.K. Guha

National Programme Officer
UNIFEM South Asia Regional Office, New Delhi

UNIFEM South Asia Regional Office works with governments, NGOs and other stakeholders in the subregion (Bangladesh, Bhutan, India, Maldives, Nepal, Pakistan and Sri Lanka) to promote gender mainstreaming in the development process, based on the definition in ECOSOC 1997/2: "Mainstreaming a gender perspective is the process of assessing the implications for women and men, of any planned action including legislation, policies or programmes, in any area and at all levels" to achieve gender equality.

Gender mainstreaming: Why?

Decisions about allocations of development resources and opportunities are made by an interrelated set of dominant ideas, development directions and organizations: collectively referred to as the Mainstream (ideological component and institutional component both reinforcing each other) which decides who gets what and also provides a rationale for the allocation of societal resources and opportunities. Therefore, if gender equality has to be achieved, it is essential to address those larger processes, paradigms, and institutional structures that constitute the mainstream.

Gender mainstreaming: How?

There are two aspects of gender mainstreaming:

Technical dimension: In order to be successful, mainstreaming requires reliable data, sound theoretical underpinnings and people with the ability to spot opportunities and interpret gender equality requirements to varied groups.

Political dimension: Promotion of women as decision makers and supporting women's collective efforts to redefine development agendas; in other words, not increased participation alone in an unequal development process, but enabling women to collectively assess their situations and express their priorities and concerns, and strengthening women's voices, participation and influence, to reset agendas and redefine paradigms.

Instruments of gender mainstreaming

- Policy coordination
- Legislation
- Training and sensitization
- Gender analysis
- Institutional development
- Advocacy and awareness generation
- Engendering planning
- Monitoring of policy and programmes
- Sex-disaggregation of data
- Building gender competence as a legitimate area of specialization
- Capacity development in gender analysis in different sectors
- Countering gender-based violence and engendering the justice systems
- Engendering process of resource allocation
- Ensuring women's participation at all levels of decision-making
- Access to information at different levels
- Adopting a human rights framework
- Decentralization of decision-making processes
- Gender-sensitive plans and policies
- Gender-sensitive enforcement and justice systems

For effective gender mainstreaming

Clear strategies for gender mainstreaming

Clear political will, clear action plans, clear accountability mechanisms

Clearly defined management responsibilities for gender mainstreaming

Strong links between gender mainstreaming and other organizational priorities

Qualitative and quantitative targets

Networking with NGOs – Alliance Building and Partnerships with women's movement in the country and the International Women's Movement

Institutional development for gender mainstreaming

Gender mainstreaming to be reflected in human resource management

Accountability mechanisms

Fostering competence

Vignettes of gender mainstreaming efforts
in countries of South Asia

Maldives

As institutional mechanisms, the Maldives has the Ministry of Women's Affairs and Social Welfare and the National Women's Council at the national level and the Island Women's Committee and the Ward Women's Committee at the local level.

In terms of major plans, policies and programmes, since 1997, the Action Plan for the Implementation of the Platform for Action is in place. It should be noted that the National Policy of Action for Women's Development is currently being finalized and the national family law is being drafted to enhance women's status. Sex-disaggregated data collection is in practice since 1995 and special focus is given to women in technical education and credit.

UNIFEM supported the engendering of the Third Development Plan. It also assisted the Ministry of Planning and Environment to conduct a national survey on sex-disaggregated data for the first time in collaboration with the Department of Women's Affairs. UNIFEM provided consultancy services towards drafting the framework and programmes for gender mainstreaming in Male (the capital) and atolls. The drafts are being finalized. UNIFEM also supported the publication of a directory of women senior government positions in 1996 and, after the Beijing Conference, the publication of the biannual magazine *"Hiyala"* on women's issues.

Pakistan

Efforts have been made to mainstreaming gender in the planning process. The Information Network for Women in Development (INWID) group was set up by UNIFEM to incorporate gender concerns in the Eighth Five-Year Plan of Pakistan. This comprised WID focal points of all donor agencies and the United Nations bodies. INWID held dialogues with the Planning Commission and helped in drafting the chapter on women in development of the Plan as well as drawing a gender check list for the Plan. It also helped to identify a list of resource persons and women's organizations to look at the gender aspect of all chapters.

INWID had received the legitimacy to be included in the advisory board of the Government of Pakistan for the preparation of FWCW. INWID was renamed Information Network for Gender and Development (INGAD) and exists as a consultative forum.

ESCAP and UNIFEM assisted a national programme on compiling and dissemination of sex-disaggregated data, including an analysis of law for the project, "Work of the Human Rights Commission and the Gender and Laws", and gender sensitization of the 1998 Census Process.

Nepal

In order to mainstream gender considerations into national development, the National Planning Commission (NPC) was supported to examine the structural obstacles to women's full participation in the development process and to identify corrective measures in policy, institutional responsibility and legal frameworks. Different methodologies were adopted for this task. First, previous (sixth, seventh and eighth) Five-Year Plans were reviewed with special attention to the sectoral WID policies so that WID priorities could be integrated into other sectoral plans. Second, the databases of several sectoral ministries (Agricultural, Tourism, Trade and Industry, Water and Power) were examined. Third, a comprehensive review of the Constitution of Nepal was conducted. Reviews of the institutional framework and legal frameworks have also been conducted.

ADB and IFAD assisted a programme on "Extending Production Credit to Rural Women" and UNIFEM complemented it with a project to "Build Gender Issues in Development Planning and Credit Programmes". They contributed to mainstreaming gender considerations into the national development and benefit monitoring and evaluation assistance.

The Agriculture Perspective Plan was extensively reviewed as a priority in order to examine the linkages between the macrolevel policies and microlevel projects and, importantly, to examine the need for it to reflect WID components. Consultations were held by the project team with sectoral ministries, NGOs, donors and stakeholders. Gender sensitization sessions and workshops were conducted by the team for various offices of the government, including the NPC as well as with NGOs. Gender Advocacy was a constant exercise of the team in its interaction at all levels with the government, NGOs and donors.

India

The Fourth World Conference on Women in Beijing created a ground swell for determined efforts towards gender equality and demand for women's participation in decision-making. In this context and in order to make women's voices heard in the national policy and planning process in general and, to complement the efforts of the Planning Commission to engender the Ninth Plan of India in particular, a "Think Tank Process" with sector expertise was initiated.

After the Ninth Plan Initiative, follow-up activities are ongoing, in particular on violence against women, including the "Zero violence zone project" and campaigns to eliminate gender-based violence. A Resource and Information Centre was established.

The Steps:

Think Tank operates in steps

Formation of the Think Tank

Think Tank had the initial interaction with
the Department of Women and Children Development (DWCD)

Lobbying   Think Tank carried out Sectoral Studies on   Advocacy
Environment, Politics, Employment, Violence, etc.

Think Tank interacts with the Planning Commission
before finalizing the Approach Paper

CALCUTTA: Regional Meetings with NGOs,   PUNE:
Basic needs and   Government representatives,   Gender-based violence
empowerment   Planning Commission etc.   and health

CHANDIGARH: National Meeting with Planning   SHILLONG:
Agriculture, Human   Commission and the Government   Status of women in
Resource Development,   areas affected
Political Empowerment   by insurgency

Detailed cross-sectoral   BANGALORE:
recommendations   Urbanization and
the urban informal
sector women

The Ninth Plan Document

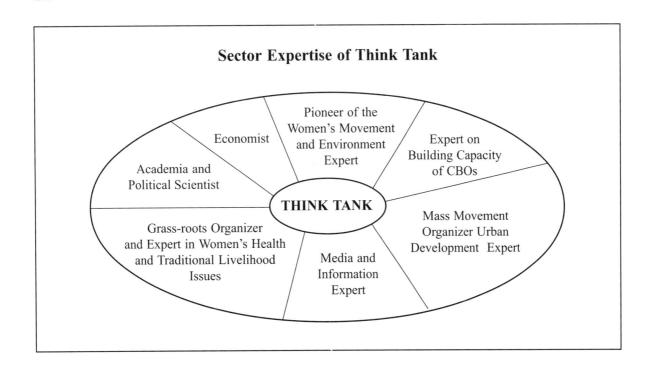

Sector Expertise of Think Tank

Economist

Pioneer of the
Women's Movement
and Environment
Expert

Expert on
Building Capacity
of CBOs

Academia and
Political Scientist

THINK TANK

Mass Movement
Organizer Urban
Development Expert

Grass-roots Organizer
and Expert in Women's Health
and Traditional Livelihood
Issues

Media and
Information
Expert

Sri Lanka

Sri Lanka has the Ministry of Women's Affairs which was established in 1997. As institutional mechanisms it also has the Women's Bureau, the National Committee on Women, Focal Points in all ministries and Women's NGO Forum. UNIFEM supported a project to strengthen the national machinery for the advancement of women.

In terms of major plans, policies and programmes, the National Plan of Action (1996) is the key. For women's economic empowerment, the Women's Bureau operates the Revolving Fund to provide women with low interest and collateral free credits, while the State Poverty Alleviation Programme recognizes spouses as the joint recipients. The reform of the penal code aims to criminalize incest and sexual harassment. Women's Desks were established in main police stations. In the area of politics, a proposal was made to reserve 30 per cent quota for women in the Assemblies.

* * *

GENDER MAINSTREAMING AT THE PACIFIC ISLANDS FORUM SECRETARIAT

Ms. Patricia Sachs-Cornish
The Pacific Islands Forum Secretariat

Introduction

The Pacific Islands Forum Secretariat (PIFS) adopted a Gender Policy in support of its commitment to mainstream gender through PIFS' work programmes and its policy advice to Forum Islands Country members and the Council of Regional Organizations of the Pacific (CROP) and inter-agency working groups.

The Gender Policy guides PIFS' efforts to mainstream gender and to achieve gender-balanced participation in development. The Policy argues that it is essential not only for promoting social justice, but it is also a matter of good economics and sound sectoral management. Worldwide experience clearly shows that supporting more equal participation by women contributes to the economic growth of their communities and improves the welfare of their families. Investing in gender equality is central to sustainable development and to the management of regional resources.

PIFS' gender mainstreaming approach takes into account the different knowledge, roles and responsibilities of women and men and recognizes that, to effect long-term positive change in the conditions of communities and nations, actions and attitudes about men's and women's roles and rights in society must change. Thus gender mainstreaming is a critical and cross-cutting consideration in development planning. Failure to strive for gender equality in all social and economic activities creates an opportunity cost ill afforded by Forum Island Countries, as sustainable economic growth is reliant on maximizing the potential of all its human resources, regardless of gender, age, ethnicity or class.

The Pacific region developed a Pacific Platform for Action (PPA) for the Advancement of Women, which was adopted in 1994 by all Forum members as part of the Noumea Declaration. PPA formally recognizes the importance of women's participation in national and regional development activities. It identifies the critical areas of concern affecting the full and equal participation of women in the region including all aspects of economics and politics. Additionally, PIFS and many Forum members are using CEDAW as a guide for promotion of gender equality and mainstreaming.

Policy vision

The Gender Policy seeks to contribute to optimum political leadership through the Forum by promoting comprehensive social and gender analysis and fully informed decision-making on issues concerning the Forum and the mandate of the Secretariat. PIFS' approach to gender mainstreaming includes gender analysis and promotion of gender equality in emerging policy issues. Some examples of this work during 2001 include promoting:

- Gender equitable access within the draft Regional ICT Policy

- Gender as a cross cutting issue in the Regional Submission to the World Summit on Sustainable Development (WSSD) and advice provided to CROP Rio+10 working group and NGOs on other natural resource management issues

- Gender issues in the International Property Rights Strategy

- Gender equality as an integral part of the Regional Basic Education Action Plan to develop human resources in the region

PIFS also published a number of papers on gender mainstreaming, such as "Women, Peace and Security for Melanesia" presented at a UNIFEM subregional meeting. Further work to develop gender indicators to facilitate gender mainstreaming in education and to monitor the inclusion of gender equality in these developments will be undertaken.

Policy principles, goals and strategies

The Policy seeks to reflect the commitment of Forum members, and hence the Secretariat, to the values of inclusiveness, equity, respect and a sharing of responsibility for sustainable and equitable development in the region.

The achievement of gender mainstreaming is guided by the following principles:

Principle one: *Recognition of the weight and importance of national and international commitments to gender equity made by Forum Island Countries.*

- Policy goals: To provide support to members as they work to fulfil gender equity commitments made at national and international levels;

- Strategies: (i) Ensure that Secretariat staff are aware of member countries' commitments in the area of gender equity and how these are relevant to divisional work; and (ii) Ensure through professional development and training that all Secretariat staff can respond with effective and appropriate analytical and technical skills to assist countries to meet their commitments to gender equity.

Principle two: *Recognition of the varied and valuable roles played by men and women, and other social groupings, in sustaining traditional and contemporary culture and in contributing to the ongoing positive development of their countries.*

- Policy goal: To analyse and document how men's and women's gender differentiated roles are relevant to, or may be impacted by, the mandate of the Forum and the work of the Secretariat.

- Strategies: (i) In all studies and programmes, staff will be encouraged to integrate an analysis of the value that the contributions of different groups can make to policy, as well as the differential impacts that policies may have on the practical needs and strategic interests of different social groups, *inter alia*, men and women, people of different ages, ethnic origin, religion; (ii) Sex-disaggregated data will be made available in all Secretariat publications which provide statistical information about people and their activities in the region (iii) Based on the two previous strategies, the Secretariat Executive and staff will aim to include social and gender analysis statements in reports to the Forum Economic Ministers Meeting, Forum Officials Committee and Forum Meetings.

Principle three: *Promotion of democratic access to development initiatives.*

- Policy goal: To promote equitable participation of women and men in all programmes stemming from Forum initiatives and the divisional work programme of the Secretariat.

- Strategy: The Secretariat will encourage members to achieve a balance of qualified men and women to participate in meetings and programmes organized by the Secretariat.

Principle four: *Promotion of open communication to ensure that balanced information is collected from all components of society and integrated into comprehensive analyses of issues relevant to the region.*

- Policy goal: To provide assistance and advice to governments to ensure balanced communication with all sectors of their societies.

- Strategy: To work with members to develop acceptable procedures to facilitate effective interaction with the private sector, communities and NGOs where these groups represent specific viewpoints relevant to achieving the annual workplan objectives of the Secretariat. For example, recent work has been undertaken to support and advise the consultant with a study on Gender Issues relevant to the Development and Management Plans for the Fiji Tuna industry.

The Gender Issues Adviser (GIA) of PIFS and UNDP Programme Analyst on Gender and Poverty coordinate an Informal Gender Working Group, which includes CROP gender focal points (GFPs), regional intergovernmental agencies and donors. The aim of the gender working group is to coordinate, collaborate and network on gender issues and developments in the region. Four meetings have been held this year to contribute to the Review of the Secretariat of the Pacific Community (SPC)/Pacific Women's Resource Bureau (now renamed the Pacific Women's Bureau, PWB), and to participate in the UNIFEM Profiling and their review of the Women and Politics Project.

Principle five: *Recognition of the importance of modelling best practices and learning from experience.*

- Policy goal: Forum Secretariat will apply the principles of this policy to the organization itself as well as to its mandated workplan.

- Strategies: (i) It will review corporate and human resources policies of the Secretariat to ensure that they do not discriminate against anyone on the basis of sex and that they encourage equitable opportunity in hiring; and (ii) establishment of a monitoring and review process for the gender policy and procedures to ensure effectiveness of the policy and achievement of goals; (iii) documentation of best practices for gender analysis and production of training materials on gender and policy analysis.

PIFS human resource development strategies

Gender Policy statements are to be included in circulars, job advertisements and consultant's reports. PIFS actively encourages member governments to nominate balanced numbers of qualified women and men to attend meetings, workshops and events. It is an equal opportunity employer and encourages both women and men to apply for its positions. Consultants are requested to ensure that their written work uses gender inclusive language and that wherever possible, all research and reporting considers and reflects the situations and experience of both men and women. Wherever data on people is collected, it is expected that it will be disaggregated by sex.

GIA Work programme 2002

PIFS has a GIA funded by the Department for International Development, United Kingdom. She provides advice from a gender perspective alongside other policy advisers in line with the PIFS mainstreaming approach, on emerging priority regional policy issues: for example, population, poverty, regional statistics development, social impact of trade agreements, health, and investment.

GIA is also involved with assisting Forum staff and CROP organizations to mainstream gender and to undertake gender analysis and develop capacity through training programmes within the Forum and with CROP. The 2002 work programme in particular is designed to facilitate the implementation of the CROP Gender Strategy. The following recommendations were the outcome of a recent PIFS workshop for CROP GFPs on Gender Action Planning and Gender Strategy Reporting. The workshop participants identified further work to be carried out with each CROP agency. They recommended that:

GIA provide Technical Assistance to review the status for the CROP Gender Policy and Gender Strategy, and make recommendations on the implementation of it within each CROP organization.

GIA undertake a review of each CROP organization's implementation of the gender strategy during 2002. Each review will include:

(i)   Discussion with the Executive and Management to build the commitment and advice on processes which will create an enabling environment for implementation of the gender strategy;

(ii)   Discussion on the Terms of References and draft reporting strategy and the role of the GFP;

(iii) An assessment of training needs to assist implementation of the gender strategy; and

(iv)   Undertaking and advising on capacity building to increase gender awareness on achieving gender equality with each CROP agency,

- GFPs agreed to review PWB gender training material for use in CROP agencies to facilitate gender integrated planning and comment of the guidelines for gender integrated training.
- SPC[74] and PIFS review the role of SPC in facilitating implementation of the Gender Strategy and technical assistance and make recommendations to the Heads of CROP if changes are required to the existing CROP Gender Strategy.

Guidelines for implementation

The divisional mandates are currently under review. The policy is to be monitored in order to bring significant results or findings to the attention of the Executive.

A subcommittee of staff, representing each division and including both men and women is to be established. The Subcommittee will be charged with interpreting the Gender Policy in light of each division's responsibilities and commitments as defined by annual workplans and the corporate mandate of the Secretariat.

Development of indicators of success to measure progress in achieving policy goals will continue. PIFS has recently introduced a performance management system which will lend itself to monitoring and evaluation of the implementation of the Gender Policy and the gender mainstreaming approach.

---

[74] Secretariat of the Pacific Community, based in Noumea, New Caledonia.

SESSION 8:

CLOSING OF THE REGIONAL SYMPOSIUM

CLOSING ADDRESS

Ms. Keiko Okaido

Deputy Executive Secretary
Economic and Social Commission for Asia and the Pacific

As the Asia-Pacific Regional Symposium on Gender Mainstreaming comes to its conclusion. I would like to express my appreciation of your hard work and congratulate all of you on the communiqué which you have just unanimously adopted.

I note with appreciation that the communiqué is a crystallization of your intensive and interactive deliberations during this symposium. It reaffirms the importance of the gender mainstreaming strategy to promote gender equality and covers new thinking on the effective implementation of the strategy. In your deliberations on alleviating poverty in a globalization world, you have drawn attention to the inadequacy of focusing only on income poverty and have called for a human poverty perspective which recognizes the multiple deprivation and the violation of the rights and entitlements of women. You have also pointed out the need to bridge the gap between macroeconomic policies and social policies which seek to achieve the goals of social justice and gender equality.

I also note that you have made value-added contributions to the important subject of gender budgeting as a means to link policy commitment to resource allocations. The interconnection which you have pointed out of the development of technical capacity for gender budgeting and the need to support this process politically especially through civil society advocacy is also very enlightening.

The institutionalization of gender mainstreaming approaches is another key area which you have addressed. Many important issues have also been raised in ensuring accountability and responsibility for gender mainstreaming. I thank those who have shared with the symposium good practices and lessons learned from your own experiences of developing and operating various innovative approaches.

The sharing of gender mainstreaming practices in various sectors has proved to be an exercise helpful for us to reflect upon the gaps between theory and practice. Innovative concepts can be considered useful, feasible, sustainable, and effective only when they prove their worth in the field. Such information would be available only from those of you who have taken the initiative to explore the potential of different approaches in reality and frequently in uncharted territory. In your working groups, I understand that you had the opportunity to look at gender mainstreaming in sectors outside the governmental arena, and also in emerging issues, including in post-conflict nation building. This has been an invaluable forum to learn from one another and to strategize on improved approaches.

In our rapidly globalizing and interconnected world, subregional and regional bodies are becoming increasingly important in shaping policy directions, and your deliberations has shed light on the various measures which intergovernmental bodies have taken to address gender mainstreaming and the useful role which these entities can play in promoting common standards and norms, and in intercountry cooperation.

As the only intergovernmental body in this region, ESCAP for its part stands ready to move forward with you in promoting gender mainstreaming as a key instrument for gender equality.

I wish to convey our most grateful thanks to the Government of Japan for its financial support, and governments and agencies that have sponsored resource persons' presentations, and all other donors and supporters that have contributed to the success of this symposium.

I would also like to thank Ms. Angela King, Ms. Carolyn Hannan, the staff of the Office of Special Advisor on Gender Issues and Advancement of Women and the Division for Advancement of Women for their collaboration with ESCAP. We would like to convey our best wishes for the upcoming four symposia that will be jointly organized with other regional commissions. It is our sincere hope that this Asia-Pacific Regional Symposium has been a successful first step in this global endeavour.

I hope you have found this symposium useful in providing you with new ideas, knowledge and information. I wish you every success in pursuit of the goals and strategies developed in this symposium to mainstream gender in all sphere of your work.

Thank you very much once again for your very valuable contributions. I wish you safe journey as you return home and look forward to continuing collaboration with you for the goal of gender equality, development and peace.

* * *

CONCLUDING COMMENTS

Ms. Carolyn Hannan

Director, Division for the Advancement of Women
United Nations

We have now reached the conclusion of four very full and interesting days of discussion on gender mainstreaming in the Asia-Pacific region. The objectives of the symposium were to stimulate dialogue and exchange of experience and good practice on gender mainstreaming between different actors in the region, particularly between Governments; to provide inputs into the work of the Commission on the Status of Women on gender mainstreaming; and, as one of five regional symposia to be held over the coming five years, to provide an input into the 10-year review of the Beijing Platform for Action in 2005.

I believe that the symposium has provided an important forum for facilitating dialogue and exchange of experience, as well as for identifying constraints and remaining challenges and some of the possible means of overcoming these. It is clear, however, at the end of these four days that, in this region as in others, there are different levels of understanding of gender mainstreaming and thus also of implementation and identification of good practice.

The communiqué has highlighted some of the key findings and I would like in this short concluding comment to raise some others.

Some **important insights** have emerged from the discussions which will help us move forward:

The importance of taking a broad focus on gender mainstreaming was emphasized, including not only the government but also the private sector, academia, religious institutions, and the media; and within government, not only the executive branch but other branches such as the judicial branch.

The importance of incorporating gender perspectives in the overall macroeconomic framework for development was highlighted. The need to move beyond individual sectors to the larger economic development framework; and to situate discussions of micro-credit and the work on gender mainstreaming in national budgets in the broad macroeconomic context, was emphasized.

Issues of good governance – in particular participation, transparency and accountability, were identified as critical in gender mainstreaming.

The importance of a rights-based approach was highlighted in many discussions and the value of CEDAW, as a framework for promoting gender mainstreaming, was emphasized by many presenters.

There is need for new examples of how and why incorporating gender perspectives into policies and programmes supports the achievement of goals in all areas of development.

Organizational change in support of gender equality can only be successful if grounded in the broader goals of development, peace and equality, as expressed through women's mobilization on the ground. Organizations cannot promoted gender mainstreaming effectively in isolation from the women's movement at the national level.

Gender mainstreaming is very much about identifying and challenging existing gender biases, for example in relation to values and norms within organizations and in macroeconomic frameworks.

Gender mainstreaming cannot be seen simply as a technical issue, involving the development of strategies, methodologies and skills. There are important political dimensions to be taken into account. Specific capabilities need to be developed to address both the political and technical dimensions.

A number of **key constraints** to gender mainstreaming were also highlighted:

There still remain huge gaps between policy commitments and resource allocations within organizations, and this negatively affects implementation of gender mainstreaming on the ground.

Many organizations still have cultures which are not supportive of the promotion of gender equality; and even where policy commitments are in place, adherence to these is not mandatory and there are no sanctions for non-compliance. Neglect of gender perspectives in policies and programmes is not questioned by senior managers.

Gender analysis and incorporating of gender perspectives is not yet done as a matter of course within organizations.

There are still serious and unacceptable gaps in the availability of sex-disaggregated data.

In the area of **institutional development** some progress could be reported:

Efforts have been made to move the responsibility for gender mainstreaming out of gender units and into line ministries and other bodies.

National machineries and gender units within organizations are increasingly working in a catalytic manner.

A broad range of mechanisms have been adopted in support of gender mainstreaming. These include use of gender focal points, task forces, high-level advisory groups; training – including for top management; development of analysis methodologies and strategies for making use of analysis mandatory; development of action plans; carrying out audits; and establishing reporting mechanisms, such as to Parliaments.

In developing strategies and methodologies for gender mainstreaming it is important to focus clearly on the goals and outcomes and not become over-focused on the process.

Institutional development is a critical element related to establishing a core set of values which should inform a body of policies and strategies, where gender perspectives are incorporated as an integral dimension.

Accountability mechanisms will be critical to successful implementation of gender mainstreaming, but there are as yet few examples of good practice in this area.

Indicators of progress in gender mainstreaming, with emphasis on outcomes, need to be developed to facilitate effective monitoring.

Although these were not specifically addressed in the symposium, I would like to raise some **risks** which need to be kept in mind.

There is a risk that the means become the end; or in other words that the focus on the process takes over from the critical focus on goals and outcomes. This was made clear in discussions with macroeconomists on gender mainstreaming in national budgets. Their interest was in what the exercise was expected to achieve and what difference this work made to outcomes on the ground. While the goals of many gender mainstreaming initiatives in relation to budgets are clear, to date there is little information to provide on the concrete outcomes. Much of the focus in discussions of gender mainstreaming in budgets has been on the process rather than the outcomes.

It is also important to take care that the processes, procedures and methodologies we put in place to support gender mainstreaming are not too complicated. There is a risk that professional staff in organizations feel that gender mainstreaming requires such high levels of gender knowledge and skills that it can only be done by specialists. In fact, gender mainstreaming should be an integral part of what professionals are already doing, and is often very much a matter of common sense. It requires identifying relevant gender issues; identifying entry-points in work programmes; and establishing means of addressing the gender issues in these entry-points.

Using the symposium to promote change

I would like to conclude by briefly describing how the results of the symposium will be utilized. The communiqué just adopted is available to all participants to use immediately in any way which will support the implementation of gender mainstreaming in their organizations. This could be to initiate a discussion on gender mainstreaming within their organizations; brief senior management on the outcomes and the implications for their organizations; or disseminate information more broadly to the general public through the media.

A short report will be prepared for submission to the Commission on the Status of Women (CSW) in March 2002. A supplementary report containing copies of all the presentations will also be made available. All of these documents will be available on the WomenWatch web site.

To ensure that there is adequate discussion of the importance of gender mainstreaming and the concrete experience in the region at CSW, delegates from Member States in the region could also include reference to the symposium and their work on gender mainstreaming in their national statements to the plenary. Copies of all the documents mentioned will also be made available to delegates at CSW. Hopefully it will also be possible to bring the symposium and its outcomes to the attention on the Economic and Social Council and the General Assembly later in 2002.

The Office of the Special Adviser, the Division for the Advancement of Women and ESCAP will continue to collaborate to find ways to effectively follow-up on the symposium and support the implementation of gender mainstreaming in the region.

Conclusion

Finally, I would like to thank ESCAP, in particular the Executive Secretary, Mr. Kim Hak-Su, for hosting and organizing the symposium. A warm thanks also goes to Ms. Thelma Kay and her team for their efforts. We all know the amount of hard, usually thankless, work that goes into the organization of such a meeting. I would like to offer my congratulations and thanks to the Chair of the Symposium, Ms. Shanti Basnyat; the Vice-Chair, Mr. H. Yousef Supiandi, and the Rapporteur, Ms. Gayle Tatsi-Misionyaki. I would also like to thank all participants for their engagement over the past four days; the presenters for willingness to share their national experiences, including constraints and challenges; and the moderators for their expertise and skills so generously shared.

The Asia-Pacific symposium was the first in a series of five regional symposia on gender mainstreaming. It is not always easy to be first. We have learned a number of important lessons which will be of value in planning the remaining symposia. I sincerely hope that you all have found the symposium a learning experience. I wish you all great success in your implementation of the gender mainstreaming strategy in your countries and in the region as a whole.

PART II

Report of the Symposium

I. INTRODUCTION

Gender mainstreaming was endorsed as a global strategy for the promotion of gender equality in the Platform for Action from the Fourth World Conference on Women (Beijing, 1995). A definition of gender mainstreaming and clear directives on what the implementation of gender mainstreaming implies were provided in the ECOSOC agreed conclusions 1997/2. Gender mainstreaming is defined as: *"...the process of assessing the implications for women and men of any planned action, including legislation, policies or programmes, in all areas and at all levels. It is a strategy for making women's as well as men's concerns and experiences an integral dimension of the design, implementation, monitoring and evaluation of policies and programmes in all political, economic and societal spheres so that women and men benefit equally and inequality is not perpetuated. The ultimate goal is to achieve gender equality"*.

The mandate for gender mainstreaming was further reinforced in the twenty-third special session of the General Assembly in June 2000. In 2001, ECOSOC resolution 2001/ 41 called for greater attention to gender mainstreaming in the work of ECOSOC and its functional commissions, including through follow-up to the implementation of the ECOSOC agreed conclusions 1997/2.

Efforts are underway within the United Nations to encourage greater attention to gender perspectives in the work programmes of all entities in the system and to support the efforts of Member States at national level. The regional commissions support implementation of the gender mainstreaming strategy at regional and subregional levels.

Experience from both the United Nations and Member States contexts has shown that the provision of opportunities for exchange of ideas, experiences and good practice on gender mainstreaming is a fruitful means of increasing awareness, commitment and capacity to implement the strategy. During a five-year period, 2001-2005, symposia on gender mainstreaming would therefore be organized in all regions to encourage increased dialogue and exchange of experiences on gender mainstreaming within the regions. The symposia would be organized through a collaboration between the Office of the Special Adviser on Women and Gender Issues and the Division for the Advancement of Women in New York and the five regional commissions.

The regional symposia on gender mainstreaming aim to:

- Establish greater links between the gender mainstreaming work of the United Nations and efforts at national and regional levels;

- Provide a more operational focus on gender mainstreaming – identifying entry-points and approaches, methodologies and tools, including through the documentation of good practice examples – to support gender mainstreaming at the national level and in intergovernmental processes at the regional level;

- Identify potentials and remaining constraints and challenges to gender mainstreaming in the regions;

- Support the work of the regional commissions on gender mainstreaming and increase reporting from the regional level to the Commission on the Status of Women.

The first regional symposium on gender mainstreaming was organized for the Asia-Pacific region in Bangkok from 10 to 13 December 2001. It was hosted by the Economic and Social Commission for Asia and the Pacific (ESCAP).

II. ORGANIZATION OF WORK

Attendance

The regional symposium brought together 80 representatives of Governments (from 26 countries and one associate member of ESCAP), regional-level intergovernmental organizations, NGOs and civil society groups and academia, as well as United Nations personnel, for a constructive dialogue on gender mainstreaming in the region. Countries and areas represented included Australia, Azerbaijan, Bangladesh, Cambodia, China, Fiji, Hong Kong (China), India, Indonesia, Japan, Kazakhstan, Lao People's Democratic Republic, Malaysia, Nepal, Netherlands, New Zealand, Pakistan, Papua New Guinea, Philippines, Republic of Korea, Sri Lanka, Tajikistan, Thailand, Tonga, Uzbekistan, Vanuatu and Viet Nam.

Documentation

The documentation for the symposium was comprised of presentations prepared for each of the sessions. The participants endorsed a Communiqué at the conclusion of the symposium, in addition to this report.

This report and all other documentation will be available on-line at the WomenWatch web site: http://www.un.org/womenwatch/osagi/regionalsymposia.htm.

Programme of work

At its opening session on 10 December 2001, the meeting adopted the following programme of work:

- ❏ Opening of the Symposium

- ❏ Election of officers and adoption of the programme of work

- ❏ Introduction to the symposium

Presentation and discussion of papers on each of the agenda items:

- Theme of the 46th session of the Commission on the Status of Women: Eradicating poverty, including through the empowerment of women, throughout their life cycle in a globalizing world

- Institutional change for gender mainstreaming

- Gender mainstreaming in national budgets

- Responsibilities and accountabilities for gender mainstreaming

- Strategies for gender mainstreaming – case studies

- Gender mainstreaming in intergovernmental processes

❏ Conclusions and recommendations

❏ Adoption of communiqué

❏ Closing of the Symposium.

Election of Officers

At its opening session, the Symposium participants elected the following officers:

Chairperson: Ms. Shanti Basnyat, Under-Secretary, Ministry of Women, Children and Social Welfare (Nepal)

Vice-chairperson: Mr. Yusuf Supiandiu, Deputy for Gender Equity, State Ministry for Women Empowerment (Indonesia)

Rapporteur: Ms. Gayle Tatsi-Misionyaki, Director, Women's Services Division, Department of Social Welfare and Development (Papua New Guinea).

Opening statements

The symposium was opened by the Executive Secretary of ESCAP, Mr. Kim Hak-Su, who pointed out that, despite the long history of efforts to promote the advancement of women, many obstacles remained which prevented the attainment of gender equality. Women in many parts of the region continued to face *de jure* and de facto discrimination. Mr. Kim emphasized as key constraints the feminization of poverty, the differential impact of globalization on women and men and the low levels of representation of women in decision-making. The importance of gender mainstreaming for producing the transformative change required to effectively promote gender equality was highlighted. Mr. Kim commended in particular the focus of the symposium on poverty eradication and globalization and on gender mainstreaming in national budget processes.

A message of support to the symposium from Ms. Angela E.V. King, Assistant Secretary-General and Special Adviser to the Secretary-General on Gender Issues and Advancement of Women, was read to participants by Ms. Carolyn Hannan, Director of the Division for the Advancement of Women. Ms. King welcomed the fact the first of the five regional symposia on gender mainstreaming was held in the Asian and Pacific region because of the long history of innovation on gender equality in the region. In her message Ms. King emphasized the commitment of the United Nations system to gender mainstreaming and outlined some of the work being done by individual entities in the United Nations and by the Inter-agency Meeting on Women and Gender Equality. She also highlighted the role of the Commission on the Status of Women and pointed to efforts being made to increase attention to gender perspectives in intergovernmental processes, for example, in the preparations for the International Conference on Financing for Development and through follow-up to Security Council resolution 1325.

The Minister for Women and Veteran's Affairs of Cambodia, Ms. Sochua Mu, delivered a keynote address on gender mainstreaming, building on the experience in Cambodia. Ms. Sochua Mu pointed to the importance of gender mainstreaming for ensuring that women were included in national development as actors and not just as recipients. Gender mainstreaming was seen as a means to ensure that women and men work together for development in all areas – in political, social and economic development. It should ensure that women as well as men have access to resources and opportunities to make important decisions and choices in their lives. Ms. Sochua Mu further emphasized that gender mainstreaming should transform policy commitments into changes on the ground. Gender mainstreaming in the area of poverty eradication must be seen as a political process. Changing society was very much about changing attitudes and practices of both women and men.

Ms. Sochua Mu provided an overview of the remaining challenges to gender equality in the Cambodian context and the catalytic work of the Ministry for Women and Veteran's Affairs. The vision of the Ministry was outlined as enabling women and men to work together to build a peaceful society, based on law and order, good governance and freedom from violence. Four priority areas were identified for the gender mainstreaming work of the Ministry: empowerment of women, education, health and legal protection. The Ministry perceived that it had an important role in monitoring Government commitments, promoting greater participation of women in all areas, influencing the development of important policies and laws and working collaboratively with NGOs in all these areas. Considerable progress had been made in local politics with 12,000 women (of 75,000 candidates) registered for forthcoming local elections.

The Director of the Division for the Advancement of Women, Ms. Carolyn Hannan, provided an overview on learnings on gender mainstreaming. Ms. Hannan highlighted some of the areas where there was considerable clarity on gender mainstreaming. These included the explicit intergovernmental mandates, both general mandates and more specific mandates on different sectors/issues; the understanding that gender mainstreaming was not an end in itself but an approach, a strategy, a means to achieve gender equality; the fact that incorporating gender perspectives would contribute effectively to the achievement of other development goals; the awareness that gender mainstreaming should involve a process of transformation – that increasing the representation and participation was not enough since the mainstream agenda could only be transformed when the contributions, priorities and needs of both women and men inform the design, implementation and outcomes of policies and programmes; and finally the understanding that commitment to gender mainstreaming did not eliminate the need for targeted activities for women and for the promotion of gender equality, or the need for gender specialists within organizations.

Two common misconceptions related to gender mainstreaming were also refuted. Firstly, gender mainstreaming was not about gender balance within an organization but was focused on the incorporation of relevant gender perspectives into the work programmes of organizations. Secondly, separate targeted activities for women were not gender mainstreaming activities, but were important complements to gender mainstreaming. Gender mainstreaming was the strategy utilized in programmes where the principal objectives were related to other development goals than gender equality, such as improving health, increasing agricultural production or reducing poverty. Gender mainstreaming involved linking the goal of gender equality to these other development goals, in the context of "mainstream" development policies and programmes.

Ms. Hannan pointed out that although gender mainstreaming was now well established as a global strategy for promoting gender equality, there was still considerable work to be done before gender perspectives were routinely incorporated into all areas of development. Trying to bring the realities of both women and men – their contributions, perspectives, needs and priorities – to bear on data collection, analyses, policy development, planning, implementation and monitoring in all areas of development, required specific knowledge and capacity. Two key obstacles were a lack of real understanding of what gender mainstreaming actually meant and the fact that the practical implications of gender mainstreaming were not fully understood in many areas of development, for example, in economics or in more technical areas.

An important starting point in the implementation of gender mainstreaming was ensuring that the initial definitions of issues/problems across all areas of activity were done in a manner which allowed for the identification of gender differences and disparities. Assumptions that issues/problems were neutral from a gender equality perspective should never be made – gender analysis should always be carried out, separately or as part of existing analyses. All analytical reports and recommendations on policy or operational issues should take gender differences and disparities fully into account. Plans and budgets should be prepared in such a manner that gender perspectives and gender equality issues were made explicit and could be specifically addressed.

Practical steps for improving the implementation of gender mainstreaming were outlined. The first step required was an assessment of the *linkages between gender equality and the issue or sector being worked on,* that is to identify the gender implications of, for example, poverty elimination, good governance, enterprise development, and peace and security issues. Secondly, once these gender perspectives have been identified in different areas of development, the *opportunities and entry-points for addressing these* in the regular processes and procedures within work programmes should be identified. Thirdly an *approach or methodology* had to be identified for successfully incorporating gender perspectives into these work-tasks in a manner which facilitates influencing goals, strategies, resource allocation and outcomes. Different strategies will be required for different types of activities, such as research and data collection, policy development, planning and implementation of programmes, training.

Finally, the importance of creating a conducive institutional environment for gender mainstreaming was highlighted. This included clarifying roles and responsibilities, establishing accountability mechanisms, developing guidelines, utilizing gender specialists and providing competence development for all personnel. Overall responsibility for implementing the mainstreaming strategy should rest at the highest levels within Governments and other organizations.

III. SUMMARY OF PRESENTATIONS AND DISCUSSIONS

A. CSW theme: Eradicating poverty, including through the empowerment of women through their life cycle in a globalizing world

To initiate discussion on this theme, presentations were provided on the outcome of the United Nations Expert Group Meeting on "Empowerment of women throughout the life cycle as a transformative strategy for poverty eradication" held in India from 26 to 29 November 2001 (Ms. Rashmi Chowdhary), the work of BRAC (Mr. Salehuddin Ahmed), as well as experiences with poverty eradication in India (Ms. Kalyani Menon-Sen) and China (Ms. Wang Xinxia). The discussions were moderated by Ms. Pawadee Thonguthai (Thai WomenWatch). The discussion is summarized below.

The discussions highlighted the increasing evidence that the impact of the ongoing processes of economic and political restructuring in the region in the context of globalization had been uneven. Some countries have managed to integrate into the global market economy while at the same time reducing poverty; others had been less successful. The correlation between economic growth and financial liberalization and poverty reduction remained problematic. In many cases, women's vulnerabilities had been heightened and had led to an expansion and intensification of women's poverty. National governments often responded to the evidence that women were over-represented among the poor through women-specific poverty programmes and targeted interventions for the empowerment of women. While participants accepted that many of these programmes were positive for the groups of women targeted, concerns were raised that by narrowly focusing attention on women-specific interventions, this approach might have hindered the incorporation of gender perspectives into mainstream policies and programmes, particularly in sectors which were critical for gender-sensitive poverty eradication strategies, such as agriculture and manufacturing. It was also considered problematic that women themselves became the target of attention rather than the gender-biased structures and processes within different sectors.

The importance of developing capabilities as a critical strategy for poverty eradication was, however, emphasized in the discussions. It was pointed out by some participants that there was still a need for women-specific inputs, particularly those that were explicitly targeted to developing capabilities of women. Without this targeted support it would be difficult to close critical gender-specific gaps. The conclusion was that gender-sensitive poverty eradication strategies would need to be complemented with targeted programmes for women.

It was highlighted that mainstream poverty eradication policies and programmes did not always address the root causes of women's poverty and were often based on the unjustified assumption that improvements in economic status and wellbeing at household and community levels would automatically lead to gender equality. Although it was increasingly recognized that poverty was a complex and multidimensional problem requiring a holistic approach, many programmes continued to address income poverty in isolation, and did not recognize the fact that poor women face human poverty through multiple deprivations and violations of their rights and entitlements. A human poverty perspective (or capability perspective), with explicit attention to gender equality issues, should be incorporated into the design and implementation of all mainstream programmes for poverty alleviation. Participants emphasized that poverty eradication did not simply require technical solutions but was very much about political decision-making. The socio-economic structures and processes which caused differing rates and levels of poverty among women and men, differential impacts and unequal potential for coping with and overcoming poverty, needed to be explicitly identified and addressed.

Gender mainstreaming in poverty eradication required specific support to women in a number of areas. Women needed training in economic literacy and access to viable self-employment opportunities. Equitable access to education and health services across the life cycle needed to be guaranteed. Microcredit and savings and social security were also essential inputs. Participants highlighted, however, the micro-credit, useful as it has been in some countries, should not be seen as a panacea for women in poverty. Poorly-run microcredit programmes could be disempowering for women. Attention to provision of microcredit should not detract from the need for giving attention to gender perspectives in all areas of economic development.

Discussions revealed that while the links between poverty eradication and women's empowerment were increasingly raised at the level of rhetoric, there was often little real change on the ground. Health, education and microcredit programmes were not automatically empowering for women. If women as well as men were not consulted on their perceptions, priorities and needs, and if their active involvement was not sought, well-meant policies and programmes could have negative effects on women. Issues of representation and access to decision-making, access to and control over resources, development of capabilities and self-esteem remained critical in efforts to empower women in the context of poverty eradication.

Participants expressed concern at the continuing gaps between macroeconomic policies focused on economic growth, and social policies focused on the larger goals of gender equality and social justice. Greater integration of economic and social policies was needed for successful eradication of poverty. Advocates of gender mainstreaming were also urged to engage with and influence processes of macroeconomic policy-making rather than focus exclusively on the micro-level. Women's potential to develop sustainable livelihoods could be directly undermined by financial and trade liberalization.

In the context of globalization, the need to incorporate gender perspectives in the overall macroeconomic framework for development was highlighted. The importance of moving beyond a focus on individual sectors to influencing the larger economic development framework from a gender perspective, and of situating discussions of microcredit and the work on gender mainstreaming in national budgets in the broad macroeconomic context, was emphasized. Issues of good governance – in particular participation, transparency and accountability – were identified as critical for poverty eradication in the context of globalization. They were also recognized as critical for the achievement of gender equality. In addition, the importance of a rights-based approach was highlighted in the discussions and the value of CEDAW, as a framework for promoting gender mainstreaming, was emphasized by participants.

Participants also pointed out that women's groups and gender-responsive NGOs in countries of the region had evolved alternative approaches to poverty eradication, which could provide valuable lessons for policy makers, planners and administrators. Greater collaboration between Governments and NGOs in the area of poverty eradication was important. This would not mean, however, that NGOs should become service deliverers. The critical role of NGOs in advocacy and monitoring for gender-sensitive poverty eradication policies and programmes must be maintained.

B. Institutional change for gender mainstreaming

Ms. Aruna Rao (Gender at Work Collective) moderated the discussion on developing conducive institutional environments for gender mainstreaming. Experience was shared from a number of different country contexts: Japan (Ms. Yoko Suzuki), Fiji (Ms. Banuve Kaumaitotoya), Timor Leste (Ms. Sherrill Whittington) and IFAD/AIT (Ms. Govind Kelkar). The discussion is summarized below.

Progress could be reported in a number of areas of institutional development to support gender mainstreaming. Efforts had been made to move the responsibility for gender mainstreaming out of gender units within national machineries or other organizations and into line ministries and other mainstream bodies. National machineries and gender units within organizations were increasingly working in a catalytic manner – promoting and facilitating rather than doing the work themselves. A broad range of mechanisms had been adopted in support of gender mainstreaming. These included use of gender focal points, taskforces and high-level advisory groups; training – including for top management; development of analysis methodologies and strategies for making use of analysis mandatory; development of action plans; carrying out audits; establishing strategic reporting mechanisms – such as to Parliaments; and positive collaboration with NGOs and civil society groups.

Challenges in institutionalizing gender mainstreaming approaches within organizations were discussed. Experiences shared highlighted several common issues. These included the need for an informed and vocal constituency that could demand change and hold public agencies and authorities accountable for addressing the interests of women as well as men, and the importance of developing accountability mechanisms within organizations, including sanctions for behaviours which perpetuated discrimination against women. An important constraint identified was the fact that in many organizations gender equality policies and gender mainstreaming strategies had been implemented from the top down, without adequate internalization of the values embedded in these policies by staff at lower levels. As a result, there was little progress in implementation of these policies.

In some contexts, organizations had established strong policies on gender equality and made explicit commitments to gender mainstreaming but then assumed that implementation would be automatic. Monitoring and evaluation mechanisms were not put in place and this reduced the potential for constructive self-criticism and further development. There were many ways in which good policies and strategies could be subverted within organizations, especially in contexts where there was little explicit management support, over and above the existence of these policies and strategies. Active support and demands for accountability from all management levels was essential for successful gender mainstreaming. Commitment of top leadership and management would take various forms such as developing clear directives and articulation of support for gender mainstreaming in the work of the organization, and demanding and supporting the development and implementation of gender action plans with clear time-frames and targets.

Although it was recognized that accountability mechanisms would be critical to successful implementation of gender mainstreaming, there were few examples of good practice in this area to share. Development of accountability mechanisms must be a priority for the future. Indicators of progress in gender mainstreaming, with emphasis on outcomes, needed to be developed to facilitate effective monitoring. Without incentives and sanctions for non-compliance, informal processes within organizations could jeopardize the implementation of very positive policies. The specific constraints, particularly related to oversight and accountability, of institutionalizing commitment to gender mainstreaming in large countries with decentralized systems were raised in the discussions.

Institutional development was related to establishing a core set of values within organizations that should inform a body of policies and strategies, in which gender perspectives were incorporated as an integral dimension. Gender-biased institutional norms were not always immediately visible or explicit but were embedded in the hierarchies, work practices and beliefs of organizations. Unchallenged gender biases and gender stereotypes within organizations could seriously constrain efforts to implement gender mainstreaming. While there had been progress in setting up the infrastructure to support gender mainstreaming in many organizations, little had been done to combat deeply embedded organizational values that discriminate against women in subtle and insidious ways. There was a clear need for strategic action to develop more conducive institutional environments for gender mainstreaming.

One concrete example of efforts to produce a more conducive institutional environment for promoting and securing accountability for gender mainstreaming was discussed. This involved the mandatory institutionalization of a methodology for gender analysis. The process involves establishing the basic gender equality principles on which work programmes should be based; clarifying the responsibilities of all actors; and stipulating the gender analysis provisions to be implemented. The methodology required that in the planning and implementation of programmes the specific roles and situation of women and men should be taken into account, so that the potential differential impacts were understood. Although emphasis was placed on the value of gender mainstreaming for programme efficiency and effectiveness and the gains in terms of transparency and accountability were outlined, one of the most difficult constraints to overcome remained the attitude that incorporation of gender analysis made processes burdensome and that there was a risk of sacrificing project efficiency in the process. The need to emphasize the value added of incorporating gender perspectives for the achievement of overall development goals as well as sector-specific goals in this context was highlighted. Constraints identified included weak gender analysis capabilities within line ministries and inadequate accountability mechanisms, both in terms of incentives and sanctions. The importance of the national machinery retaining a catalytic and supportive role and developing effective partnerships with line ministries and other actors, to ensure effective institutionalisation, was emphasized.

It was also noted that there were important links between gender equality policies of the organization itself (including on equal opportunities, a gender-sensitive work environment and harassment issues within the organization) and commitment to gender mainstreaming in work programmes. Organizations which were poor performers on gender equality within their own organizations could be assumed to perform poorly on gender mainstreaming. In particular organizations with poor records on open and flexible management styles, and/or with extremely hierarchical structures, did not have potential to do well on gender mainstreaming.

C. Gender mainstreaming in national budgets

Experience in mainstreaming gender perspectives in national budget processes was provided from Sri Lanka (Ms. Patricia Alailima) and the Philippines (Ms. Ermilita Valdeavilla and Ms. Maria Isabel T. Buenaobra). A video presentation from Australia (Ms. Rhonda Sharp) was also shown. The discussions were moderated by Ms. Linda Miranda (CAPWIP). The discussion is summarized below.

There were still unacceptably wide gaps between policy commitments to women's empowerment and gender equality and the resource allocations to meet the goals set. Budgets at different levels were one of the most powerful instruments for bridging this gap, as well as for promoting women's equitable access to public resources and mainstreaming gender perspectives into national development frameworks. Presentations and discussions stressed the importance of clear objectives in efforts to mainstream gender perspectives in budget processes, i.e. to develop awareness of gender perspectives in different sector areas which needed to be addressed; to establish accountability for commitments to gender equality; and to make necessary changes in resource allocations through budget processes.

Experiences of incorporating gender perspectives into budgeting processes in different countries of the region demonstrated the importance of clarity on the responsibilities and accountabilities of organizations and individuals involved. The involvement of economic and planning bodies, finance and budget departments and the legislature, as well as oversight by an informed and committed group of gender advocates, were important to the process of making budgeting processes gender-responsive. The role of the national machinery was critical for ensuring the necessary political and technical support. To be effective and sustainable, gender mainstreaming in budgets had to be supported by an active constituency for gender equality, both within government and in the civil society.

The presentations highlighted the importance of adequate research on the gender perspectives in different sector areas which needed to be taken into account in resource allocations. While gender research groups and institutions played an important role in carrying out research and making information available, experience had shown that it was also critical to develop the capacity of staff in Ministries of Finance and line ministries, to be able to identify areas where gender was relevant and know where to go to get necessary information. The importance of availability of sex-disaggregated statistics was emphasized.

Some of the strategies utilized to achieve gender-responsive budgets were discussed. To raise awareness of the gender implications of budget processes, sex-disaggregation of statistics was one important strategy. Improvement of data at household and individual level was critical, as was increased research on unpaid work. Initiatives were also needed to raise public awareness. The importance of challenging the notion of "neutrality" of particular sectors to gender equality in the budget process was highlighted. To increase accountability of budget processes to policy goals on gender equality – assessing where resources went, through which process, and with what results – a number of strategies had been developed. These included making information on budget processes more accessible to the general public; including information on budgets in reporting to CEDAW; making gender-responsive budgets an election issue; and using media effectively. One strategy which was mentioned but had not yet been utilized involved using general audit processes to monitor the gender-responsiveness of budgets at different levels. Assessing changes in the budget allocations required consistent monitoring. Assessing impacts of budget changes on the situation of women and gender equality, i.e. the extent to which women as well as men benefit from resource allocations-required systematic data collection and research, involving the full commitment of relevant line ministries.

Positive experiences reported included the fact that efforts to bring greater attention to gender perspectives in local budget processes had resulted in the empowerment of women to engage in discussions with local politicians and administrators on resource allocations. In these contexts, politicians and administrators were increasingly forced to motivate decisions taken and to increase consultation with women as well as men. At national level, efforts to bring gender perspectives to the centre of resource allocation decisions were more formalized. Requirements for the development of Gender Action Plans and regular reporting on progress by line ministries had led to the development of greater awareness, commitment and capacity to take gender perspectives into account. The fragility of the gains made, and the constant need for the national machinery and civil society groups and networks to advocate and monitor, were, however, highlighted.

Issues of good governance – participation, transparency and accountability – were raised in the discussions on budget processes. It was pointed out that there was little transparency in relation to the process of developing budgets. In most countries the final products were presented, with little information on the processes behind critical decisions on resource allocations. Empowerment of women in relation to budgets included skill development in relation to understanding the budget processes at national and local levels, in order to be able to initiate an informed dialogue with budget and finance departments and hold them accountable to policy commitments.

The need to work to bring gender perspectives to the whole of the budgets at national and local levels, rather than working to secure a portion of the budgets for specific support to women, was emphasized in the discussions. Gender mainstreaming in national budgets should aim to ensure that resource allocations were based on gender analysis of needs and priorities in all sector areas and that policy commitments to gender equality in different sector areas – health, education, agriculture, infrastructure – were backed up with resource allocations.

In the context of globalization, the importance of incorporating gender perspectives into all the issues of financing for development was highlighted, not just in relation to domestic resource allocation through national budgets. Issues of foreign direct investment, external debt management, trade and development assistance were also critical. In relation to debt, questions of what the loans were used for and who repaid and in what manner must be raised. Issues of revenue-raising, for example through taxation, were also important. Was the burden of taxation on households or individuals: was it detrimental to the poor: were there differential impacts on women and men? Social policy and social security measures were also identified as critical.

D. Responsibilities and accountabilities for gender mainstreaming

Ms. Patricia Licuanan (Miriam College, Philippines) moderated the discussion on the responsibilities and accountabilities for gender mainstreaming. Experience from within Government was provided from New Zealand (Ms. Wendy Moore), the Republic of Korea (Mr. Ji Kyu-Taek) and the Philippines (Ms. Ermilita Valdeavilla). Experience on the role of NGOs in ensuring government accountability for policy commitments was presented from Sri Lanka (Ms. Swarna Jayeera, CENWOR). The discussion is summarized below.

The participants discussed mechanisms to clarify the responsibilities for gender mainstreaming of different actors and ensure accountability. This included different actors within country contexts, such as Government (line ministries and national machineries, National Statistical Offices, Census Offices, etc.), Parliament, NGOs and civil society groups and researchers. Within organizations, responsibilities needed to be clearly spelt out – including for top management, middle-level management, programme staff, budget officers, gender focal points, etc. – and linked to overall policy commitments. Accountability at the highest levels, while sometimes difficult to build, was critical for stimulating accountability at lower levels.

The central role of **national machineries** in promoting gender mainstreaming was raised in the discussions. The critical role of national machineries was, however, a very difficult one. There was agreement among participants that national machineries should play a catalytic role in promoting gender mainstreaming – advocating, advising, supporting in different ways, without taking over responsibility, and monitoring and reporting on progress. This required the development of collaborative working styles, sound knowledge of gender analysis methodologies and special skills to promote and facilitate gender mainstreaming. A key constraint facing national machineries in their catalytic role in gender mainstreaming was the pervasive resistance of organizational cultures in many government bodies to gender equality values. The constraints to gender mainstreaming in different line ministries needed to be identified and strategies developed to overcome them.

It was recognized that national machineries should also move beyond promoting gender mainstreaming within individual sectors to identifying and promoting gender perspectives in overall development frameworks. Greater engagement with macroeconomic issues was required. New challenges such as globalization and HIV/AIDS needed to be given particular attention.

Within the region, the national machineries in some countries were well established and catalytic frameworks in support of gender mainstreaming were already in place; while in others, such as in countries in economic transition or post-conflict reconstruction, the national machineries were still under development. The importance of ensuring the development of the national machineries in these latter countries which built on the lessons learned in other countries in the region was stressed.

The importance of finding ways and means of ensuring that **line ministries** take responsibility for gender mainstreaming in their respective sector areas was highlighted. The need for specific accountability mechanisms was raised. The importance of high-level commitment within line ministries was also identified as critical. Participants shared examples, in this session and in following sessions, on ways and means of developing awareness, commitment and capacity within line ministries. These included training and capacity-building inputs, development of concrete approaches, methods and tools, and provision of technical support. Apart from developing adequate policies and strategies, the need for establishing effective oversight functions in relation to gender mainstreaming in line ministries was also noted.

An innovative approach to developing accountability for gender mainstreaming, involving the requirement of Gender Implementation Statements on all policies going to Cabinet, was discussed. The Gender Implementation Statements outline the gender implications of the policies being presented to Cabinet. These included clarification of the gender perspectives on desired outcomes and the nature and extent of potential impacts on women and men, both directly and indirectly, as well as policy options for addressing any gender implications identified. The process should involve consultation in the development of the statements and monitoring of results by collecting sex-disaggregated data. The objective was to legitimize the framework for gender analysis in areas other than social sectors. Political commitment at the highest level was critical for successful implementation of the strategy. The national machinery played an important catalytic role in the process, by providing training and information materials and tools to the departments. Constraints identified included the lack of capacity for gender analysis in departments; the lack of data disaggregated by sex and ethnicity; the failure to understand the gender approach (that it was not only about women); and the reliance on the national machinery to provide all back-up.

The importance of building new constituencies for gender mainstreaming among the **general public and NGOs and civil society groups** was highlighted. This involved broad dissemination of information on what the government had committed to in global intergovernmental processes, in treaties such as the Convention on the Elimination of All Forms of Discrimination Against Women (CEDAW) and in policies and strategies at the national level, as well as regular reporting on efforts made and concrete results on the ground. Training in advocacy and monitoring for civil society partners actors was essential.

Research organizations had particular responsibilities, as well as specific potentials, for securing accountability for commitments to gender equality. Examples of the innovative work of such organizations was shared. These included development and dissemination of regular reviews of the situation of women; in-depth research in critical policy areas and monitoring of state policies in these areas; carrying out of gender audits of organizations, including line ministries; policy dialogue and specific contributions to policy formulation; preparation of information materials, guidelines and tools; and provision of training and sensitization programmes.

Statistical bodies played a key role as access to adequate sex-disaggregated and gender-sensitive statistics were identified as essential for successful gender mainstreaming. Gender perspectives needed to be mainstreaming into all statistical areas. This involved, over and above sex-disaggregation, changes in approaches and methods for data collection, production, analysis and dissemination as well as identification of areas where gender-sensitive data was still not collected and utilized in policy and programme development.

The importance of **donors** for the effective implementation of gender mainstreaming was raised. It was pointed out, however, that there were serious gaps between policy commitments to gender mainstreaming of international organizations, including the United Nations, and their practice on the ground. The fact that many international organizations have ghettoised gender equality concerns, including the promotion of gender mainstreaming, within their own organizations is a constraint to gender mainstreaming within their partner countries. The need for Governments and NGOs and civil society groups to demand greater accountability of international organizations and donors for gender mainstreaming in their policies and programmes was emphasized in the discussions. Donors should be required to make attention to gender perspectives mandatory in all support in the region.

E. Strategies for gender mainstreaming – case studies

Case studies on development of strategies for implementing gender mainstreaming were presented from a number of sectors – education (Ms. Redya Betty Doloksaribu, Indonesia), human rights (Ms. Shanti Dairiam, IWRAW), forestry (Ms. Kanchan Lama, FAO/Nepal), development assistance (Ms. Rosemary Cassidy, AusAID, Australia), census (Ms. Suman Prashar, India), gender support methods (Ms. Polotu 'A.F. Fakafanua, Tonga), national reconstruction (Ms. Joana Vitor, Timor Leste), political participation (Ms. Shalini Bijlani, PRIA) and policy leadership and advocacy within government (Ms. Khair Jahan Sogra, PLAGE Bangladesh). The discussion is summarized below.

In discussing the different case studies – gender mainstreaming in specific sectors (education and forestry), through census exercises, development cooperation activities, efforts of national machineries and other government bodies, as well as in relation to human rights, political participation and in post-conflict situations – a number of generic approaches were identified, as will be outlined below.

Participants pointed out the importance of access to **gender specialists** to advocate, advise, support and monitor progress on gender mainstreaming. Specialist expertise was particularly essential for the development of strategies and action plans for gender mainstreaming and providing competence development for staff. At the project level gender specialists were considered important to assist in the identification of relevant gender issues, support consultation with women as well as men, and recommend strategies for overcoming barriers and obstacles to the equitable participation of women. Use of gender focal points within organizations had increased, although there were constraints to their effective utilization. Their roles and responsibilities needed to be made very clear – particularly the fact that they were resources rather than those with full responsibility for gender mainstreaming. In many cases gender focal points were not experts and were not provided with adequate training to allow them to play an effective role. In community level projects, grass-roots motivators, organizers or promoters could be effective catalytic agents – ensuring increased consultation with women as well as men, increasing equitable participation and highlighting discriminatory attitudes and practices at the local level. These groups need, however, needed considerable support.

Gender training was also identified as an essential element in strategies to promote gender mainstreaming. Training was required at all levels to increase awareness and knowledge on gender issues, ensure commitment and develop capacity. Training programmes needed to focus on developing necessary leadership, communication and problem solving skills for working with gender equality issues. Experience had shown that capacity development for gender mainstreaming would involve a long process. A one-off training programme of one or two days produced few changes. More innovative process-oriented methods needed to be developed, including different types of follow-up training. Capacity development could also be achieved through the development of methodologies, guidelines and toolkits, particularly if done in a participatory manner. Training should also be offered to top and middle-level management levels.

Development of **gender analysis methodology** was highlighted as critical for effective gender mainstreaming. Some capacity for gender analysis was required for all professional staff, not only gender specialists or gender focal points. Gender analysis should be applied to all sector areas. In some areas particular skills were required. Professional staff also needed to know where they could go to get support if they were not able to carry out the analysis themselves. Gender analysis could be carried out as a separate analysis or included as an integral part of other analyses being undertaken. Gender analysis findings should be fed into the design and formulation stage of project development. Access to sex-disaggregated data was critical.

Gender mainstreaming guidelines – general overall guidelines, handbooks or manuals or such tools for specific sectors – had proven useful for promoting greater implementation of the strategy. Participatory development of such tools increased the "ownership" of the tools and potential for their utilization.

Strategies for gender mainstreaming needed to include efforts to increase **consultation with and participation of** women as well as men. Networking to provide ongoing support to women and gain access to their perceptions, priorities and needs, was also an important strategy at the grass-roots level. Sharing of experiences between different groups of women was also an important strategy.

Establishing effective **monitoring mechanisms** was also identified as vital for successful gender mainstreaming in different sector areas. At the project level participatory monitoring procedures were important. Ensuring access to information was essential for participatory monitoring processes. Accountability was reported as a constraint, and even with built in monitoring mechanisms, ensuring compliance was often a problem.

The importance of a **rights-based approach and effective use of CEDAW** was highlighted. The effective utilization of different treaty bodies and human rights rapporteurs should be increased. CEDAW provided an excellent framework for assessing gender mainstreaming, emphasizing equality of opportunity, access and results.

The low participation of women in **political decision-making** was identified as a constraint to gender mainstreaming. Innovative strategies for incorporating gender perspectives into governance and public administration needed to be developed. The mainstreaming of gender perspectives in local governance in the context of decentralization remained a huge challenge. Experience in the region had shown that even where increased participation of women was made mandatory, considerable supportive inputs were required to ensure that women could participate in an equitable and effective manner. Systematic monitoring was necessary to identify constraints.

In **complex emergencies**, including conflict and post-conflict situations as well as natural disasters, incorporation of gender perspectives could meet resistance because of the attitude that gender mainstreaming was only relevant when all major problems were solved, as well as the perception of women as primarily victims. Greater emphasis needed to be put on the gender perspectives in both the emergency assistance inputs as well as more long-term development activities. The perception of women as key actors and agents of change should be promoted. The opportunities for changing the situation of women and gender relations in these post-conflict and post-disaster situations needed to be identified and capitalized on, particularly through providing access to information and training as well as job opportunities. The equitable participation of women should be promoted in all areas. The need for a strong focus on human rights was highlighted as well as for support to the development of an active role for women's groups and networks.

The example of gender mainstreaming in **census** exercises was discussed. Ways and means of eliminating male biases in the processes, caused by inadequacies in methodology and instructions for and training of enumerators, were discussed. Effective strategies to make the census more gender-sensitive included ensuring that the Master Trainers were gender-sensitive; training of all enumerators on gender issues; hiring of more female enumerators; modifying the forms for collection of information at household level; including a specific chapter on women in the instructions; and raising awareness among the general public through posters, banners, advertisements and radio and television programmes.

F. Gender mainstreaming in intergovernmental processes

To highlight the importance of incorporating gender perspectives in intergovernmental processes, the experiences of ASEAN (paper prepared by Ms. Moe Thuzar and delivered by Ms. Vilayvanh Dilaphanh), ADB (Ms. Anita Kelles-Viitanen), Forum Secretariat (Ms. Patricia Sachs) and of support to Member Countries in SAARC (Mr. S.K. Guha, UNIFEM South Asia) were presented. Ms. Thelma Kay (ESCAP) moderated the discussions. The discussion is summarized below.

In the discussion it was noted that in the context of globalization there was increased interdependence within regions and subregions. Many emerging issues required intergovernmental collaboration, for example trafficking, migration, HIV/AIDS and trade. Intergovernmental processes at regional and subregional levels had become increasingly critical.

Participants pointed out that intergovernmental mandates – both global and regional – provided important political support for gender mainstreaming and were essential instruments for securing necessary financial resources. The importance of expanding the use of intergovernmental processes, and the intergovernmental mandates emanating from them, to ensure increased and sustained attention to gender mainstreaming was raised. The intervention frameworks of intergovernmental organizations were determined by their respective governing bodies, and these were often focused on a few strategic issues. Work programmes were determined by global mandates and international instruments. Efforts must be made to more broadly disseminate the Platform for Action, the outcome of the twenty-third special session of the General Assembly and CEDAW as critical mandates for all intergovernmental bodies.

It was noted that many Governments and donors still perceive gender equality as a marginal issue and therefore a campaign to keep gender mainstreaming on the agenda, at the highest political level, especially through intergovernmental mechanisms, must be continued and reinforced. Participants pointed out that strategic allies had to be identified on various intergovernmental bodies, including in subcommittees or working groups; stronger collaborative initiatives needed to be developed by different actors to influence intergovernmental bodies; and constant contact and communication needed to be maintained with constituents and support groups in civil society.

The need for specific gender expertise within intergovernmental bodies to support gender mainstreaming through catalytic roles was stressed. Those servicing intergovernmental bodies needed gender training in order to be sensitized and equipped with the necessary professional skills and expertise to mainstream gender perspectives into their substantive work.

The role of donors in facilitating gender mainstreaming in intergovernmental processes was discussed. This role should be primarily catalytic, supporting the efforts of individual Member States as well as their collaborative efforts in intergovernmental contexts. Donors could also play an important role by facilitating the creation of space for inputs from NGOs and civil society groups, as well as for bringing critical stakeholder together for dialogue on the implementation of the Platform for Action and the outcome of the twenty-third special session of the General Assembly.

IV. CONCLUSIONS AND RECOMMENDATIONS

General insights

The importance of taking a broad focus on gender mainstreaming was emphasized throughout the discussions. Stakeholders should include not only Governments but also NGOs and civil society groups, the private sector, academia, religious institutions, the media and other actors in society. Within government the focus should not only cover the executive branch but all other branches, including the judicial branch. The need to incorporate gender perspectives in the overall macroeconomic framework for development was highlighted time and again as critical for effective gender mainstreaming – moving beyond individual sectors to the larger development framework.

Gender mainstreaming was seen to be very much about identifying and challenging existing gender biases, for example, in relation to values and norms within organizations and in macroeconomic frameworks. Gender mainstreaming could not be seen simply as a technical issue – involving the development of strategies, methodologies and skills. There were important political dimensions to be taken into account. Specific capabilities needed to be developed to address both the political and technical dimensions.

Issues of good governance – in particular participation, transparency and account-ability – were identified as critical for gender mainstreaming. The importance of a rights-based approach was highlighted in many discussions and the value of CEDAW, as a framework for promoting gender mainstreaming, was emphasized by many presenters.

While there was increased understanding that incorporating gender perspectives into different areas of development supported other development goals as well as promoting gender equality, there was a need to provide new examples of how and why incorporating gender perspectives into policies and programmes would supported the achievement of sectoral goals. Good practice examples were needed in this respect – with clear evidence that the incorporation of gender perspectives provides a "valued-added" impact.

Organizational change in support of gender equality within Governments, donor organizations, NGOs and other bodies could only be successful if grounded in the broader goals of development, peace and equality, as expressed through women's mobilization on the ground. Organizations could not promote gender mainstreaming effectively in isolation from the women's movement at the national level. The voices of women had to be heard and their expressed priorities and needs taken into consideration. Consultation with women as well as men was essential for successful gender mainstreaming.

The need to always link the strategy of gender mainstreaming to the overall goal of promoting gender equality was highlighted throughout the discussions. The importance of placing the goal of gender equality in a broad socio-economic context was also raised. Gender equality could not be seen in isolation from other socio-economic criteria such as race, class, poverty levels, and age.

Participants encouraged further work on promoting, facilitating and monitoring gender mainstreaming at both regional and subregional levels and highlighted the important role of ESCAP in this process.

A number of **key constraints** to gender mainstreaming were also highlighted in the discussions:

There still remained huge gaps between policy commitments and resource allocations within many organizations, and this was negatively affecting implementation of gender mainstreaming on the ground. Many organizations still had cultures which were not supportive of the promotion of gender equality. Even where policy commitments were in place, adherence to these was not mandatory and there were no sanctions for non-compliance. Neglect of gender perspectives in policies and programmes was not questioned by senior managers.

Gender analysis and incorporation of gender perspectives in policies and programmes had not yet been done in a systematic manner within organizations. There were still serious and unacceptable gaps in the availability of sex-disaggregated data. Indicators of progress on gender mainstreaming had not yet been developed. Those indicators which did exist were very much process indicators focused on the organization itself rather than on outcomes and impacts.

Recommendations

The meeting called on Governments, regional intergovernmental bodies and civil society actors, with support of international bodies and donors as appropriate, to work towards the following goals:

General promotion of gender mainstreaming

- Ensure that the principles of gender equality and a rights-based framework, as embodied in CEDAW, are mainstreamed into policies, programmes and activities of all actors in development.

- Promote people-centred analyses of Government policies and programmes, that make visible their economic and social impacts and outcomes, particularly in terms of their congruence with larger national goals of gender equality and social justice.

- Broaden the focus on gender mainstreaming within Governments, to include branches other than the executive branch, and emphasize the role of other actors such as the private sector, academia, the media, political parties, trade unions and religious organizations.

Gender mainstreaming in specific areas

- Incorporate gender perspectives into the conceptual frameworks and processes of macroeconomic planning and decision-making, in order to address the multiple dimensions of human poverty of women as well as men.

- Support gender equality advocates to gain a basic understanding of macro-economics, including planning and budgeting processes, to enable them to engage in informed dialogue at all levels on economic issues and national policies from a gender perspective.

- Support gender-responsive budget analyses, through developing and disseminating methods and tools that build on existing experience and good practice.

- Ensure that the principles of gender equality and non-discrimination, as embodied in Security Council Resolution 1325, are mainstreamed into United Nations peace support operations, including conflict prevention, peace-building and post-conflict reconstruction.

- Incorporate gender perspectives in governance, through promoting participation, transparency and accountability.

Institutional development for gender mainstreaming

- Develop capacities to address the political dimensions of promoting and sustaining gender mainstreaming and provide the necessary technical support to initiate and expand gender mainstreaming in strategic sectors and issues.

- Enhance and strengthen the range of mechanisms for supporting gender mainstreaming, including gender focal points, taskforces and high-level advisory groups; training – including for top management; strategies for making gender analysis mandatory; action plans; accountability mechanisms and monitoring and reporting mechanisms. Develop indicators for gender mainstreaming – on process, outcomes and impacts.

- Build new constituencies to deepen and sustain gender mainstreaming, including among men.

The role of national machineries on gender mainstreaming

- Support the development of increased partnerships with NGOs and civil society groups and support the development of both political and technical skills required by these groups for promoting and monitoring gender mainstreaming.

- Play catalytic roles in developing the political and technical skills for gender mainstreaming in line ministries, other government bodies and other actors in societal development.

- Develop capacity to address new challenges in the region from a gender perspective including globalization, post-conflict reconstruction, governance, trafficking and HIV/AIDS.

- Develop capacity to play the critical monitoring role in relation to gender mainstreaming, and hold line ministries accountable.

Documentation of good practice

A number of potential good practice examples were identified in the discussion which would require further investigation and documentation. These included, but were not limited to:

1. Promoting of women's participation in local elections in Cambodia;

2. Incorporating gender perspectives into the census in India;

3. Efforts to ensure gender-sensitive resource allocations in the Philippines;

4. Mandatory use of Gender Implication Statements in New Zealand and Gender Impact Assessment and Evaluation (GIAE) in Japan.

V. CLOSING OF THE SYMPOSIUM

The Deputy Executive Secretary of ESCAP, Ms. Keiko Okaido, made a closing statement on behalf of ESCAP. Ms. Okaido congratulated the participants on the adoption of the Communiqué and the reaffirmation of the importance of the strategy of gender mainstreaming. She highlighted the importance of the focus on poverty eradication, the impact of globalization and national budget processes and the importance of regional and subregional bodies in ensuring that gender perspectives were given adequate attention. Ms. Okaido emphasized ESCAP's commitment to work with Member States and NGOs in the region in promoting gender mainstreaming as a key instrument for gender equality.

In her concluding comments, the Director of the Division for the Advancement of Women, Ms. Carolyn Hannan, drew the attention of the participants to the objectives of the symposium. She concluded that the symposium had been successful in facilitating dialogue on knowledge, experience and good practice and thanked participants for their active contributions to discussions. A number of important recommendations had been made through the Communiqué. Ms. Hannan pointed to two methodological issues that would need to be kept in mind in implementing gender mainstreaming. Firstly, that focus on process or the means should not detract from the necessary focus on the end, or the goal of gender equality. Secondly, the processes, procedures and methodologies put in place to support gender mainstreaming should not become too complicated. Otherwise professional staff may feel that only highly skilled gender specialists could implement gender mainstreaming. The goal was for all professional staff to take gender perspectives into account in the work they were already doing. In conclusion, Ms. Hannan assured participants that the outcomes of the regional symposium would be brought to the attention of the forty-sixth session of the Commission on the Status of Women in New York in March 2002.